BATTLE OF THE BULGE

THE FIRST 24 HOURS

BATTLE OF THE BULGE

THE FIRST 24 HOURS

DAVID JORDAN

amber
BOOKS

Published by
Amber Books Ltd
Bradley's Close
74–77 White Lion Street
London N1 9PF
www.amberbooks.co.uk

ISBN 0-9544356-5-6

Project Editor: Michael Spilling
Design: Jerry Williams
Picture Research: Natasha Jones
Maps: Peter Harper

The analysis, opinions and conclusions expressed or implied in this book are those of the author and do not necessarily represent the views of the JSCSC, the United Kingdom Ministry of Defence or any other government agency.

PICTURE CREDITS
(I.W.M. = Imperial War Museum; U.S.N.A. = United States National Archives)

Amber Books Ltd: 14, 179

Aerospace Publishing: 10, 67, 75, 78, 106, 115, 130

POPPERFOTO: 62, 66, 70–71, 74, 118, 119, 122–123, 129, 134, 177, 181

Süddeutscher Verlag: 9, 24, 43, 45, 49, 53, 54, 65, 68, 73, 76, 79, 81, 93, 114, 121, 132–133, 144, 149

TRH Pictures: 6–7, 11, 13, 15 (U.S.N.A.), 16–17, 18 (U.S. Army), 25, 26–2, 28, 29 (I.W.M.), 30, 31, 32–33, 34–35 (Bundesarchiv), 36, 37 (I.W.M.), 38, 39, 41 (U.S.N.A.), 42, 50, 51 (U.S.N.A.), 55, 63, 69 (U.S.N.A.), 72 (U.S.N.A.), 84–85, 88–89, 104, 108–109, 110–111 (I.W.M.), 113, 116, 120, 125, 126, 127, 128, 136, 137, 140, 141, 142, 146–147, 152–153, 158, 160, 161, 164–165, 167, 168, 169, 170, 173 (U.S. Army), 174, 175, 176, 184–185, 186, 187

The U.S. National Archives: 40, 46, 52, 57, 58–59, 61, 64, 77, 80, 82, 86, 91, 92, 95, 96, 98, 99, 101, 102, 103, 105, 107, 139, 145, 151, 155, 157, 163, 178, 180

Printed and bound in Italy by: Eurolitho S.p.A., Cesano Boscone (MI)

Contents

CHAPTER ONE

REACHING THE ARDENNES

Following the astounding successes of the Blitzkrieg, Hitler's attempt to secure domination in Europe had stalled. By early 1944, Germany had been forced onto the back foot, and worse was to come. A second front was opened in the early summer, and the German army was forced back towards its own frontiers. As the year drew to a close, the question was not if the Allies would win, but when.

By December 1944, World War II had been under way for more than five years. The anti-fascist alliance headed by the 'Big Three' of the United States, the Soviet Union and Great Britain had recovered from earlier reverses against a seemingly invincible German army to inflict a steady series of reverses on Adolf Hitler's forces. On the eastern front, Soviet forces had launched a winter offensive in the Ukraine on Christmas Eve 1943 and this had led to disaster for the Germans. In mid-February, the battle of Korsun–Shevchenkovsky ended with the rout of substantial elements of the retreating German forces: thousands of men drowned in a panic-stricken attempt to cross the Gniloi Tikitsch. The Sixth Army suffered fearful attrition in the Nikopol salient, and the once-unstoppable German army was in the unenviable position of suffering two major reverses at once.

German Panzer Mark IIIs and IVs, the mainstay of the Panzer force in the early years of the war, roll though the streets of a French town. The German use of Blitzkreig tactics, a major development in all-arms tactics, swept all before them in the early part of the war.

GERD VON RUNDSTEDT

Gerd von Rundstedt was born the son of an old Prussian military family in 1873, and it was inevitable that he too would become a solider. He was commissioned into the German army in 1893, and was a staff officer by the outbreak of World War I. He continued to hold staff positions throughout the conflict, ending it as the Chief of Staff to XV Corps. He remained in the army after the Versailles settlement, and held a series of commands until his retirement in 1938. He was recalled in June 1939. Von Rundstedt commanded Army Group South in France, and then in Russia. He resigned in December 1941 to pre-empt his dismissal by Hitler, and retired once more. It was a brief retirement, as he was recalled again in March 1942 to take over as Commander-in-Chief, West and – temporarily – as Commander of Army Group B. He was relieved of command in July 1944 after disagreeing with Hitler over the need to withdraw in the face of the Allied advances in Normandy. In the aftermath of the July Bomb Plot against Hitler, he supervised the court of honour that dealt with the officers suspected of complicity in the assassination attempt against Hitler – although he did this out of a sense of duty to the army rather than to the Führer, of whom he had a low opinion.

Hitler reappointed von Rundstedt as Commander-in-Chief West, but more as a figurehead than a commander with any real decision-making powers. After the Battle of the Bulge, von Rundstedt commanded his forces in the defence of Germany, but was dismissed again in March 1945. He was captured in May 1945 by the Americans, and spent three years in a prison camp in Britain before being allowed to return home. He enjoyed a quiet retirement until his death in Hanover in 1953.

Despite this, Stalin still worried that the Germans would launch new offensives in the summer of 1944 if the Allies did not open the second front in Europe, while optimism at German headquarters rose as the Soviet offensives petered out. Although the rise in morale was notable, it did not mean that the Germans thought that the advantage was swinging back in their direction. They were uncomfortably aware that an invasion of Europe was likely and had to plan for dealing with this threat, settling for the plan of holding in the east while throwing the Anglo-American invasion back into the English Channel. This was not just an idle dream, since preparations to defend the French coast had been in hand since March 1942.

FORTRESS EUROPE

One of the key turning points for the war in Europe came in December 1941, when Germany declared war on the United States in the aftermath of the Japanese attack on Pearl Harbor. The United States, having found itself at war with Japan, was not certain to enter the European war, but Hitler – for reasons that remain unclear – decided the issue, announcing that Germany was at war with America three days after the Japanese attack. This presented a series of planning challenges to the German high command, the Oberkommando der Wehrmacht (OKW), which was already reeling from a totally unexpected Soviet offensive against their forces in Russia on 5 December 1941. The OKW was forced to accept that the appearance of the United States as an enemy, coupled with the efforts of a reinvigorated Red Army on the eastern front, would militate against a short war: they would have to plan for a conflict that would last for some years.

The United States did not represent an immediate threat to the German position in Europe, since its army was relatively small and would take time to build up. The Germans anticipated that it would be early 1943 before American troops arrived in Britain, the only place from which an invasion to open a second front could be launched. The logical conclusion to be drawn from this was that the main German effort would remain on the eastern front. While the fighting continued there, it would be necessary to establish defences along the coastline of occupied Europe to deal with any attempt to land in the West.

This decision was formally recognized in March 1942, when Hitler issued a directive ordering the construction of an immense line of fortifications stretching from the Franco-Spanish border up to the North Cape in Norway. At the time, Hitler was convinced that the British would attempt a landing in Norway so that they would be in a position to protect their Arctic convoys from the depredations of the U-boats. He gave instructions that the Norwegian coastline was to be given top priority in the construction of shore defences, and his instructions were carried out to the letter: by the end of 1943, Norway had the most heavily fortified coastline in the world. The effort expended on building the Norwegian defences meant that the French coastline received relatively little attention. Construction work began at a comparatively leisurely pace, and the defences at Dieppe were only partially completed when British and Canadian troops staged a landing there on 18 August 1942.

The Dieppe raid was not a success, and the British learned a number of extremely valuable lessons. Hitler issued another directive calling for the construction of widespread fortifications along the French coast but, while he decreed that the work should be undertaken with great vigour, those responsible for implementing the order were convinced that he was overly concerned – after all, they reasoned, a major raid had been driven off with half-completed fortifications manned by inexperienced and over-age reservists, and this suggested that the pace of building need not be frenetic. This complacent attitude had changed by autumn 1943, after the Allies had staged successful landings in Tunisia, Sicily and Salerno by the end of September. Hitler responded with yet another directive, ordering the creation of a series of fortifications to ensure that any invasion was defeated 'before, if possible, but at the latest upon the actual landing'. On 1 January 1944, his concern about the state of the defences led to him dispatching Field Marshal Erwin Rommel to inspect the so-called Atlantic Wall, simultaneously appointing him commander of Army Group B, with operational command over the German forces in northern France . By this point, it was clear that the Allies would be in a position to launch an invasion in the near future, although no one knew exactly when, or even more importantly where, it would be.

Rommel found himself in almost immediate dispute with the Commander-in-Chief West, Field Marshal Gerd von Rundstedt, over the way in which the coast should be defended in the event of an Allied invasion. Von Rundstedt wished to allow the Allies to land before attacking them with six panzer divisions as they were establishing their beachhead. Rommel was unconvinced by this idea: he was all too aware of the effect of air attack on armoured columns from his time commanding the Afrika Korps, contending that the panzers would be destroyed by bombing and naval gunfire as they headed for the beachhead. The only way of defeating an invasion, Rommel argued, was to destroy the landing forces as they came ashore.

This bitter dispute between von Rundstedt and Rommel led to the direct intervention of Hitler, who suggested a

Hitler and Von Rundstedt study the situation at the front. By the middle of 1944, Hitler took little notice of the views of his generals, insisting that his orders be followed to the letter. Hence their valid objections to increasingly grandiose schemes were ignored, with disastrous consequences.

compromise: the panzers would be placed under his direct control, and he would give the order to move them. This was accepted, but it meant that operational control in the face of an Allied landing risked being confused and less effective than it might have been. Rommel's views on the need for strong fortifications prevailed, however, and by early spring 1944 the defences were beginning to emerge. The question remained: when and where would the landings take place? The general answer to the first question could be given: 'soon'. Unfortunately for German defensive planning, however, the Allies were not going to reveal their plans.

MEDIUM TANK M4 'SHERMAN'

The Sherman was the mainstay of the Allied tank force during the last two years of the war, although it first appeared in September 1941. In the aftermath of the attack on Pearl Harbor, it was rushed into service at the start of 1942. It first saw action with the British at El Alamein in October 1942, causing the Germans considerable difficulties because its 75mm (2.95in) gun was able to defeat any German tank then in service. The arrival of the Tiger tank and then the Panther meant that this period of advantage was short. When the European campaign began in June 1944, the Sherman was outclassed by several German tanks, but the Allies had so many Shermans that the weight of numbers told. While the M4 suffered from drawbacks such as lack of armour protection and main armament that could not compete with the German tanks, the vast number available to the American and British forces meant that they were able to make widespread use of their armour, often with decisive results as they advanced towards Germany itself.

PLANNING THE INVASION

The Anglo-American invasion plans were first drawn up f ollowing the meeting between Prime Minister Churchill, President Roosevelt and their Combined Chiefs of Staff at Casablanca in January 1943. Two months later, the 'Trident' conference in Washington laid down that the landings should take place on 1 May 1944 under the codename Overlord. Planning responsibility was given to the British Chief of Staff to the Supreme Allied Commander (COSSAC), Gen Sir Frederick Morgan. Morgan's title was somewhat misleading, since no supreme commander had then been appointed. Undaunted, Morgan and his Anglo-American staff set about working out the details of an invasion.

The first task for COSSAC was to work out where the invasion should take place. Three locations in France suggested themselves: the Pas de Calais, Brittany and Normandy. Although the Pas de Calais offered the shortest route across the channel (with the attendant benefits for continual air cover and the logistics to support the invasion force once ashore), it was rejected. The topography of the area was far from ideal, and the Pas de Calais was so obvious an area for assault that the Germans had begun to fortify the region with some vigour. Brittany enjoyed a brief period of favour among some of the American planners owing to its good beaches, but was rejected on account of the logistical difficulties presented by its position far to the west of the Low Countries, which would extend the supply lines as the Allies broke out. The Royal Navy also passed some choice comments about the appalling weather and the hazardous nature of the surrounding waters. Thus Brittany fell from favour and Normandy was chosen.

Once the location was decided upon, preparations began. The number of troops arriving in England increased, and their training became more intensive. Landing craft were built, maps were prepared, and specialist tanks that could swim, clear mines or fire heavy demolition charges were constructed. By May 1944, there were

An M4 Sherman Medium tank. The Sherman provided the bulk of British and American tank formations from 1942 onwards: 53,362 were built in three years, with updated designs.

over three million soldiers, sailors and airmen from Britain, America, Canada, New Zealand, Australia, Poland, France, Belgium, Norway, the Netherlands and Czechoslovakia waiting in England for the instruction to launch an invasion.

COSSAC also had a supreme commander to work for. After some indecision, Gen Dwight D Eisenhower was finally appointed as the supreme Allied Commander for the invasion on 7 December 1943 – although Winston Churchill had loyally pressed the case for a British commander, he was aware that the vast contribution being made by the United States would mean that the man for the job would have to be an American. Eisenhower set about preparing for the invasion of Europe. These preparations merit an entire book of their own, but it is worth noting some of the key elements of the build-up to Operation Overlord (as the invasion was to be codenamed). One of Eisenhower's first tasks was to deal

German soldiers man a machine gun position on the French coast after France's capitulation. The weapon is an MG34, the first ever 'general purpose' machine gun, which could be fired from a bipod in the light machine gun role, or from a tripod for sustained fire.

> One of our best equipped infantry divisions was sent to the Channel Islands late in 1941 and they were never returned to me during the entire course of the Western campaign. So long was this formation stationed in Jersey, Guernsey and Alderney that rumour had it that they were soon to receive arm bands inscribed with the words 'King's Own German Grenadiers'.
>
> *Field Marshal Gerd von Rundstedt,*
> *on Hitler's control of troop dispositions prior to D-Day*

GENERAL GEORGE S PATTON

Probably the most flamboyant American general of the war, George S Patton distinguished himself in World War I as an officer in the American tank corps. His first action in World War II came in North Africa, where he commanded II Corps. He was then given command of the US Seventh Army for the invasion of Sicily. Although this was a success, Patton was dismissed after a visit to a military hospital, when he struck a soldier who had been admitted for battle fatigue. Patton accused the man of cowardice, and the press furore led to his loss of command. When he was re-employed as Third Army commander, he found himself serving under his former subordinate Omar Bradley, but their relationship worked well. During the course of the Normandy campaign, Patton maintained his reputation for advancing swiftly. Third Army fought across Europe and was ultimately to play a decisive part in the Battle of the Bulge. In the spring of 1945, Patton's forces crossed the Rhine and drove towards Czechoslovakia. Political pressure forced him to withdraw, and he found his post-war assignment as a military governor dull in the extreme. He was killed in a road accident in December 1945.

with the clashing egos of his subordinate commanders: since these included Gen Bernard Montgomery and Gen George S Patton, this was no easy task.

By early June 1944, everything was in place. After a postponement of 24 hours, due to poor weather conditions, the assault began just after midnight on 6 June 1944.

D-DAY

The first actions of the invasion were not carried out on D-Day itself, but on the previous evening by members of the French Resistance alerted to their missions by cryptic messages broadcast by the BBC's French language service. Shortly after midnight, an aerial armada of transport aircraft and gliders was heading for France. Although the air drop was marked by confusion as paratroopers landed miles from their drop zones (and often miles from other elements of their units), the airborne troops set about attacking the Germans. The air drops were followed by the actual landing of the amphibious force. The landings went relatively smoothly, except at Omaha Beach, where for a while it appeared that the landing would have to be suspended, but Brigadier General Norman Cota, the assistant divisional commander of 29th Division, managed to make sense of the confusion on the beach. He gathered together a company-sized force from the men on the beach, drawn from a mix of Rangers, engineers and infantrymen and led them forward from the beach to a fold in the bluffs, from where they were protected from machine-gun fire. Cota established shore-to-ship communications, and then sent his men to attack German positions. By 1100, these attacks had succeeded in capturing the Vierville exit to the beach; within half an hour determined attacks had captured the Saint-Laurent exit and the Americans were moving off the beach in strength. Elsewhere the British and Canadians had moved forwards from Sword, Juno and Gold beaches, while American forces at Utah Beach had endured a far less torrid time than their comrades at Omaha.

The German reaction was confused. The first parachute landings were interpreted as supply drops to the Resistance, while the appearance of the invasion fleet was considered to be a diversionary move, with the real assault coming in the Pas de Calais area. Von Runstedt could not be shaken from this view, and nor could Hitler. The Führer was reluctant to order the release of the armoured units, although 21st Panzer Division's commander had begun to engage the airborne troops around the Orne bridges on his own initiative. By nightfall on 6 June, the German response was more coordinated, but the Allies were firmly ashore.

BREAK-OUT

Establishing a beachhead was just the first part of the Allied invasion – once ashore, they then had to break out into the countryside beyond, and this proved to be an extremely difficult matter indeed. A major reason for this was the nature of the countryside. Between Carpiquet and the Cotentin peninsula lay the bocage – narrow, sunken lanes surrounded by tall, thick hedges that led to small, well built villages or individual stone farmhouses. In short, the bocage was a defender's delight. The Allies' first attempts to exploit the success of their landings met hard resistance along the line. The experience of the British 7th Armoured Division demonstrates the nature of the bitter struggle that followed in the Normandy campaign.

Montgomery decided that he would use the 7th Armoured Division (the famed 'Desert Rats') to punch through the gap in the area of Villers-Bocage. This would enable the division to link up with the 51st Highland Division and encircle Caen. Thus, on 10 June, 7th Armoured moved from Tilly towards Villers-Bocage. The area was defended by the Panzer Lehr

Division, which was understrength but still a formidable opponent in the difficult countryside. The decision by the 7th Armoured Division commander to attack on a relatively narrow front assisted the Germans, who would have found it difficult to resist an attack all along their over-extended line. As it was, a bitter battle developed with fierce fighting. It took 7th Armoured Division three days for its lead elements to enter Villers-Bocage. Once these forces had passed through the town, they were ambushed by a lone Tiger tank commanded by Michael Wittmann, a panzer 'ace' from the eastern front. Wittmann was credited with the destruction of 117 enemy tanks up to 13 June 1944, and was about to add to his tally. He began by destroying the lead tank from the 4th County of London Yeomanry (Sharpshooters) and, having cut off an easy escape route for the column by destroying the lead and rear tanks, began to move along the column picking off the British tanks as he went. A rescue force in the form of tanks from the 8th Hussars was given a similar mauling before a shot from a 6-pounder anti-tank gun (to which the Tiger's main armour was impervious) knocked a track from Wittmann's mount, rendering it immobile. He was forced to escape on foot (later succumbing in the battle when an air strike delivered by RAF fighter-bombers destroyed his tank), but left carnage behind him. Later that afternoon, a counterattack by the Panzer Lehr Division drove 7th Armoured Division back to Tilly: in the fighting the British lost 25 tanks, 28 other vehicles and a large number of men. The pattern was to be repeated as the Germans fought doggedly over every inch of French soil. The British forces faced a considerable proportion of the German army, making their advance difficult and costly, a pattern that was to be repeated for the rest of the Normandy campaign.

British troops come ashore at Gold Beach on D-Day, 6 June 1944. The sea is obviously choppy, and this caused serious problems with sea-sickness on many of the Allied landing craft as they approached the French coast.

By the start of July, neither the Allied nor the German high command was content: the Allies were not progressing as quickly as they had hoped, while the Germans were faced with a serious problem – their attempt at a counteroffensive had failed. On 3 July, Hitler removed von Rundstedt from his command, replacing him with Field Marshal Gunther von Kluge, who had a reputation as a 'yes man' and was unlikely to dissent from Hitler's increasingly unrealistic demands to hold fast in the face of heavy Allied pressure. The greatest immediate danger to Hitler, though, was not from the Allies or generals wishing to retreat, but from those who sought a more direct means of removing the Führer's hands from the command structure.

If we succeed in throwing back the invasion, then such an attempt cannot and will not be repeated within a short time. It will mean that our reserves will be set free... If we don't throw the invaders back, we can't win a static war in the long run...Therefore the invader must be thrown back at his first attempt.

Adolf Hitler, early 1944

20 JULY

On 20 July 1944, in keeping with his usual custom, Hitler held a planning meeting at his command centre near Rastenburg, East Prussia (now Ketrzyn, Poland). Known as the 'Wolf's Lair' (as a play on Hitler's use of the codename 'Wolf' in the early days of the Nazi party's activities), this was buried deep in a forest and its gloomy location seemed to be something of a metaphor for the progress of the war at this time. The buildings were also in a state of flux. Hitler's normal location was in a concrete bunker some feet beneath the forest floor, but the recent introduction of deep penetration bombs by the RAF had led to concerns that the bunker might be vulnerable to attack. As a result, workmen were busy strengthening the bunker's roof, and conferences were being held in a large wooden hut instead. The conference on 20 July was also a little different in that it took place an hour earlier than was normal: Hitler had a luncheon engagement with Benito Mussolini and had brought forward the proceedings.

The conference began on time, but without Field Marshal Wilhelm Keitel, the head of the German high command (OKW). Keitel's absence was explained when he arrived a few moments later with Col Count Claus von Stauffenberg, the representative of the Training and Replacement Command, who was scheduled to provide a report on the raising of new divisions. Keitel gave a formal introduction for von Stauffenberg, even though Hitler had met him before: there was little chance of the Führer forgetting the new arrival's appearance, since grievous wounds sustained on the eastern front had cost von Stauffenberg an eye, a hand and some fingers of the remaining hand. Von Stauffenberg took his place at the conference table, placing his distinctive yellow leather briefcase beneath it. After a few moments, he muttered an apology to the man next to him, explaining that he had to go and make a telephone call. He left the hut just as Hitler was beginning to expound upon the situation on the eastern front. A few minutes later, Keitel was becoming anxious at von Stauffenberg's absence: the discussion about the eastern front was drawing to a conclusion, and the missing officer was due to make his presentation next.

In camouflage fatigues, a member of an SS Panzer division carries an MG42 machine gun. The MG42's design was of such high quality that the weapon returned to production (in a different calibre) for the Federal German Army as the MG3.

As Keitel began to fret, the Führer's thoughts on the situation in the USSR were interrupted by a deafening explosion. Keitel saw a blinding flash of light near Hitler and watched transfixed as a light fitting descended from the ceiling, landing on top of the dictator. The noise of the explosion brought men running. The first survivor they saw was Keitel's adjutant, who picked himself up and moved a little unsteadily away from the hut: he was first out by virtue of having been blown through the window by the blast. Another figure followed through the window, then some more emerged from the door. Finally Keitel himself appeared, supporting Hitler as the two men left the wreckage. Hitler was bleeding from wounds on his face, and his trousers were shredded and smouldering from the blast; doctors later removed from his legs hundreds of splinters from the table.

While the doctors were treating him, Hitler pondered the blast. His first reaction was that the hut had been hit in an air raid, but he was soon disabused of this notion: there had been no bomb-

A British Sherman Firefly moves through the French countryside. The Firefly was fitted with a 17-pounder anti-tank gun, making it a match for most opposition; the most notable problem with the Firefly design was that there were never enough of them available.

ing in the area. This turned his thoughts to an assassination attempt and the conclusion that there had indeed been some sort of improvised explosive device in the hut. Following up the logical guess that it must have been planted there by one of the workmen brought in to work on the bunker, he sent a party of officers to look for the remote-control cable that must have been used to detonate the bomb. The search party found nothing , and began to look more closely at the hut. They concluded that the explosion appeared to have occurred inside the hut itself, probably under the map table around which the conference was being held.

The investigations into the blast now gained momentum: suspicion was already falling, correctly, on von Stauffenberg. He had disappeared, apparently to a nearby airfield, and pieces of his briefcase – they had to be from his, since they were yellow leather – were being retrieved from all over the remains of the conference room. Von Stauffenberg's background also made him suspect. He was from the pre-Nazi officer corps, was a Catholic and an aristocrat. Just one of these attributes would have raised suspicion as to his dedication to Hitler; all three of them, in conjunction with the devastated briefcase and his disappearance, made him the prime suspect. Having been informed of this, Hitler first decided that von Stauffenberg, an officer with several reasons

> The battlefield at Falaise was unquestionably one of the greatest 'killing grounds' of any of the war areas... Forty–eight hours after the closing of the gap, I was conducted through it on foot, to encounter scenes that could be described only by Dante. It was literally possible to walk for hundreds of yards at a time, stepping on nothing but dead and decaying flesh.
>
> *General Dwight D Eisenhower*

Hitler shows the deposed Italian dictator Benito Mussolini the damage caused by the bomb intended to kill him on 20 July 1944. The failure of the plot convinced Hitler that he was destined to be victorious in the war, and this inspired him to launch the Ardennes offensive.

to oppose him, had made an attempt on his life and then flown to Moscow. This rather implausible conclusion was overtaken by the reality of events.

In the middle of the afternoon, the Wolf's Lair began to receive copies of signals emanating from Berlin and claiming that an unscrupulous group of officers and politicians had assassinated the Führer, and that the government had declared a state of emergency. During the period of emergency, full authority would be vested in the signatory of the telegram, Field Marshal Witzleben (who had been retired by Hitler in 1942). Von Stauffenberg's name as co-signatory of the signal demonstrated that the bomb was actually part of a coup attempt. The conspirators had control of the Bendlerstrasse headquarters building in Berlin, along with a number of other key sites. For a few hours, it appeared as though the coup might succeed: Hitler was at an isolated location, and all the commanders loyal to Hitler were, naturally, at the battlefront. It looked as though the coup would succeed through lack of opposition.

CONSPIRACY FOILED

Fortunately for Hitler, his run of luck had not ended with surviving the bomb blast. Just after 18:30, he received a telephone call from Joseph Goebbels, the propaganda minister. With some difficulty, Goebbels reported to the still-deafened Hitler that he had with him a Major Renner, the leader of the only combat unit then in Berlin, a guards battalion. He was, Goebbels explained, confused: he had received one set of orders instructing him to place members of the government under house arrest and another telling him to arrest Witzleben and von Stauffenberg. Goebbels wondered if Hitler would like to talk to Renner. Hitler said he would. He told Renner that he was to restore order in Berlin, and to shoot anyone who stood in his way.

Renner carried out his orders diligently. By midnight, von Stauffenberg and three other conspirators were dead. Field Marshal Ludwig Beck, who was implicated in the plot, killed himself at the second attempt, and a wave of arrests began. Suspects were brutally interrogated, sometimes implicating those who had little, if anything, to do with the plot. The names included that of Erwin Rommel, who was given the choice of committing suicide, followed by a state funeral and the honouring of his name, or a trial that would lead to much unpleasantness for his family. Rommel chose the option of a poison pill. Subsequently, Rommel's proponents have argued that he alone might have saved Germany from utter and irredeemable defeat, but this is a moot point. The bomb plot cost Germany one of its most capable commanders, and had one further important effect: it reinvigorated Adolf Hitler.

Only an hour or so after the blast, Hitler was entertaining Mussolini to lunch. He spoke excitedly about how his survival clearly demonstrated both his true destiny and that of Germany. Divine providence meant that, whatever the current unfavourable circumstances facing Germany, she

would ultimately prevail. Witnesses said that, far from being shaken by his narrow escape, Hitler was euphoric, convinced that he would triumph after all. This renewed confidence also brought about other results. He no longer trusted his military commanders, with one or two notable exceptions, and would take an even greater level of control over military operations. He began to accept even less advice from the army, and displayed an unwillingness to listen to any suggestions that contradicted his own perceptions of the situation on the battlefield. This was to have important repercussions for the future conduct of the war. The current situation, though, was bad enough, and the Allies finally started to make the breakthrough they had been looking for after weeks of bitter fighting.

OPERATION COBRA

Gen Montgomery hoped that Operation Goodwood, launched from the British sector, would provide the Allies with the breakthrough for which they were searching, but he was to be disappointed. Goodwood failed in its objective and, to make matters worse, about a third of the British tank strength in Normandy was knocked out of the fighting. The offensive managed to make a penetration of just 9km (6 miles), but achieved more than these figures suggest: as well as inflicting attrition upon already overstretched German forces, the offensive convinced the Germans that the main Allied effort would come from the British sector.

Gen Omar Bradley, commander of the US First Army, proposed the outline for Operation Cobra after it became clear that the German defences lacked any real depth, especially in the American sector. Cobra was to start with carpet-bombing the German forces in front of the US VII Corps, commanded by Gen 'Lightning Joe' Collins. VII Corps would then advance towards the Germans' main line of resistance and seek to break through, with the aim of concluding the first phase of Cobra by being in a position to enable American units to push into Brittany to seize the ports. Such a break-out would demand the use of more units, which would appear in the form of Gen Patton's Third Army.

Cobra was meant to begin with bombing attacks at 1300 on 24 July, but a heavy overcast sky above the battlefield prompted the decision to call off the attack. This did not prevent confusion when some bombers did not receive the recall message; more than 300 dropped their bombs, and one unit accidentally released theirs on elements of the 30th Division, inflicting 25 fatalities and injuring more than 100 men. Bradley was furious, not only because of the casualties, but because he feared that it would alert the Germans to the offensive. As it happened, the Germans did not change their plans. The commander of the German Seventh Army, Gen Paul Hausser, did not appear particularly concerned when he reported the events of the day to von Kluge; the commander of the Panzer Lehr Division, Fritz Bayerlein, was convinced

A column advances near Fontainbleu during the Normandy campaign. Only one man spares a glance at the dead German: all had seen enough bodies to make one more unremarkable. Despite their American uniforms, the men are members of the Free French forces.

that his men had repulsed a major American attack, not realizing that the sound and fury to which his men had responded had been generated by falling bombs rather than advancing troops.

COBRA KICKS OFF

Cobra began again shortly after 09:30 the next day with strafing attacks by P-47 Thunderbolt fighter-bombers, followed by just under 1500 B-17 and B-24 bombers. These dropped more than 3000 tons of bombs, and were in turn followed by 380 B-26 medium bombers that added another 1400 tons of high explosive to the fray. The German defences were shattered. More than a thousand of the defenders were killed, with around the same number wounded or so badly dazed that they were incapable of resistance. The bombing also disrupted the communications network – but it did not manage to deal with all of the defenders evenly. Many of the German troops nearest to the American positions escaped unscathed, along with their tanks; and once again bombs fell short, killing 111 men and wounding 490, including Lt Gen Lesley McNair, the head of Army Ground Forces.

The ground attack began at 11:00 and ran into stiff resistance in those areas where the bombing had not inflicted much damage. This meant that the first day proved to be disappointing for the Americans, who had gained about a mile rather than the three miles that were anticipated. Collins decided that he would commit his armoured forces the next day, rather than continuing the infantry attack alone. This decision paid off as the armoured forces broke through, and Collins continued to apply pressure by also attacking through the night of 26/27 July. By the end of 28 July, the German defences were in disarray, their hopes of an orderly withdrawal dashed. This prompted the Americans to refine Cobra: where a period of consolidation had been planned after the breakthrough, it was decided to exploit the apparent collapse of the German forces. The continuing advance prompted Hitler, who would not accept that the German forces were in a dire state, to intervene with plans for an operation that were most unlikely to succeed.

Operation Lüttich was intended to begin in the area around Mortain, striking at Avranches. Avranches was the key to the American advance, since it was the hub through which all supplies to Patton's Third Army had to pass. Hitler believed that an attack here would dislocate the entire American effort, and had grandiose ideas for cutting off the forward American divisions. The attack began on 7 August and penetrated almost 16km (10 miles) into the American lines. Some American units were cut off and it appeared that Hitler's plan might work. However, Hitler's belief that God was on his side after the events of 20 July was ill-founded. When dawn broke, the weather was fine, and by the middle of the morning the sky was teeming with fighter-bombers. The advance had to stop as the Germans sought cover, and for the next three days they would attack only at night. Bitter fighting followed, but the Germans made no significant gains, much to Hitler's fury.

On 8 August, the first elements of Patton's Third Army reached Le Mans. Eisenhower ordered them to turn north and head towards the British sector. At the same time, the Canadian II Corps planned to attack south towards Falaise: if they succeeded, they would link up with the Americans and cut the Germans off. Just after nightfall on 8 August, more than a thousand heavy bombers plastered the flanks of the corridor leading to Falaise with high explosive; the Canadians then began to advance down the corridor, heading for Falaise under the auspices of Operation Totalise.

The Germans attempted to stop the advance, launching a counterattack just before midday on 9 August. This was thrown back by 1400, but, just as the Canadians and the accompanying Polish forces were about to resume their advance, the sky was filled with 500 B-17 Flying Fortresses from the USAAF. The plan was to repeat the bombardment of the night before, but this went disastrously wrong. Many bombs fell short, killing friendly forces and damaging or destroying many tanks.

The next day, a Canadian battle group managed to lose its way and blundered into two panzer groups. To make matters worse, the Poles were engaging the panzers and took the Canadians under fire as well. Although progress was being made on Totalise's objectives, it was in danger of crawling to a halt as the Canadian and Polish forces ran into increasingly heavy opposition. The Americans, however, were having a better time and pushing towards Argentan. The prospect of linking up with the Americans added new impetus to the British forces, and a development of Totalise was swiftly introduced.

OPERATION TRACTABLE

The new plan, Tractable, was intended to be a massive assault against the Germans, preceded by a devastating artillery bombardment. As the bombardment crept forward, more than 300 tanks and four infantry brigades followed behind it. At this point, however, disaster struck when many of the 800 heavy bombers providing air support began to drop short of the Germans and onto the Allied forces. Although the troops pressed on, the dust and smoke kicked up by the bombing

North Sea
XXXXX
21
MONTGOMERY
Brussels
Namur
BELGIUM
Antwerp
XXXX
9 SIMPSON
XXXX
1 CRERAR
The Hague
XXXX
2 DEMPSEY
Rotterdam
Neder Rijin
Neerpelt
Maas
Waal
Maastricht
XXX
I
XXXX
25 CHRISTIANSEN
XXX
XII
Eindhoven
NETHERLANDS
XXX
VIII
XXX
XIII
XXX
SS XII
XXX
II
Roermond
XXX
LXXXI
XXX
II
XXX
XXX
Grave
Venlo
Nijmegen
Arnhem
Krefeld
XXXX
1 SCHLEMM
Rhine
XXXXX
H
STUDENT
Wesel

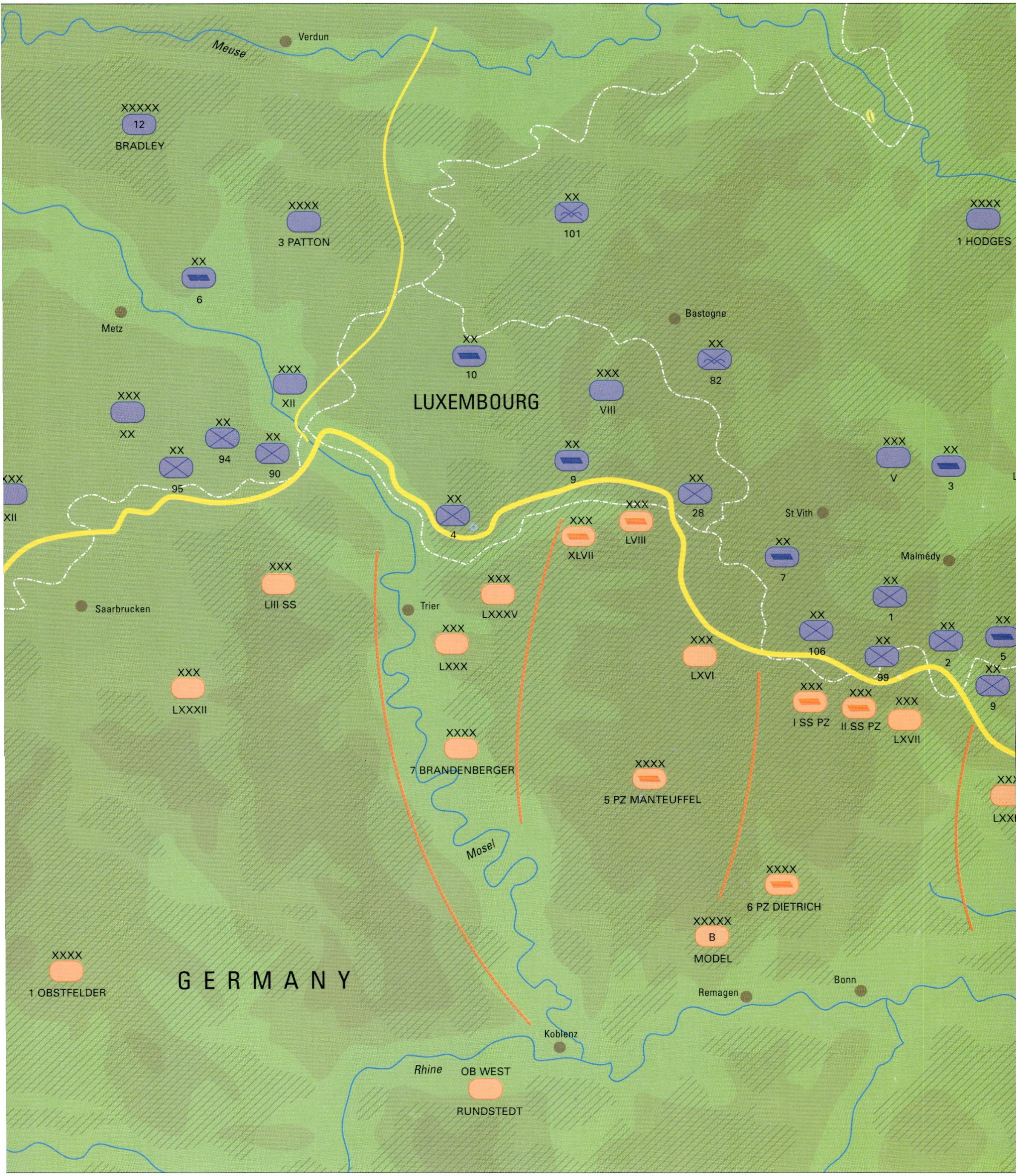
Verdun
Meuse
XXXXX
12
BRADLEY
XXXX
3 PATTON
XX
101
XXXX
1 HODGES
XX
6
Metz
Bastogne
XX
10
XX
82
XXX
XII
XXX
VIII
LUXEMBOURG
XXX
XX
XX
94
XX
90
XX
95
XX
9
XXX
V
XX
3
XXX
XII
XX
4
XX
28
St Vith
XXX
XLVII
XXX
LVIII
XX
7
Malmédy
XXX
LIII SS
Saarbrucken
Trier
XXX
LXXXV
XX
1
XX
106
XX
99
XX
2
XX
5
XX
9
XXX
LXXX
XXX
LXVI
XXX
LXXXII
XXX
I SS PZ
XXX
II SS PZ
XXX
LXVII
XXXX
7 BRANDENBERGER
XXXX
5 PZ MANTEUFFEL
Mosel
XXXX
6 PZ DIETRICH
XXXXX
B
MODEL
XXXX
1 OBSTFELDER
GERMANY
Remagen
Bonn
Koblenz
Rhine
OB WEST
RUNDSTEDT

A Tiger Tank rolls down the road. These, the most formidable German tanks of the war, were better armed and armoured than the Allied tanks, but were vastly outnumbered: in the battles of attrition during the European campaigns, it was numbers that made the difference.

and the artillery was so intense that it became almost impossible for them to see where they were going. Tanks and armoured personnel carriers began colliding with one another and the advance fell into disarray. The confusion was compounded when the armour encountered a narrow stream in its path, not too wide for them to worry about, but with steep banks that the tanks were unable to traverse. The armour was finally able to move on after engineers dropped fascine bundles into the stream, but the advance had slowed irreversibly. Once again, the Canadians found themselves making a slow, hard advance, eventually entering Falaise on 15 August.

Although the Allies were clearly gaining the upper hand, Hitler remained convinced that he could defeat them through a series of armoured counterattacks. He passed orders to von Kluge that the pressure on Avranches was to be maintained, while further operations against Falaise and Argentan were to be launched at once, with the intention of keeping the American and Canadian forces apart. It was at this point that von Kluge's willingness to obey Hitler's every whim failed him. As he was travelling to inspect forces in the Falaise–Argentan pocket, his staff car was strafed by fighter-bombers. Von Kluge managed to reach his destination, shocked but uninjured. He concluded that Hitler's orders were impossible to fulfil, and signalled Berlin with the fateful information that the German forces were no longer strong enough to defeat the Allies. Without waiting for a reply, von Kluge ordered the troops in the pocket to begin a withdrawal.

News of the withdrawal sent Hitler into an apoplectic rage. He sacked von Kluge immediately and ordered him to return to Berlin. Rumours that von Kluge would find himself implemented in the bomb plot (with the consequences that entailed) must have found their way to the unfortunate Field Marshal; he poisoned himself rather than make the journey to face Hitler's wrath. On 17 August, Hitler replaced von Kluge with Field Marshal Walther Model, knowing that Model was a loyal Nazi who would obey orders. Model may have been loyal, but he was not a fool. As soon as he took over, he appreciated that the position was hopeless, and that the only sensible course of action was to continue to withdraw. He was astute enough, however, to do so while using whatever remnants of armour were available to make thrusts against both Falaise and Argentan: if he failed to make a breakthrough (as he knew he would), he could at least point to the fact that he had carried out Hitler's instructions as best he could. By 19 August, the Germans were in a desperate state – artillery and air strikes were decimating the retreating German columns; two days later, those forces remaining in the pocket were trapped as the jaws of the trap closed. Free French forces raced for Paris, despite Eisenhower's initial orders that they should not, and within days the city had fallen to them. By 29 August, American troops were marching down the Champs-Elysées as part of the liberation celebrations. The Normandy campaign was over – but a long, hard slog still lay ahead.

Men of the headquarters group of 1st Airborne Division prepare to move off from the Horsa gliders that landed them near Arnhem, in September 1944. The wing of the glider has clearly sustained a heavy impact with an obstacle (probably a tree) on landing.

ARNHEM

The Allied advance continued at considerable pace after the fall of Paris, and by the end of August the Germans were being driven back on all fronts. On 2 September 1944, British tanks entered Belgium, reaching Brussels, to wild acclaim, in the balmy early evening of the 3rd. At this point, the Allies became perhaps too optimistic in their outlook, believing the war to be all but won. In addition, the egos of some Allied generals began to surface, with Montgomery making himself particularly unpopular with the Americans owing to his constant efforts to command the land battle

despite being under Eisenhower's direction. In fairness, this did not stop Montgomery thinking about how to win the war – and on 10 September he proposed a plan of great daring. It hinged upon the Dutch town of Arnhem.

Montgomery proposed that a single thrust towards Berlin might cause the Germans to collapse. He suggested achieving this by using the First Allied Airborne Army to seize a corridor of 100km (60 miles) from the Belgian frontier to the Rhine. Twenty-First Army Group (Montgomery's command) would then rush down the corridor, outflanking the Siegfried Line and gaining a bridgehead over the Rhine. The operation would be codenamed 'Market Garden' and Eisenhower gave approval for it to take place a week later, on 17 September.

A StuG assault gun of the 9th SS Panzer Division moves past three British soldiers captured at Arnhem. Of 10,000 men who landed at Arnhem, only 2000 returned to British lines when the paratroopers were evacuated from the town on the night of 25/26 September 1944.

What Montgomery and Eisenhower did not discuss was the fact that relations were fraught between the commander of First Allied Airborne Army, the American Gen Lewis Brereton, and his British deputy, Lt Gen Sir Frederick 'Boy' Browning. This meant that the planning for Market Garden was conducted in a tense atmosphere, but by 15 September a workable plan was in place. Bridges at Eindhoven, Nijmegen and Arnhem would be seized, the first two by the 101st and 82nd Airborne Divisions respectively, and the third by Maj Gen Roy Urquhart's 1st Airborne Division. Browning had his doubts about the seizure of Arnhem, confessing to Montgomery that he worried that they 'might be going a bridge too far' – a line that gained immortality in later years.

Market Garden began on Sunday 17 September 1944 with the departure of a vast aerial armada from English airfields, carrying paratroops or towing gliders. Twenty thousand troops had been landed along the corridor by 1400. After this, almost nothing went right for the 1st Airborne Division. Unfortunately for the Allies, Field Marshal Walter Model was having lunch just 3km (2 miles) from the landing zone and reported the landings to Hitler within minutes, before arranging for the 9th and 10th SS Panzer Divisions to head for Arnhem and Nijmegen. The British XXX Corps, spearheading the advance to support the airborne troops, lost time due to German opposition and a congested road, and then ground to a halt 16km (10 miles) south of Arnhem after the Germans reacted with great vigour to their arrival. This meant that the 1st Airborne Division was cut off and spent the next few days fighting against incredible odds, waiting for relief. This did not come, and although elements of 21st Army Group finally reached the south side of the river Waal, the main branch of the Rhine, they could not cross it. On 24 September, Montgomery ordered the evacuation of the remaining members of the 1st Airborne Division. Of the 10,005 men who had flown into Arnhem, only 2163 made it back across the river. The war would drag on.

BACK TO ATTRITION

The failure at Arnhem was a blow to the Allies, and it was clear that the Germans were still some way from being defeated, even if they were in serious difficulties. Worse still for the Allies, the Germans gained renewed confidence from the successful thwarting of Market Garden. Although they were now forced back on their frontiers, they were at least falling back to prepared defensive positions that would be

> Two and a half months of bitter fighting, culminating for the Germans in a blood-bath big enough even for their extravagant tastes, have brought the end of the war in Europe within sight, almost within reach. The strength of the German Armies in the West has been shattered, Paris belongs to France again, and the Allied armies are streaming towards the frontiers of the Reich.
>
> *Intelligence Summary, Supreme Headquarters Allied Expeditionary Forces, 26 August 1944*

Gen. Bernard Montgomery, flanked by Gen. Omar N Bradley (US First Army) and Lt General Sir Miles Dempsey (British Second Army). Montgomery commanded all the land forces in France until September 1944, when Eisenhower assumed his post as overall land commander.

difficult to break through, while they had short lines of communication. The Allies were not in such a good position. Their logistical organization was marked by corruption and by self-interest on the part of the senior officers responsible for it, while the Germans had only just been evicted from the port of Antwerp (on 4 September). This meant that the Allies would be ill-placed to win the sort of struggle by attrition that was now inevitable until the logistics improved.

Although Antwerp had fallen, it could not be brought into use until the German Fifteenth Army had been dislodged from the banks of the Scheldt estuary, which controlled the entrance to the port. Montgomery had, understandably, been distracted by the operation at Arnhem, and had given the task of clearing the estuary to the Canadian First Army. On 8 October, Admiral Sir Bertram Ramsay, commanding naval operations for northwest Europe, told Eisenhower that the Scheldt would not be cleared until at least 1 November, since the Canadians had encountered stiff opposition and were short of supplies, particularly ammunition. Eisenhower was most perturbed and ordered Montgomery to clear the Scheldt estuary. An unseemly dispute then broke out as Montgomery refused to accept that this task was anything more than an attempt to consign him quietly to a backwater, enabling the Americans to 'steal' the glory that was rightfully his; he also suggested that Arnhem had failed since Eisenhower had an unsatisfactory campaign plan. At this point, Eisenhower felt that he had no option but to remind Montgomery who was in command: if Montgomery had no confidence in his handling of the matter, they must 'refer the matter to higher authority'. It soon became clear to Montgomery that such a referral would be a disaster for him, since it was impossible to conceive of a situation where Roosevelt would side with Montgomery and remove Eisenhower; it would be politically unacceptable in an election year for the American President to side with a foreign general over an American hero. Churchill would be bound to concur with Roosevelt – despite his status, Montgomery would have to be sacrificed to the smooth running of the alliance. Montgomery carefully withdrew from his position and gave orders placing the clearing of the Scheldt as the top priority for his forces.

CLEARING THE WAY

By the time Montgomery was persuaded of the need to give priority to the Scheldt, operations were well under way. The Polish Armoured Division, in concert with the Canadians, had managed to remove the Germans from about 32km (20 miles) of the southern bank of the Scheldt, but they had still covered less than half the distance. The Germans were well aware of the significance of the Scheldt to the Allies, and their defences at the mouth of the river were formidable, particularly on the island of Walcheren, where 12,000 men occupied well-fortified positions supported by some fifty heavy guns. The town of Flushing had been transformed into a fortress, with homes having been turned into strongpoints to provide withering layers of defensive fire against any attackers.

A tank landing craft heads for the beach during operations to take Walcheren island. Although much of the island was underwater after Allied bombing had breached the dykes, the Germans put up fierce resistance, and it took several days for the British to gain control.

The British and Canadian forces began to assault the positions in terrible weather that negated the air cover vital to operations, since aircraft were grounded or found their targets almost impossible to locate. The Canadian 3rd Division fought their way down the Scheldt using amphibious armoured fighting vehicles until they finally captured the last strongpoint at Knokke on 2 November. The Canadian 2nd Division attacked along the Beveland peninsula on 24 October as the British 52nd Division crossed the Scheldt and launched an attack to force the Germans into the Canadian forces. By the end of October, the Germans had been pushed back onto Walcheren.

ASSAULT FROM THE AIR

The difficulty of assaulting the island was addressed by using air power. The planners for the operation decided that the best way of dealing with the island was to flood it by breaching the Westkapelle dyke. Mosquito and Lancaster bombers made the first attack on the dike on 3 October, following this with more attacks on 7, 11 and 17 October. By the time the bombers had finished, most of the island was underwater, except for the coastal dunes and the towns of Middelburg and Vlissingen. Another two days of bombing and naval gunfire were used to soften the defences of the remaining areas, and on 1 November British Commandos landed at Westkapelle and Vlissingen (Flushing). A Canadian attack across the causeway was beaten back, and there was fierce fighting for the next two days, with the advantage swinging back and forth. Flooding caused by the bombing meant that the Commandos had a slightly easier task: a series of small islands stood in their way, which they took one at a time. Vlissingen was a much more difficult proposition, but after heavy fighting the German forces were persuaded to surrender on 4 November. On the same day, the Royal Navy began to sweep the Scheldt of mines: over the next three

German troops push into place one of the gates forming part of the West Wall (or Siegfried Line) defences. Designed to prevent tank movement, the concrete 'dragon's teeth' added to the difficulties faced by Allied troops , but did not prevent them from entering Germany.

American troops dig in to new positions in Belgium during October 1944. These solid dugouts and defensive positions proved of great value during the German artillery bombardment that preceded the attack on the opening day of the Battle of the Bulge.

weeks, ten minesweeping flotillas were required to remove the threat of mines. On 28 November, the first convoy of ships arrived safely, and by early December the port was operating fully. This meant that the Allies now enjoyed a dramatically improved logistic situation; having had too little port capacity for months, there was now a surplus, which would make the battles to come easier to sustain, if not to fight.

AMERICAN ADVANCES

While the British were busy clearing the Scheldt, the American First Army (now commanded by Gen Lewis Hodges following Bradley's elevation to command of Twelfth Army Group) launched an assault against Aachen on 12 September. Bitter fighting ensued, and the defenders determined to follow Hitler's orders to fight to the last man. Six days of intensive street fighting saw the German perimeter pushed back to a small area of the city by 22 October. The Germans were finally left holding a four-storey air raid shelter. The Americans took it under fire with 155mm (6in) howitzers and, after twelve hours of bombardment, the German forces surrendered. The battle for Aachen was particularly bloody, but it was overshadowed by the incredibly bitter fighting that took place in the forests of the Hürtgenwald (or Hertogenwald in Flemish).

The Hürtgenwald, almost 20km (12 miles) wide, stretched from near Verviers in Belgium to Düren in Germany and was intersected by part of the Siegfried Line (or West Wall). The Americans launched a series of assaults between September and November, taking 33,000 casualties in the process. Finally, on 8 December, the Americans reached the banks of the Roer river. While the First Army had been struggling in the Hürtgenwald, Patton had led the Third Army against Metz, which had surrendered on 21 November. By early December, the Third Army overlooked the West Wall, but had suffered 55,182 casualties. The Allied armies appeared to have lost momentum and Montgomery was pressing Eisenhower to find a means of forcing the Germans into mobile warfare, thereby ending the war of attrition that was taking place.

Although there was some gloom at the realization that the war was going to drag on into 1945, the Allies had at least managed to drive the Germans back across the entire front, even if this had been very difficult and still left the obstacle of the West Wall defences to breach. Also, bringing Antwerp into use meant that the logistical problems dogging the campaign since the summer had been overcome – the Allies could start to think about how to bring about the defeat of Germany. However, it could not be ignored that the strategy employed thus far seemed to have run out of steam. At a meeting with Montgomery on 28 November, Eisenhower admitted that his plan had ceased to deliver the hoped-for results. Montgomery's idea about mobile warfare seemed to provide a possible solution: the question was how to bring it about. The Allies pondered how to proceed. On 16 December, Hitler gave them the answer – he launched a massive offensive in the Ardennes.

CHAPTER TWO

PLANS AND PREPARATIONS

As the military situation grew worse, German military commanders became disillusioned with the leadership of Adolf Hitler. His overoptimism and refusal to accept the reality of the situation drove senior army officers to despair, as they were unable to convince Hitler of the serious flaws in his strategy. As the Allies pressed on towards Germany itself, Hitler produced another plan to restore his fortunes. He would, he thought, win the war by attacking on a front that had brought success before: the Ardennes.

DESPITE THE DIRE SITUATION in which the German army found itself, Hitler refused to see anything other than a victory for the Third Reich as the final outcome of the war. Realizing that defensive operations were unlikely to provide this, he turned his thoughts to more aggressive options. On 19 August 1944, Hitler first mentioned his intention to launch an offensive later in the year. He explained to the small group of trusted advisers that he would aim to begin the fighting in November, when the weather was likely to be so bad that it would impose serious limitations on the ability of the Allied air forces to operate in support of their armies. Within a fortnight, he had summoned von Rundstedt to his headquarters at the Wolf's Lair, and asked him to resume his duties as commander-in-chief in the West. Hitler's request was not a recognition of the fact that von Rundstedt had been correct in his judgement of the situation in Normandy, nor that his sacking had been unjust. Hitler disliked von

Less than two hours after the attempt to assassinate him on 20 July 1944, Hitler strolls through his headquarters, clutching his injured arm. The plotters hoped that killing Hitler would end the war, but their failure convinced him that his ultimate victory was ordained.

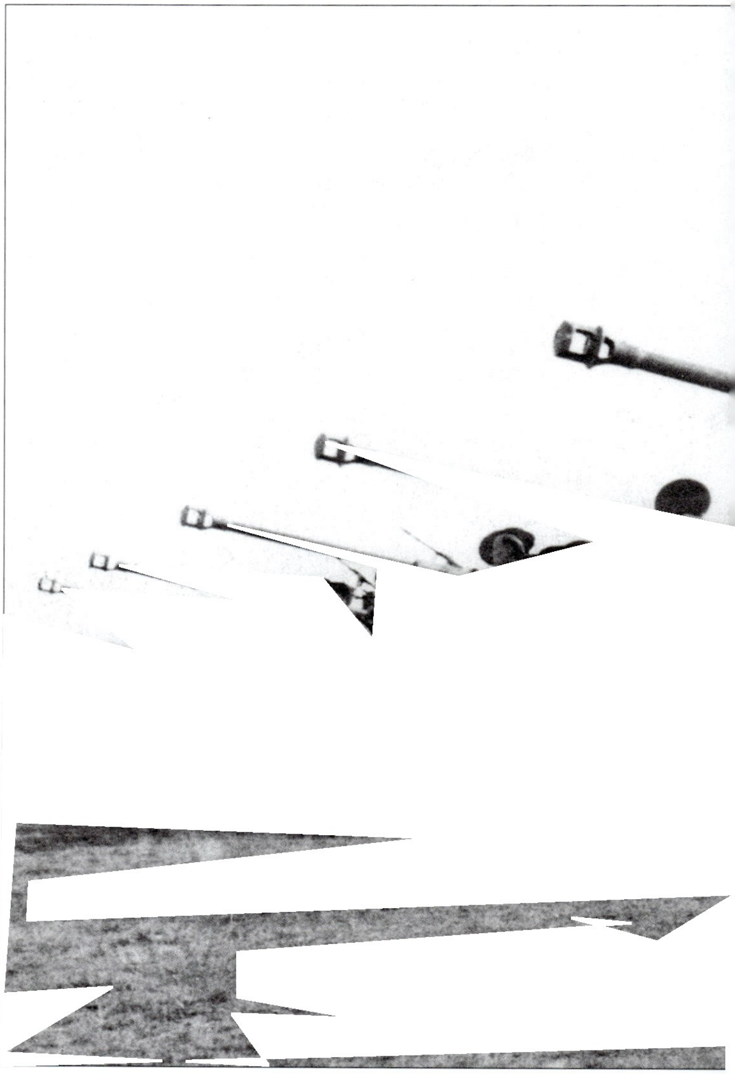

Members of the SS stand in front of their Panzer Mark IV tanks prior to an inspection. The Mark IV was one of the most versatile tank designs of the war, undergoing continual updating so that it remained effective until the end of the conflict.

Rundstedt intensely, seeing him as the embodiment of the Prussian officer corps that regarded the Führer with such disdain: it was no secret that in private conversation von Rundstedt referred to Hitler as 'the Corporal', with obvious contempt for a former NCO promoted well above his station. This personal dislike was not enough to outweigh the utility of having von Rundstedt return. Hitler knew that most German soldiers had huge respect for the 70-year-old Field Marshal, and felt that this might inspire the soldiery to greater heights. Also, Hitler hoped that appointing von Rundstedt would mislead the Allies. They would, Hitler thought, expect von Rundstedt to follow the 'rules' of warfare, which said that an army in the same position as that of the German army should not seek to launch an offensive against such odds.

VON RUNDSTEDT APPOINTED

Von Rundstedt was, therefore, a useful tool for Hitler to employ – he had no intention of revealing his plans for an offensive, and simply told his returning Commander-in-Chief that his duty would be to defend in front of the West Wall for as long as was practicable, before falling back onto the West Wall, where the decisive battle would occur. Hitler completed his deception by telling von Rundstedt that the possibility of launching an offensive was not credible, since the strength of forces available was inadequate. Von Rundstedt left the meeting apparently contented with his reappointment; almost as soon as he had left, Hitler set about drawing up the plans for the offensive.

The appointment of von Rundstedt as a figurehead was not enough to transform German fortunes. His Chief of Staff, General Siegfried Westphal, was forced to tell the returning Field Marshal that the German position was precarious. Westphal later contended that disaster would have followed had the Allies inflicted a heavy defeat on German forces on any part of the western front. The term 'front' was, in fact, something of a misnomer, since there were gaps along its entire length. Furthermore, absolutely no steps had been taken to ensure that the Allies would have difficulty crossing the Rhine. Not one of the bridges over the river had been prepared for demolition, and it took until the middle of October 1944 for this potentially fatal omission to

> Never before in history were there coalitions like the one of our enemies, composed of such heterogenic elements with completely contradictory goals. Those we have as enemies today are the greatest extremes on this earth: ultra-capitalist states on the one side, and ultra-Marxist states on the other side; on the one side a dying empire, Britain, and on the other side, a colony striving for inheritance, the USA. There is friction between these states even today about their future goals...If a few more very hard blows are delivered, then it might happen at any moment that this artificially supported common front will collapse with one tremendous clap of thunder.
>
> *Adolf Hitler addresses his senior officers, 12 December 1944*

be rectified. German forces were perilously weak. When von Rundstedt resumed his command, there were only a hundred serviceable tanks available on the entire western front. This compared with an Allied strength approaching 8000. Thirteen German infantry divisions were considered effective, while twelve were only partially fit for renewed operations. A further fourteen were deemed to possess so little combat potential that they were, to all intents and purposes, useless as formed fighting units.

DIVINE PROVENANCE

Such disadvantages might have been slightly offset had the Germans enjoyed strength in the air. Here, too, though, they were sadly lacking. The constant battering by Allied fighters and the demands of the Eastern front meant that the *Luftwaffe* was outnumbered at a ratio of about 25:1. In sum, the impression that Germany was teetering on the brink of defeat was not inaccurate. Hitler, though, had other ideas.

Hitler's belief that divine providence had saved him from death in the bomb plot appeared to reinvigorate him. Rather than look at the terrible losses sustained in battle, he focused on what he took to be positive aspects of the situation. First, he had little to worry about on the home front. The bomb plotters had failed to provoke any signs of unrest, and the brutal manner in which Hitler had dealt with the plotters (and anyone remotely suspected of links to them) meant he was confident that the chances of an opposition movement appearing were slim.

As well as being in a position where the war effort would not be undermined by public opposition, Hitler could point to the fact that he still had nearly ten million men under arms, most (around seven million) in the army and the

Hitler's optimism was down to his belief that 1000 Me 262 jet fighters were available. However, the actual numbers were far fewer, not least because his insistence that the aircraft also be used as a bomber had required design modifications, which delayed service entry.

Waffen-SS. There was still a pool of manpower that could be exploited, which seemed to demonstrate that Germany had not yet been bled white of men for the front line. He also took heart that, although Germany had been under sustained air attack for more than two years, industry was still producing war material. Clever use of dispersal of factory locations, increased working hours, an increase in the employment of slave labourers, and savage reductions in the output of goods for civilian consumption meant that the figures for industrial output were impressive. Indeed, production was increasing rather than declining: the output of fighter aircraft, weapons and ammunition would reach a peak in the autumn of 1944. All of these factors meant that Hitler still held hopes that saving the situation was possible.

In fact, Hitler had fewer grounds for optimism than he thought. Although there were still men who could be conscripted, many of these were unlikely to make the best troops. The age for conscription had been raised to sixty; those who would previously have been declared medically unfit for service were permitted to join the army's ranks; and some of the supposed 'reserve' of manpower constituted those who had once been in the services but had been invalided out, although not crippled by their wounds. Furthermore, an increasing number of soldiers at the front line were men remustered from the navy and air force. This meant that while the army gained men with considerable training and experience, very little of this was relevant to the business of land combat.

THE FAILING LUFTWAFFE

The picture of an apparently failing Anglo-American air offensive was also misleading. The need to defend the airspace above the Third Reich meant that production of aircraft had become increasingly biased towards fighters. Although bomber aircraft were still being produced, the *Luftwaffe* was becoming an ever more unbalanced body, lacking the means of supporting the army when battle was under way. There were signs that the army was becoming steadily more bitter at the lack of air support, particularly given the increasing efficacy of Allied air attack in support of ground operations. Dispersing industry was all very well, but the bombing of communications targets meant that it was increasingly difficult for larger items to reach their intended users. As far as aircraft were concerned, the higher output was more than welcome, but the *Luftwaffe* was running short of men to fly them. Although willing volunteers could be found to replace the depleted ranks of fighter pilots, there was a serious difficulty in that the new arrivals had no experience: all too many of the new pilots flew a few missions before being hacked out of the sky by enemy fighters. Hitler held great hopes for jet- and rocket-powered aircraft, notably the Me 262, but was frustrated by the delays in their service entry. No one was able to explain to him that his insistence that the Me 262 be built as a fighter-bomber rather than a pure fighter had done much to delay the programme; nor could he quite understand that the relatively nascent technology was often less reliable than the tried and tested piston-engined fighters.

Hitler's refusal to grasp the full reality of the situation meant that he felt Germany's real problem was a lack of time – a lack of time for the jet fighters to come into service, for the increased production of weapons to filter through to the front line and for the reserves of manpower to become effective. The place where time needed to be gained was in the west, since the vast expanse of the eastern front ensured it would be some time before the Russians were able to threaten any part of Germany that was vital to the continuation of the war. The Red Army was at least 500km (310 miles) away from being in a position to inflict such a crippling blow and, besides, the latest Russian offensive was beginning to lose momentum. In the east, Hitler concluded, he had time. The west was a different matter.

In the west, the Allies would shortly be able to threaten the Ruhr and its vital industrial capacity: Hitler was painfully

A German soldier peers out of a defensive position somewhere along the West Wall. Although the fortifications along the German frontier were outdated by 1944, they still posed a difficult obstacle for the Americans to bypass.

aware that losing the Ruhr would be a stunning blow from which Germany would need a miracle to recover. Taking the Ruhr, however, would not be an easy task. At this point, of course, in the first months after D-Day, German forces were successfully holding out in the French and Belgian ports, imposing a heavy logistical burden upon the allies as they advanced further away from Normandy: as Hitler first thought about an offensive, the reopening of Antwerp was more than three months away. In addition, he knew that the Allies would have to break through the West Wall. Although the fortifications were not impregnable, the West Wall consisted of substantial amounts of concrete and barbed wire, and the terrain was not the easiest upon which to conduct operations. Again, this meant that he could justifiably conclude there was time available. The difficulty was that time of itself would not be an adequate means of winning the war. Hitler may have been prone to bouts of delusion, but he was not unaware that the Allies could bide their time: their overwhelming superiority in manpower and productive capacity would allow them to gradually crush Nazi Germany. Hitler knew that time had to be supported by action; he also calculated that this action would need to be a decisive blow against the Allies, one that would change everything and bring about a peace deal that, although probably not vastly favourable to Germany, would ensure that the thousand-year Reich would not die less than a dozen years after its inception. This demanded a return to offensive operations, no matter how unwilling his generals were to see this.

Gun positions for the Atlantic Wall are constructed in the Skoda armament works in Czechoslovakia. The Germans made great use of Czech manufacturing facilities to support their armies, but even the use of such captured facilities was not enough to help them in the end.

A FATAL BLOW

The Western front was the only reasonable choice for such a blow against the Allies, given the sheer scale of operations that would be required for a decisive attack in the east. There was a further reason for Hitler's belief that the western front would provide him with an opportunity for a stunning success. He was not afraid to observe that the alliance ranged against him was the most unusual in history, dominated by two capitalist nations and one communist, states which were diametrically opposed to one another. He identified contradictions in the relationship between the United States and Britain, perceiving the former as making efforts to bring about the collapse of the British Empire, while the British were ready to do anything to protect their imperial possessions. The Russians, meanwhile,

Josef 'Sepp' Dietrich, commander of Sixth Panzer Army for the Ardennes offensive, decorates one of his soldiers. Dietrich owed his position to his years of close association with Hitler. A reasonable commander at lower levels, he was out of his depth at the army command level.

wished to see the overthrow of capitalism, making them far more obvious enemies to Britain and America than Germany. Hitler contended that the coalition facing him was artificial and that a single, decisive strike in the west would blow it apart. The western allies would, he thought, be prepared to secure a separate peace, allowing Germany to turn all its resources to crushing the communists – something that the capitalist nations would surely welcome.

This misunderstood the nature of the anti-Hitler alliance. While there was some mistrust between the British and the Americans (and even more between the Americans and the Soviet Union), the tensions between them were as nothing compared to their determination to defeat Germany. When referring to the unpleasant nature of Stalin's regime, Winston Churchill had observed that if the devil joined the Allies, he would make favourable references to him as long as he remained committed to fighting Germany. Tensions between the Allies could wait; and Hitler's simplistic view utterly failed to grasp this. Nonetheless, it inspired Hitler's thoughts towards the decisive offensive in the west: by the end of August, he knew what it was that he had to do.

CREATING THE MEANS

Since Hitler was not prepared to trust his Commander-in-Chief West, he gave Goebbels the task of finding enough

manpower to build no fewer than 25 divisions: this was hardly part of the propaganda minister's regular portfolio, but Hitler trusted Goebbels far more than he was prepared to trust army officers in the aftermath of the bomb plot. Hitler then ordered the four SS panzer divisions on the western front to leave the front line for re-equipping. He did not tell von Rundstedt why he had ordered this, but at first glance it appeared that the Führer was simply ensuring that his favourites were the first to receive new equipment. This, of course, was not Hitler's plan – he wanted the panzer divisions to form the armoured spearhead of his offensive. To control them, he created a new headquarters, the Sixth Panzer Army, headed by SS-Obergruppenführer Josef 'Sepp' Dietrich.

DIETRICH APPOINTED

Sepp Dietrich was an unlikely general officer, owing his position more to friendship with Hitler from the early days of the Nazi Party than to any great military prowess: he had reached the rank of sergeant in World War I, which had appeared to be the limit of his service career. He had then fallen in with the Nazis, taking command of Hitler's bodyguard in 1928. This was renamed the *Leibstandarte Adolf Hitler* in 1934 and had been the lead unit of the *Waffen-SS*, seeing extensive action in Poland, France and Greece before transferring to the eastern front. It had returned to the western front in time to face the invasion on 6 June, by which time Dietrich had risen to command I SS Panzer Corps. On the day after the invasion, Hitler ordered his old comrade to drive the Allies back into the sea. Dietrich was faced with an impossible task, as he had just two divisions. Rather than drive the Allies back, it was I SS Panzer Corps that was defeated, being decimated in the process. It is possible that Dietrich was already disillusioned with Hitler's leadership, but the events of 7 June 1944 seem to have confirmed his suspicions that the Führer was not a military genius. Nevertheless, he remained one of the most trusted of Hitler's generals, which made him a natural choice for the command of the vital Sixth Panzer Army (this unit was given the honorific title of Sixth SS Panzer Army in 1945, and is often referred to as such in accounts of the Battle of the Bulge, although this is strictly incorrect). There were, however, questions about his ability. Many acknowledged that Dietrich was a reasonably competent divisional commander, but felt

A lone GI walks along a woodland road in the Ardennes. It was believed that this dense forest made the area unsuitable terrain for an offensive. Certainly, it ensured that control of the road system was important, as cross-country manoeuvre was extremely difficult.

During the 1940 campaign against France, an early-model Panzer Mark IV with a short-barrelled 75mm (2.95in) gun rolls on through terrain. The fact that the commander is out of the turret suggests the photograph was taken when the threat of enemy action was negligible.

that command of an Army was a greater responsibility than he was capable of bearing; the less kind suggested that it would have been better had he remained a sergeant.

Having found his commander, Hitler now needed to find the location for his proposed masterstroke against the Allies. He did not have to look very far.

THE ARDENNES

Hitler decided that the main aim of his offensive should be the Belgian port of Antwerp. There were good reasons for this, not least the fact that the Allies had recently managed to bring it into operation, thus dramatically reducing their supply lines. Also, a drive on the city would split the British and Canadian armies from the Americans, and enable them to be destroyed. While this all sounded perfectly sensible to Hitler, it took little account of the ferocious difficulties that such a course of action would face. Hitler was not to be swayed from this dramatic objective, and this shaped the planning process. The shortest distance to Antwerp was from the German positions in the north, along the boundary between the American and British forces north of Aachen. Hitler appreciated that it would be best to give his forces the shortest possible distance to cover, but the terrain around Aachen was impossible for a swift offensive. The ground was bisected by rivers and canals – major obstacles to the tanks that were to drive through the Allied positions. This forced Hitler to look closely at the Ardennes as the area for his offensive, and he found it to his liking.

The Ardennes had been a favourable area for the Germans before, most recently in 1940, when the French high command had been stunned by the audacity of the German invasion through the woodland. The French refused to believe that such an assault was possible, given the terrain, and had devoted much (but not, as is popularly supposed, all) of their defensive planning considerations to building up the Maginot Line. Hitler thought that there was little danger of the Allies regarding the Ardennes as an area from which the enemy would launch a major offensive, and the gains to be made from an assault here appeared to be enormous. Although the terrain was restrictive for manoeuvring forces, the Germans had amply demonstrated that armour could move through the area rapidly, and Hitler had little doubt that it could do so again. There were other aspects of the Ardennes that

> The Führer spoke of the material and personnel issues... Prepare to take the offensive in November when the enemy air force cannot fly. Main point: some 25 divisions must be moved to the West in one to two months.
>
> *Generaloberst Alfred Jodl, Diary Entry 19 August 1944*

Below: German troops rush to man an 88mm (3.45in) Flak gun. The famed '88' proved lethal in the anti-tank role. Massed ranks of '88' were used during the Allied strategic air campaign against Germany – but were unable to defeat the offensive.

Right: Hitler, Keitel and Jodl make a show of studying a map for the camera. The scene suggests that the Führer is consulting with his senior officers: by 1944, however, he took less regard of the professional soldiers, and would not accept any efforts to amend his plans.

commended it for the offensive. Just over the border from the Ardennes, the forests in the German Eifel region would disguise the build-up of an attacking force from aerial reconnaissance. Once the offensive was under way, the distance to Antwerp was little more than 160km (100 miles). This relatively short distance was not the only attraction, for if the attack were successful it would cut off the British and Canadians and ensnare the American First and Ninth Armies around Aachen as well. Hitler quickly realized that if he attacked through the Ardennes, he could obtain a victory against the Anglo-American forces so decisive that they would be forced to sue for peace; the offensive would trap half the Allied forces, eliminate the imminent threat to the Ruhr and allow Hitler to turn his attention to the eastern front by withdrawing troops from the west. The prize was fantastic. Hitler decided that he would be in Antwerp within a week. His mind was set: the offensive would be in the Ardennes.

Hitler knew that this offensive would not be like that in 1940. Germany no longer possessed the advantages that it had enjoyed four years before, when France and the Low Countries had fallen with relative ease. While the *Luftwaffe* had enjoyed air superiority in 1940, it most certainly did not by autumn 1944; he was well aware that the lack of air superiority was a crippling blow to ground operations, since the Allies were able to use their fighter-bombers almost at will against columns of troops and armoured formations. Unable to depend on the much-reduced *Luftwaffe* to defend the troops on the ground from the depredations of air attack, he therefore proposed for the offensive a timing that sought to enlist a different form of defence: the weather. It would take time to refit and train the divisions needed for the offensive, which meant that the offensive would have to take place in November. This would almost certainly ensure that the Allies would be unable to fly many sorties before German troops were in Antwerp.

UTMOST SECRECY

On 25 September, Hitler held another meeting at the Wolf's Lair, where he gave out more details about his plans. The assault would be preceded by an enormous artillery barrage, followed by an infantry assault to break into the Allied lines. Once this was achieved, the first echelon of panzer divisions would pass through, driving towards the Meuse to seize the all-important bridgeheads. They would be followed by the second wave of armour, which would be followed by infantry divisions that would move to protect the flanks of the advance. Sixth Panzer Army would deliver the main effort of the offensive, while the panzer divisions of the Fifth Panzer Army, commanded by General Hasso von Manteuffel, and the infantry divisions of General der Panzertruppen Erich Brandenberger would support the operation. Hitler instructed Generaloberst Alfred Jodl, the Chief of Staff to the OKW, to conduct an analysis of the plan. As secrecy was of paramount importance, all those undertaking the analysis were forced to sign a pledge of secrecy (a breach of which would lead to execution), while von Rundstedt and the field commanders who would actually be conducting the offensive would be made aware of the plan only when necessary. This was all a little ironic, since Hitler had proudly told the Japanese ambassador that he intended to launch a large-scale offensive in the west some weeks before. The ambassador had reported this to Tokyo, little realizing that his signal would be intercepted by the Americans (although, as we shall see, their interpretation of this intelligence gift was lacking).

THE GENERAL STAFF

Although Hitler had instructed the General Staff to analyze his plan, they did not have much room to manoeuvre: their task was to mould the outline into a workable scheme that the Führer would accept. This meant that they could not reject the plan out of hand, nor could they modify it beyond recognition. There was sufficient flexibility within this relatively rigid system for them to mould an effective plan, although a key sign that all was not as it should be was the fact that, despite his status as the head of the OKW, Field Marshal Keitel was entrusted with nothing more than estimating the amount of fuel and ammunition that would be needed for the assault.

The General Staff developed Hitler's outline into a planned offensive that would begin at some point between 20 and 30 November 1944. The offensive would take place in the sector of the Ardennes between Monschau and Echternach (Luxembourg), with the initial aim of taking bridgeheads over the Meuse. From here, the offensive would aim for the ultimate objective of Antwerp. In the course of the fighting, the British and Canadians would be engaged north of the line Antwerp–Liège–Bastogne, with the intention of destroying their combat power. The staff officers concluded that, although risky, Hitler's plan was feasible and offered a good chance of success once planned fully (which was not something that could be said of all of Hitler's ideas during the war). They moulded the concept into five possible courses of action, of which the staff recommended the first two, Operation Holland and Operation Liège-Aachen, as being most likely to deliver the result Hitler wanted. Operation Holland called for a single-axis attack to be

Hitler studies a progress report as Keitel looks on. Keitel's obedience to Hitler was complemented by a tendency to tell him what he wanted to hear. These traits were among the reasons Keitel became head of the high command, not his prowess as a military commander.

launched from the Venlo area, aiming for Antwerp, while Liège-Aachen suggested a two-pronged assault on the Allies. In this scenario, the main effort would drive in a northwesterly direction from northern Luxembourg, and would then turn to meet the second attack that would be launched from the sector lying to the northwest of Aachen. Hitler was attracted to both courses of action, eventually deciding that the two-pronged assault was his preference in a meeting with Jodl on 9 October. He ordered that the staff should develop a draft plan to draw the two courses of action together. There was a serious problem, however, of which the General Staff were well aware: the resources to undertake such a plan were simply not available. Jodl was in a difficult position. On his own, he could not expect to persuade Hitler to modify the plan: for this, he needed the opposition of the field commanders, but as yet they were blissfully unaware of what the Führer had in store for them. Consequently Jodl could not call upon them to try to talk Hitler into aiming for less dramatic objectives.

Jodl therefore began to lay down the plan that would be followed for the offensive. It was to be launched on a front some 96km (60 miles) wide from Monschau (32km southeast of Aachen) to Echternach. The Sixth Panzer Army would attack between Monschau and the Losheim Gap; the Army would pass south of Liège, cross the Meuse and then head for Antwerp. On the left of the Sixth Panzer Army, the Fifth Panzer Army would attack through St Vith, cross the 'Skyline Drive' and then head for the Meuse. They would cross the river a few kilometres upstream from Namur and then turn

FIELD MARSHAL WALTHER MODEL

Walther Model was the son of a music teacher, born in 1891. He decided upon a career in the army, and was commissioned in 1909. He served in a variety of staff positions in World War I, and was invited to remain in the post-war army. Model was impressed with Hitler (as a politician, if not as a military commander) and joined the Nazi party. He was a loyal member for the rest of his life. Model commanded IV Corps in Poland, the 3rd Panzer Division in France and then XXXI Panzer Corps in the early fighting in the USSR. He was then given command of Ninth Army between 1942 and 1944, when he took over as commander of Army Group North in the Ukraine. He briefly commanded Army Group Centre from June 1944, before taking over Army Group B in August. Hitler had high regard for Model (not least since he was not from the traditional background associated with most senior officers), and his constant use of Model to deal with difficult situations led to Model's nick-name of 'the Führer's Firefighter'. Model was astute enough to appreciate that arguing with Hitler over some of his less sensible decisions rarely succeeded, and simply carried out the Führer's instructions. He did so, however, by interpreting these orders in the loosest possible sense, which meant that he could go some way toward reconciling Hitler's ideas with reality. Model continued to command his Army Group after the Battle of the Bulge was over. It was surrounded in the Ruhr pocket in April 1945, and forced to surrender. Walther Model decided that he was not going to surrender, and on 21 April 1945, he shot himself.

Field Marshal Walther Model, 'The Führer's Firefighter'. Model did not have the traditional background of a German officer; coupled with his outstanding military skills, this meant that Hitler held him in higher regard than he did most of his other generals.

to the northwest. In so doing, they would bypass Brussels and provide security for the Sixth Panzer Army's southern flank. Brandenberger's infantry-dominated Seventh Army would attack on both sides of Echternach, heading west; it too would use some of its strength to secure the southern flank.

THE FIFTEENTH ARMY MOVE

Two days after these opening moves, the Fifteenth Army was to be prepared to attack around Aachen, with the aim of pinning down any American units that were attempting to reinforce the Ardennes; if everything went to plan, though, the Fifteenth Army would continue its advance to the south, reaching the Meuse at Liège and trapping the Americans around Aachen in the process. This part of the plan was not especially detailed, and left several unanswered questions as to how the Fifteenth Army was to operate. This may have been a result of the General Staff recognizing that the question of how to defeat the one million Allied troops who were to be cut off so easily was not one to which they could give an answer, and which the Führer was happy to ignore.

The staff sent this revised plan for Hitler's scrutiny; he approved. He gave the plan the codename *Wacht am Rhein* (Watch on the Rhine) with the intent of making it sound as though the scheme was one of defence rather than attack. Jodl also sent a message to all the commanders on the western front informing them that they should work under the assumption that no offensive action would be likely, or indeed possible, for some time to come.

With this deception in place, the planning continued. It was at this point that the field commands would need to be informed, since the way in which German military planning was conducted meant that the General Staff would produce the basic outline of the plan, stating the objective and other key factors, but would leave the job of adding the fine detail to those charged with carrying out the plan. As a result, instructions were sent out to von Rundstedt and Model, requesting the presence of their respective chiefs of staff to the Wolf's Lair. The assumption in both headquarters was that Hitler intended to make clear his displeasure at the fact that the Americans had recently captured Aachen. Siegfried

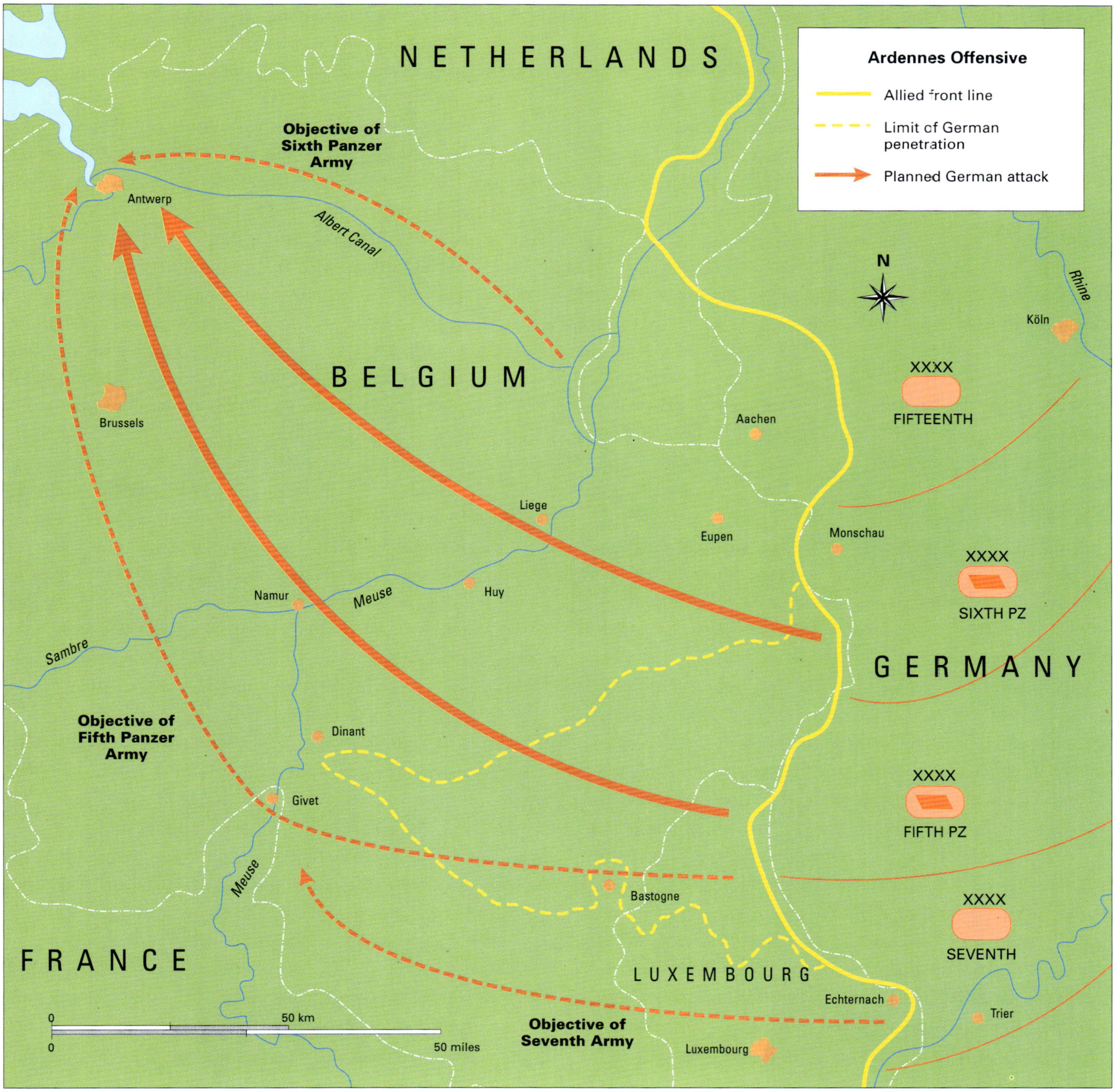

The extent of Hitler's ambitions can be fully appreciated from this map. The goal of Antwerp was unobtainable, and the resulting bulge in the Allied lines was exactly what Hitler's generals had warned him of.

Westphal duly headed to the Wolf's Lair from von Rundstedt's headquarters, while Model sent General der Infanterie Hans Krebs. They met at the entrance to the Wolf's Lair, but before they were able to proceed any further they were required to sign a security pledge. Both men were puzzled, but signed the pledge – doubtless noting the rider that anyone who broke it would be shot. They then went in to Hitler's daily situation conference, where he failed to say anything about the fall of Aachen. The conference went on as normal, but at its conclusion, 15 of the assembled party (including Krebs and Westphal) were asked to remain behind. Hitler took the floor and began to speak, laying out the details of the proposed offensive to his stunned audience.

Hitler's enthusiasm was clear – he explained that there would be 30 divisions involved, supported by at least 1500 aircraft from the *Luftwaffe*. Krebs and Westpahl were not convinced, even though Hitler's speech was inspiring and dramatic. They understood that nine of the divisions would have to be drawn from von Rundstedt's command, and would need to be withdrawn from the line, re-equipped and brought up to strength before they could be ready to take their part in an offensive. In the interim, the fight against the Allies was to be continued with great vigour, even though preparing for the offensive would mean that none of the formations to be employed in the assault in the Ardennes would be available to assist.

THE GENERALS REACT

When Krebs and Westphal returned to their respective chiefs, they were not surprised that both were appalled. Von Rundstedt acknowledged that Hitler's plan had an element of genius about it, but that was about the only good thing he had to say about it. He considered it was simply far too ambitious, noting that the plan to hold the Allies back while preparations for the attack were under way would be just the first of their difficulties. As for reaching the Meuse, von Rundstedt felt that there was little chance of this happening; if, by some incredible good fortune, they should manage this, the flanks would be more vulnerable than Hitler anticipated as the forces headed for Antwerp. Finally, Hitler seemed unable to accept that the Allies would be likely to launch a counteroffensive in response to the German attack. Based on their performance so far, there was nothing to suggest that the Allies would suddenly fall into a state of shocked paralysis, unable to react as the Germans swept to victory. All in all, von Rundstedt felt that the offensive would be likely to cause a bulge in the Allied lines, but do no more. Worse still, this limited success would be bought at the price of high casualties that the German Army could ill afford.

Reaction at Field Marshal Model's headquarters was similar. Model told Krebs that the plan did not have 'a leg to stand on' when he heard Krebs's description of what Hitler had said at the meeting. As a result, both von Rundstedt and Model began to try to find ways of adjusting the plan to fit the resources that they had available. Von Rundstedt proposed that the attack should cross the Meuse between Liège and Namur, joining with a simultaneous attack from the north (thus trapping American forces around Aachen), while Model suggested a similar scheme, but attacking in only one direction. Von Rundstedt subsequently invited Model to his headquarters, along with the three army commanders who would be involved. Dietrich, Brandenberger and von Manteuffel were astounded to learn of the plan. They talked for several hours, and it was clear that none of them was happy. Von Rundstedt and Model raised their alternative plans, both of which appeared to be much better than Hitler's grand scheme. Von Rundstedt concluded the meeting by telling Model to resolve the differences between their two plans, so as to enable them to approach Hitler with coherent – and, it was to be hoped, persuasive – opposition. This was a significant move since, although Model was nominally under von Rundstedt's command, the two men had little time for one another. Von Rundstedt appreciated that he was himself a figurehead, complaining that the only thing he had any control over was the changing of the guard outside his HQ; Model understood this, since his status as a Field Marshal gave him the right to approach Hitler without any reference to his nominal commander. In effect, Model could operate independently of von Rundstedt, although the two men took care to observe the formalities that were appropriate to their supposed relationship. As if to demonstrate that the two were, for once, of the same mind, Model responded to von Rundstedt's directive by altering his plan so that it was almost the same as that of the Commander-in-Chief West's.

On 3 November, Jodl visited Model's headquarters, where he was assailed by von Rundstedt, Model and von Manteuffel (invited by Model to add weight to their objections), each pointing out the problems inherent in the plan. Von Manteuffel told Jodl that, although he was confident the Meuse could be reached, it would depend upon everything going to plan, and would require that the Seventh Army be greatly strengthened. Although Jodl may have sympathized, he told the men that Hitler's plan was 'irrevocable'. This was confirmed a week later when Hitler issued the formal operational directive for *Wacht am Rhein*; it was identical to his original plan. Hitler fended off another attempt by von Rundstedt and Model to modify the plan, but he did agree to postpone the attack from 25 November to 10 December when it became clear that preparations could not be completed in such a short space of time. Von Rundstedt made one final effort. On 2 December he sent Westphal, von Manteuffel and Hitler's old friend Dietrich to a meeting at the State Chancery in Berlin, hoping that they might change Hitler's mind. This objective was not realized. Dietrich said nothing, while von Manteuffel was able to secure only some minor changes to the plan at a tactical level. The only alteration that Hitler would allow was to change the name of the plan from *Wacht am Rhein* to *Herbstnebel* (Autumn Mist), the name for Model's alternative scheme. The die was cast: the Ardennes offensive would take place according to Hitler's conception, not that of his generals.

German tank crews look up at the sound of an aircraft. The extent of Allied air superiority meant that the movement of the supplies had to take place in bad weather, at night, or through heavily forested areas so that enemy air reconnaissance did not reveal the increased rail activity.

THEORY VS REALITY

This presented von Rundstedt with a number of problems. As noted in Chapter One, the Allies were hardly idle when Hitler was planning his masterstroke in the Ardennes. This meant that there would be a considerable gap between the theoretical strength of the forces assigned to Operation Herbstnebel and their actual order of battle when the campaign began. Hitler's plan suggested that an impressive array of forces would be engaged in the offensive. There would be four armies, eleven army corps, fifteen motorized or mechanized divisions and twenty-three infantry divisions. To support them, there would be nine artillery corps and seven brigades equipped with rocket artillery (the famed *Nebelwerfer*). This sounded impressive, but von Rundstedt and his subordinates could be forgiven for wondering exactly where these forces would be coming from. To take the Fifteenth Army as an example, its assignment to the offensive meant that, on paper, six divisions were added to the attacking force. Since it was already engaged around Aachen,

German workers unload fuel from rail wagons, while debris from air raids litters the ground. By 1944, the Germans were desperately short of fuel for aircraft and armoured vehicles, and by the end of the war, much of the Luftwaffe was grounded for want of gasoline.

however, it would not be able to join the battle until the Allied forces facing it had reacted to the offensive and headed to reinforce other units. The Fifteenth Army, therefore, could send its divisions into the fray only once the Allies had moved away significant numbers of their troops. In addition, the definition of what constituted a division had become rather more flexible by late 1944. Two of the Fifteenth Army's divisions had been merged to provide one unit that was somewhere near proper strength. The 49th Infantry Division had been absorbed by the 246th Volksgrenadier Division, and had ceased to exist. This would have been unremarkable had the General Staff removed the formation from their lists, but they did not. Thus, the Fifteenth Army was credited with one more division than it actually possessed. The 89th Infantry Division still existed, but could muster only enough men to form a battalion. The obvious course of action – suggested by both von Rundstedt's staff and officers at Army Group B headquarters – was to disband the unit and move the men elsewhere to fill gaps in the line in other formations. However, Hitler turned down the recommendation. As a result, the 89th Infantry Division appeared on the plan as being a full-strength division, when it was actually able to carry out only the tasks of a much smaller formation.

Further administrative sleight of hand occurred with the panzer divisions. The 21st Panzer and 17th SS Panzergrenadier divisions had been engaged in action since June, and had not

> If we had had ten more good divisions, we might have thrown you over the Meuse, but how we could have held the big salient thus created is not clear. Our strategic position would have been worse rather than better.
>
> *Generaloberst Alfred Jodl, Head of the OKW, interviewed 1945*

been withdrawn from the line. They had been so badly weakened by the fighting that their combined strength was below that of a single division. Nonetheless, they appeared on the plan as two panzer divisions. The 10th SS Panzer Division was heavily engaged around Aachen and its strength was considerably reduced. Model attempted to remove it from the line for rest and re-equipment, but was forbidden to do so since the proposed replacement unit was assigned to *Wacht am Rhein*. Since 10th SS Panzer Division was also meant to be employed in the offensive, yet another formation would be operating well below its paper strength. Nor was this the end of the problem: although von Rundstedt, Model and other senior officers were deeply suspicious about the veracity of the order of battle for the offensive, they were unable to make this clear in the orders that were circulated to lower formations. In their turn, these formations made plans on the assumption that the troop lists were accurate.

> Should the attack be stopped at the Meuse due to lack of reserves, the only result will be a bulge in the line and not the destruction of sizeable enemy forces.
>
> *Field Marshal Walther Model, 23 November 1944*

All of this was bad enough, but the Allies simply added to the difficulties by continuing to attack. Within hours of the US Third Army launching an attack on 8 November, Hitler had sent a signal reminding von Rundstedt that he was not to

Pilots of P-51 Mustang fighter aircraft of the US Army Air Force are briefed before a bomber escort mission over Germany. The provision of escorts meant that the Luftwaffe found it difficult to engage the bomber formations, and suffered severe losses.

call upon those units assigned to *Wacht am Rhein,* even if this meant that his forces had to fall back. This was all very well, but von Rundstedt was painfully aware that the attack around Metz risked splitting the German First and Nineteenth Armies. He felt that his only option was to retain at the front some of the panzer units intended to be sent for rest and refit; by 21 November the situation had deteriorated further, and the Panzer Lehr Division was ordered from its assembly area to lead a counterattack (which was later called off). The American attack meant that two of the divisions assigned to *Wacht am Rhein* were caught up in the fighting before they were able to leave the front line, while the Panzer Lehr Division had also been badly mauled by the time it was sent back to its assembly area.

The beginning of the Third Battle of Aachen on 16 November caused even more difficulties, and Model was forced to deploy his only reserves, the XLVIII Panzer Corps: this, of course, was to little effect, since Aachen fell shortly afterwards. Von Rundstedt was left in a situation where the need to despatch reserves was so great that he would draw upon those units kept in reserve for the offensive, send them into battle for a few days and then withdraw them. The fighting also meant that the ammunition stocks reserved for *Wacht am Rhein* were depleted as desperate commanders were forced to break into them. By early December, von Rundstedt and Model were even more convinced that the grand objectives for *Wacht am Rhein* were unattainable. Model went as far as to suggest that the plan be reduced in size, only for Hitler to send a reassuring message that the promised units would be made available. From where, and by what means, he did not say.

TINKERING WITH THE PLAN

The Allied attacks meant that it was impossible to prepare the units for the offensive in the proposed timescale, even after Hitler had agreed to move the date from 25 November to 10 December. On 7 December it became clear that the attack would have to be delayed for a few more days. Goebbels had been reasonably successful in forming new divisions from a

Along the German frontier during autumn 1944, two American tanks pass a knocked-out German assault gun. The Ardennes offensive delayed the advance into Germany, even though the Allies continued their attack around the Roer river area for the first hours of the attack.

mix of sailors and airmen transferred to the army and those who had previously been exempt from call up, but the process had been slow. Some final preparations were still needed, and it seemed wise to allow a little extra time. In addition, there were worrying reports about the fuel situation. The armoured and mechanized units had consumed more fuel than had been estimated, and there was a need to replenish their stocks. These factors conspired to push the start date back to 14 December. It became clear that even more time was required, and the date was then postponed another 48 hours to 16 December. Even at these late stages, the plan was not fixed. On 8 December, Hitler suddenly displayed enthusiasm for a vague idea put forward by Model that paratroops should be dropped behind Monschau to seize the road leading across the upland region of the Hautes Fagnes. This would provide a blocking force that would prevent American reinforcements from moving into the battle zone until Dietrich's units joined them. For this task, Hitler decreed that a battalion of more than a thousand men was required.

Troops from a German anti-tank squad pass an abandoned Sherman tank. Note the assortment of weaponry: at the rear, a Panzerfaust rocket; two MP40s,; and a Raketenpanzerbüsche, *better known as the* Panzerschreck *('Tank Terror'), which could knock out any Allied tank.*

This was a more difficult task than Hitler imagined. After the staggeringly high losses inflicted upon German paratroops in Crete, they had been used purely in an infantry role. This in turn meant that many of the paratroops had not, in fact, learned to jump out of aircraft. The commander selected for the mission, Oberstleutnant Friedrich August Freiherr von der Heydte, pointed out that finding his men was going to be a particularly difficult task. Hitler responded by ordering that every parachute unit should send its 100 best men to join the force. This, of course, was almost guaranteed to ensure that commanding officers went around selecting misfits, troublemakers and poor soldiers for the new force. Von der Heydte could at least count on 250 men who had been under his command before, and whose regard for him was such that they descended on his battalion asking to be included in the mission. Using Hitler's decree, von der Heydte managed to retain all 250: if they were that eager to participate, he reasoned that he could rely on them.

This was about the only cheering news for von der Heydte. When he reported to Dietrich, he found that the commander of Sixth Panzer Army was rather drunk, and not open to persuasion. Dietrich was concerned that a parachute drop would destroy the element of surprise, and told von der Heydte that the drop would have to take place just before the ground assault began. Von der Heydte was horrified and pointed out that this would mean that his men were dropping at night onto moorland broken up by heavily wooded areas. This was a formidable proposition for a trained unit, but it seemed almost impossible given that many of his men would have made perhaps only a single practice jump by the time of the attack. Dietrich would not accept a request to reconsider, and von der Heydte was forced to head back to his men and to try to provide them with at least some of the skills that they would require.

FINAL PREPARATIONS

The final part of the planning process, of course, was the positioning of the required forces opposite the area from which they would launch their attack. As noted above, the fact that many of the units required for the offensive had to be thrown into battle as the Americans advanced greatly hindered German preparations. It is true that the German railway system was capable of dealing with the burden placed upon it as units were moved around, but this was no simple process. Men, tanks and artillery – and associated supporting equipment – had to be moved to the concentration area from East Prussia, the Netherlands, Norway, Denmark, Austria and Poland (a sign of just how thinly spread German manpower

Below: A Panther is prepared for transit to the holding area just behind the front. Of the German tanks used in the offensive, the Panther was probably most effective. It did not have the manoeuvrability problems of the Tigers, and was better armed and armoured than the Panzer IV.

Right: A railway line takes a direct hit from air attack. The Allied campaign against rail movement was a serious hindrance to the Germans. Hence a carefully worked-out plan was needed to move equipment for the Ardennes offensive without being spotted by Allied reconnaissance.

was at this time). In a number of cases, some of the forces assigned to the assault had to be conveyed away from the front line to enable them to rest and re-equip, before being moved on to the concentration area. All of this depended on the rail network in Germany, the efficient administration and operation of which could not be questioned. The German Army had come to regard rail as its key mode of transport, and for good reason. Germany was not short of coal, and its industrialization in the last years of the nineteenth century had seen enormous amounts of rail-related construction. The railways were militarized (many of the routes were laid down following instructions from the General Staff rather than being the result of civilian requirements) and they ran at high levels of efficiency. Although Allied air attacks had inflicted enormous levels of damage and destruction to its rolling stock, the sheer scale of the German state railway meant that these losses could be made up.

What the railway management could not do, however, was to control the level of Allied air attacks on its facilities. Fortunately for the Germans, Allied policy decisions meant that the railways were not the highest priority for bomber forces. British and American bomber leaders were never able to agree about which were the best target sets for their forces. Air Chief Marshal Sir Arthur Harris, the Air Officer Commanding-in-Chief of RAF Bomber Command, was convinced that bombing key German cities would bring about the collapse of the German war effort, while his US counterparts contended that attacking oil targets would create the same result. Transportation targets were not regarded as being of primary importance, and prior to D-Day Eisenhower had implied that he would resign if the bomber commanders continued to resist his wishes that transportation targets be hit. (The threat worked – the bomber leaders appreciated that, given a choice between them or the Supreme Commander, the politicians would find in favour of him). Although Harris remained deeply sceptical about the value of transport targets until his dying day, Bomber Command was therefore compelled to place them reasonably high on its list of priorities. The Americans remained convinced that oil targets were the best option. Indeed, railways were given lower priority than ordnance depots and motor vehicle production, and it took considerable pressure from the British to raise railway targeting to the second priority, behind oil.

PANZERKAMPFWAGEN IV MEDIUM TANK

The Panzerkampfwagen (PzKpfw IV or just 'Panzer Mark IV') served the German army all through World War II, undergoing continual upgrading in its main armament and armour protection. Some 9000 were built, and it was the most commonly encountered German tank, in contrast to the popular myth that almost all German tanks by 1944 were either Panthers or Tigers. The Panzer IV's 75mm (2.95in) main gun may have been the same calibre as that found on the Sherman, but it was notably more powerful. The sheer versatility of the Panzer IV's chassis meant that it was able to take the inevitable increase in weight as improvements were added, and this ensured that it remained an effective fighting vehicle until the end of the war.

PROTECTING THE LOCOMOTIVES

This meant that the Germans were given a degree of leeway in their rail operations: they were able to move the equivalent of 66 divisions before the Ardennes offensive. Air attack impinged on these movements on 27 occasions, but the delays imposed did not last for more than two days. Some of the units being moved lost equipment, and this would inevitably have some effect on their performance during the battle; it did not prevent them from reaching the battle zone, though. Some measures to deal with the threat of air attack against the trains themselves were put in place: to force the pilots of fighter-bombers to attack from higher altitude (with a loss of accuracy), all trains were provided with light flak guns, while the cabs of the trains were armoured to protect the crews from machine-gun fire and bomb fragments. This apparently obvious step was most important, since it had been noted that air attacks on trains often left the locomotive virtually intact, but the crew dead: without them the train (self-evidently) could not continue.

These measures were, however, last-ditch attempts to deal with air attack. The primary solution adopted was to try to avoid exposing the locomotives to attack in the first place. The majority of rail traffic was sent out at night or when the weather precluded flying operations – to assist this, the local rail stations were given links to the meteorological service so that they could react quickly to changes in the weather. To add to this strategy, the Germans were able to benefit from the heavily wooded country in the Eifel area, which prevented movement, and the fact that the rail lines went through a large number of tunnels. Careful control of train movement ensured that the Allies were unable to impose crippling damage on the network, and units and equipment

German soldiers move along the line of a barbed wire fence, early on 17 December 1944. The low-lying mist that helped disguise their movements is obvious in this picture, and meant that infiltration tactics gave the Germans an element of surprise.

were able to move to the front relatively swiftly. This should not be taken as indicating that ingenuity completely defeated Allied air attacks on the rail network: the attacks were a factor, and caused delay in the delivery of some crucial stocks. The amount of fuel and ammunition required for the offensive was enormous, and the delay and dislocation imposed on the rail networks by air attack meant that not all of this was able to get through. At this point, ammunition stocks were not greatly below the intended levels, but it must be recalled that the planning counted on a rapid advance, rather than fighting for any period: if more fighting occurred than had been anticipated (if the attack was held up in a certain sector, for example), ammunition consumption would be greater and the lack of munitions would begin to make itself felt.

Fuel and lubricants were similar problems, but by the 16 December the 4.5 million gallons required were available. That said, half of this was held in fuel dumps near to the Rhine rather than readily available to the troops. Between September and 15 December, the main concentration area received just over 2000 trainloads of troops and supplies. A remarkable achievement, this pushed the Eifel rail system to the brink of saturation: on 17 December von Rundstedt's staff had to order the reserve divisions to disembark on the west bank of the Rhine. This meant that they were further away from the fighting area than desirable, with implications for the success of the operation if they were required quickly. By the evening of 15 December, the last of the units committed to the opening assault were moving to their start lines. They were understrength, lacked equipment (or employed a sometimes bewildering variety of up to date, obsolescent or captured equipment), lacked fuel and lubricants, and were short of ammunition. They had one advantage: surprise.

Malmedy
Vith 8

CHAPTER THREE

ATTACK VERSUS DEFENCE

The Allies were aware that the Germans might stage a counterattack, but were confident they would be able to repel it. Intelligence suggested that the enemy would be hard-pressed to muster the forces needed for a major assault, and the Allies seemed to enjoy the initiative, attacking almost at will along the front. It was dangerous to underestimate the Germans, however. Their weapons and equipment were equal to those of the Allies, and in some regards, superior. They also had one key advantage: surprise.

A KEY REASON for choosing the Ardennes as the area to launch the offensive was that it would have the benefit of surprise. German forces were not strong enough to keep the Allies otherwise engaged by diversionary attacks, so they had to rely upon deception to keep the Allies off guard. They would also be helped by the failure of Allied intelligence to piece together the clues pointing to a concentration of German strength in the Ardennes. The intelligence staffs came tantalizingly near to appreciating what was about to happen, but did not make the necessary connections in time.

THE INTELLIGENCE PICTURE

Cynics often claim that the term 'military intelligence' is an oxymoron, but this is both unfair and misleading. Those responsible for ascertaining the enemy's dispositions and

Two members of Kampfgruppe Peiper on the road to Malmedy, posing for propaganda purposes. In the background are SdKfz 251 half-tracked armoured personnel carriers. The SdKfz was an extremely versatile vehicle, of which no fewer than 22 variants were produced.

plans face formidable obstacles if their opponents have any conception of the importance of operational security. During World War II, the Allies had the tremendous advantage of being able to read German signals thanks to the work of the British code-breaking centre at Bletchley Park. The Germans remained convinced that their Enigma encoding machines were invulnerable to cryptoanalysts, and cheerfully carried on dispatching top secret signals through a means that had been 'cracked' some time before. Despite this disadvantage, however, the Germans were generally good at signals security and fully aware of the benefits of deception. This meant that it was not always easy to place the Enigma decryptions into the correct context. This must be recalled when considering the way in which the Allied intelligence organization seemed to be befuddled by German plans for the Battle of the Bulge – indeed, it is not inappropriate to observe that the context in which operations are conducted will influence the deductions being made. This was certainly the case in autumn 1944.

THE HIGH COMMAND

In early September 1944, the Combined Chiefs of Staff in Washington began considering plans for bringing the war to a conclusion before the year was out. After some deliberation they were confident that they had a solution and informed Gen George C Marshall, the US Army's Chief of Staff. Marshall wrote to Eisenhower to inform him that plans for another major offensive were in hand. Eisenhower responded that he was in broad agreement with the sentiments of the Chiefs of Staff, but that he had some doubts as to whether their plans would be practicable. He noted that the Allies were having logistic problems thanks to the continued difficulties in securing Antwerp: as noted in Chapter One, the Germans held on to this vital port for some time, making the logistic situation much more awkward for the Allies. Eisenhower's reply convinced Marshall that the time was not yet propitious for another all-out assault on the Germans, and he decreed that planning should not advance further. The proposed memorandum to Eisenhower laying down the basic framework for the offensive was never issued.

The assessment of strategy was not vested in the Chiefs of Staff alone. In the European theatre, consideration of the steps required to bring about the final collapse of Germany was under way. Eisenhower had always felt that the best way to strike at the heart of Germany was to do so from the

GENERAL DWIGHT D EISENHOWER

Eisenhower's career began slowly, but culminated with his election as President of the United States in 1952. Eisenhower was born to a relatively poor family in Denison, Texas on 14 October 1890. He attended the US Military Academy at West Point, where he excelled as a sportsman. After graduating in 1915, Eisenhower held a number of training positions, and did not see service during World War I. His lack of combat experience did not hold him back, and he was clearly destined for high rank after graduating at the top of his class at the Command and General Staff School in 1926. By the outbreak of World War II, he was a Brigadier General. He did not remain in this rank for long, being promoted during the course of 1942, when he took command of the European Theatre of Operations and US Forces in Europe. Eisenhower commanded Operation Torch and then the Allied forces in the invasion of Sicily. At the end of 1943, he was appointed as Supreme Commander, Allied Expeditionary Forces in preparation for the invasion of Normandy.

Once the invasion had taken place, Eisenhower took control of ground operations as well, while retaining the supreme commander's position. His strategy of attacking all along the front came in for heavy criticism, most notably from Field Marshal Bernard Montgomery. It also meant that General Patton was denied the resources he needed for a swift drive on Germany, a further cause for contention. Nevertheless, the strategy is generally held to have been the correct one, and Eisenhower's diplomatic skills in handling his more volatile commanders cannot be ignored. Once the war was over, Eisenhower commanded the Allied occupation forces in Germany until December 1945, when he returned to the United States to become the Army Chief of Staff. He held this position until 1948, when he retired to become the President of Columbia University. He was not in this post for long, since he was recalled by President Truman in December 1950, so that he could become the first Supreme Allied Commander in Europe in the aftermath of the establishment of NATO. Eisenhower stood down from this position when he became a candidate for President. He won the presidential elections of 1952 and 1956, and oversaw a massive build up in America's armed forces as the Cold War became ever more serious. Eisenhower retired from public life when his second term concluded, and died after a long illness in 1969.

General George Marshall, the head of the United States Army, arrives for a meeting with Generals Middleton and Patton. President Roosevelt initially chose Marshall as the supreme allied commander in Europe, but realized that his services in Washington were too valuable to lose.

north, driving through the industrial heartlands of the Ruhr. He had incorporated this into his plan of campaign, which began with the landings in Normandy. The first phases of the plan had been achieved, but there was now disagreement on how best to continue with the campaign. The fifth phase of the plan was for Allied forces to wear down the German forces prior to phase six – the destruction of the German forces west of the Rhine before crossing the river in strength. It was here that the contention started, with Field Marshal Montgomery leading the opposition to Eisenhower's concept of operations. In short, Eisenhower wished to carry the attack to the enemy in both the north and to the south. The forces in the north, under Montgomery, would be given priority for supplies, while those in the south (driving towards the Saar) would have to accept that their needs would be secondary. Montgomery, however, felt that this was inappropriate. He wanted all resources to be concentrated in the north, ensuring that the main effort wanted for nothing. Montgomery was not alone in having doubts about the validity of attacking in strength in more than one place on the front, since the British Chief of the Imperial General Staff, Field Marshal Alan Brooke, was equally unconvinced about Eisenhower's strategy. The principle of attacking in more than one place continued, for, as Montgomery's 21st Army Group began to clear German forces from its sector to the west of the Meuse river, the American First and Ninth Armies began a drive towards Cologne. The US Third Army, meanwhile, headed for the Saar. This seems to have made Montgomery even less patient with Eisenhower's concept of operations, and his complaints to Brooke increased. Finally Brooke went to Churchill to inform him that the strategy of attacking all along the front was unsound (he described it as 'sheer madness'). Brooke also suggested that Eisenhower was overburdened with his dual functions as Supreme Commander and land component commander, and contended that there should be two army groups rather than the three then extant.

This almost accorded with Montgomery's thinking, apart from Brooke's suggestion that Bradley ought to be the land commander: Montgomery clearly had designs on this position himself, whereas Brooke recognized that the American preponderance in the theatre meant that the land commander would have to be an American rather than a British general. Eisenhower attempted to resolve the existing differences with a conference at Maastricht on 7 December 1944, but he was unable to persuade Montgomery of the validity of his approach of attacking all along the line in the effort to wear down the enemy.

This debate is of importance when considering Allied preparedness (or the lack of it) for the Battle of the Bulge, for it demonstrates the way in which the Allies perceived the situation as 1944 drew to a close.

PERCEPTIONS

Although there were obviously disputes among the Allies as to how best to win the war, these were never based on fears that the war would be lost; rather the question was one of how to win most expeditiously and with the fewest possible casualties. The Germans were still acknowledged as difficult opponents, but towards the end of 1944 there were many who thought that the German armies were on the verge of

Major General Sir Frederick Morgan and General Sir Bernard Montgomery in 1943. Morgan was appointed Chief of Staff to the Supreme Allied Commander (COSSAC) in 1943, drawing up the first plans for the invasion of Europe. His role in D-Day was critical but often ignored.

An M7 105mm (4.1in) self-propelled gun, in a posed picture in which crew-members sit in their travelling positions. The M7 was built upon the chassis of an M3 or M4 medium tank, and provided extremely effective fire support, being rarely (if ever) used in the assault gun role.

collapse. The results of the American offensive that began on 16 November might have been viewed as a warning that this was not the case – three weeks of fighting produced nearly 125,000 American casualties. Even these signs of resistance could be given a positive interpretation, however, and many Allied planners argued that such heavy fighting must have told much more upon the already-stretched Germans. Events to come would demonstrate that these interpretations were optimistic, but it is important to remember that they were not groundless.

At Supreme Headquarters Allied Expeditionary Forces (SHAEF), Maj Gen Kenneth Strong, the head of intelligence, noted that the fighting was costing the Germans the equivalent of a division of men every few days. With such losses, the German reserves were being thrown into battle on one front, and then moved elsewhere to assist against another onslaught. Such 'fire-fighting' meant that the reserves were suffering ongoing attrition, and the constant movement of the forces without respite meant that the men were inevitably suffering from fatigue.

There were other grounds for believing that the Germans were close to collapse. The offensive around Aachen had been met with a lacklustre response, and the intelligence officer to the US First Army noted that the German defences were clearly declining in strength. He suggested that the weight of Allied attacks might even lead to large-scale surrenders, and that steps should be put in hand to deal with the logistical problems associated with handling large numbers of prisoners of war. This was a surprising comment from an officer otherwise known to be a pessimist.

> On the morning of 16th December, I felt in need of relaxation. So I decided to fly up to Eindhoven in my Miles light aircraft, land on one of the fairways of the golf course, and play a few holes of golf… But our game was soon interrupted by a message to say that the Germans had launched a heavy attack that morning on the front of the First American Army…
>
> *Field Marshal Viscount Montgomery*

MUTUAL MISTRUST

The intelligence chief in question was Col Benjamin 'Monk' Dickson. He had served with the US Army during World War I, but had decided against taking a full-time commission at the conclusion of the conflict, correctly deducing that promotion prospects would be slim. Instead he embarked upon a successful civilian career while maintaining a reserve commission. He had specialized in intelligence work and his rise had followed that of Gen Bradley. However, when Bradley was appointed to command 12th Army Group, Dickson did not go with him: the 12th Army Group had been provided with its own ready-made intelligence staff, and Dickson remained at the First Army with Bradley's successor, Lt Gen Courtney Hodges. This created problems for the intelligence system, since it appears that the First Army staff regarded those at 12th Army Group with some disfavour. They were not slow to note that, while Dickson had a background in intelligence, the chief of the Army Group's intelligence staff, Brig Gen Edwin Sibert, was an artilleryman by profession. Dickson was at pains to reject any suggestions of animosity between the two, but there is enough evidence to suggest that a certain degree of tension existed between the staffs. Just as the First Army's intelligence officers were unimpressed with the newcomers, the staff at 12th Army Group had their doubts about the First Army. They came to regard Dickson as an alarmist, basing this belief on his propensity to list German divisions as being on the western front solely on the basis that they were no longer on the eastern front: it seemed as though Dickson forgot about the possibility of such units being in the rear areas, refitting after hard fighting against the Red Army, or even of the division having temporarily ceased to exist as a result of casualties sustained. There were one or two instances where units reported as being on the western front by the First Army staff were known to be elsewhere. Whether this was the result of Dickson being alarmist or merely overcautious was a moot point: 12th Army Group was minded to downplay almost automatically some of Dickson's assessments as soon as they arrived. This mistrust might have been overcome had there been better communications between the intelligence staffs of First Army and 12th Army Group: remarkably, there was little. Dickson and his staff tended to share information with the intelligence staff of Montgomery's 21st Army Group more frequently than they did with 12th Army Group, even though they were very much in the 12th Army Group chain of command.

General Eisenhower (left) chats with Lieutenant General Bradley (right, commander of the 12th Army Group) and Major General Louis A Craig (commander of the 9th Infantry Division) during a visit to Butgenbach, Belgium, just before the Ardennes offensive began.

Despite these difficulties, and Dickson's tendency towards pessimism notwithstanding, there were some areas of agreement between the two staffs. One of these was the unspoken supposition that a German attack in the Ardennes was most unlikely given the situation on the front and the simple fact that the area did not appear to offer anything of strategic importance to the Germans. After all, why should a battered army nearing defeat launch an attack in an area that contained nothing of importance to it?

Despite this not unreasonable point of view, it should not be thought that the Allied high command was without concerns regarding the Ardennes. Eisenhower was well aware that the Ardennes front was thinly held, and made worried noises from time to time about the dangers of a German attack, especially given their past

A Tiger tank is prepared for transportation to the front. The offensive required a large amount of armour, but the Eastern front also had its needs. As a result, the armour available to the three German armies varied: Seventh Army, for instance, had negligible armoured support.

penchant for launching attacks in this area. The other Allied generals who shared this concern included Bradley and Maj Gen Troy Middleton, the commander of VIII Corps, which was assigned to holding the front. Middleton was uncomfortable about the length of front assigned to his three divisions, since it stretched across a distance that could be held only relatively lightly. Given the general view of the state of the German forces, however, and the apparently low probability of attack, little was done.

FINDING CLUES

The clues to German preparation were there, of course, but finding them and then interpreting them was not an easy task. The first hints of events on the western front came from Bletchley Park. On 18 September 1944, staff there began to decipher a message about Sixth Panzer Army and the withdrawal of a number of units (including several SS units) from the front line. The message took some time to decode and it was nine days before its contents were revealed and passed on. Other signals were intercepted giving details of the withdrawal of units from the front line – one, from the middle of October, made clear that Sixth Panzer Army was the OKW reserve, placing it under Hitler's control rather than von Rundstedt's. The failure to appreciate fully the implications of this played a notable part in what was to follow. Also, while Bletchley Park picked up regular messages referring to Sixth Panzer Army from the start of October, intelligence staffs began to take notice of the formation only in November. The question facing them, of course, was whether the Germans planned a counterattack using the new formation and, if they did, where it would fall. Sibert argued that the Germans would attack against the First and Third Armies once they had broken through enemy lines and were heading towards the Rhine and the Ruhr. Strong agreed with this general assessment, and having seen the decryption of

Baron Oshima's signal to Tokyo (following his meeting with Hitler) he was convinced that any attack would take place in November. Had German preparations followed the unrealistic timetable laid down by Hitler, he would, of course, have been quite correct in this assessment. The intelligence staffs were now beginning to concur that the Germans would seek to launch some kind of offensive. Unfortunately, they were no nearer to divining where it would take place.

Strong, Sibert and Dickson were in general accord by 20 November that the Germans would counterattack around Cologne once the Americans had crossed the Roer river. It seemed certain that Sixth Panzer Army would be used for the attack, and information gathered about Fifth Panzer Army suggested that it too might play a part. There were, however, other signs about German preparations, and these did not fit in with the accepted pattern of what was likely to occur.

Both Bletchley Park and aerial reconnaissance sorties began to pick up signs that the Germans were organizing

General Bradley, Major-General Troy Middleton and Major General Matthew Ridgway. Ridgway, commander of the 82nd Airborne division, always carried two grenades on his webbing, arguing that he might need them. Events at Arnhem suggested he had a point.

much heavier rail traffic in the Eifel than they had done for some time. In addition, interception of signals laying down the priorities for German aerial reconnaissance bore no resemblance to the pattern of reconnaissance that would be required for a counterattack in the Cologne area. The signals revealed that the *Luftwaffe* had been instructed to pay attention to the areas around Eupen, Malmédy and the Meuse river crossings, none of which was anywhere near the proposed counterattack. This raised the question of why these areas were of such interest, but the link between the reconnaissance missions and the likely threat to the Ardennes was not established.

The Jagdpanther was one of the finest armoured vehicles to see service during the war, even though the lack of a turret meant that the traverse of its main gun was limited. It was fortunate for the Allies that production was badly affected by bombing, limiting the number available.

RECOGNIZING THE THREAT

While the signs may not have been adequately interpreted by the Allies, concern over the Ardennes increased in the last ten days of November. Although the Ardennes region was not part of the Third Army's area of operations at the time, the southern part of the Eifel would be in the path of its projected advance. As a result, Gen Patton was eager to ensure that his intelligence staff gained a full picture of what was going on in the region. His intelligence chief, Col Oscar W Koch, began to study the German dispositions in the area and soon became concerned. By 24 November his misgivings had been transmitted to Patton, who made a point of noting his view that the Germans were building up opposite VIII Corps; by 9 December Koch was so concerned that he laid on a special briefing for his commander.

At the briefing, Koch told Patton that the Germans had taken at least 13 divisions out of the line, many of them from the SS (regarded as among the fiercest opponents because of their dedication to Nazism), while another three were known to be heading for the Eifel area from Scandinavia. Koch assessed that the German dispositions pointed to one of two conclusions: either they would employ their newly arrived forces to meet American attacks, or they might even launch an attack themselves, probably in the area around the Roer river, although Koch could not be certain.

Koch was not alone in being concerned about the enemy concentration in the Eifel. 'Monk' Dickson became alarmed when a signal calling for English-speaking volunteers to join a special unit was intercepted: he was convinced that such a unit would be employed for the purposes of sabotage in an offensive. This led him to the conclusion that the Germans might, perhaps, be desperate enough to launch such an assault, and he set about drawing up an intelligence estimate to put across his views. The document, Estimate 37, became a particularly controversial document, since Dickson would later claim that it provided enough information for commanders to work out that the Germans would shortly begin offensive operations in the Ardennes. In fact, although Dickson drew attention to an offensive, he said that the focal point of the attack would be somewhere between Roermond and Schleiden, and thus well to the north of the Ardennes. Dickson presented the document on 10 December. As more information appeared over the next few days, his concerns increased and he began to change his mind as to the location of the offensive. On 14 December, VIII Corps reported that a Belgian woman, who was believed to be a credible source of

JAGDPANTHER

The Jagdpanther represented a break with convention in that it marked a shift from the policy where tank destroyers were conversions or improvisations of existing tank designs, instead being purpose-built on the best available chassis. This happened to be that of the Panther tank, which led to the name of the new vehicle. With an 88mm gun, it could knock out any Allied tank, and proved to be a superb fighting vehicle.

Panzer Mark IV tanks on the advance. Although outnumbered, the German tank force inflicted serious casualties upon the Allies. The Mark IV entered production before the outbreak of war, but remained a viable tank thanks to a series of upgrades.

information, had reported the build-up of German forces opposite the Ardennes. That evening, at the First Army staff meeting, Dickson dramatically stated that the offensive would be in the Ardennes; despite the stir this caused, he was not able to argue his case further. After the meeting he set out for Paris to take four days' leave. Dickson had not taken any proper leave for six months, and there were those who argued that much of his controversial and 'alarmist' intelligence reports stemmed from him working without a break since the Normandy landings. Whether this was correct or not, Dickson certainly deserved a short rest.

At 12th Army Group headquarters, Brig Gen Sibert was also increasingly puzzled and concerned by intercepts from Bletchley Park stating that the *Luftwaffe* had been ordered to reconnoitre the Meuse crossings. He immediately sent his deputy, Col William H Jackson, to London to obtain as much information as he could about these reports, but Jackson was unable to unearth any additional information. A discussion with his terrain expert, Maj Ralph Ingersoll, only deepened Sibert's concerns. Ingersoll, who had been studying German rail movements further south in the region of Bitburg, suggested that the Germans might in fact be building up their forces in the region by the simple expedient of withdrawing two divisions at a time and replacing them with three new divisions. It would be a relatively simple procedure to hide the third division from the Allies by careful signals security. Sibert was sufficiently impressed to tell Bradley of the possibility that the Germans were building up their forces around Bitburg. Bradley asked Eisenhower for an armoured division as a reserve for the Ardennes, but he was turned down. The Supreme Commander appreciated Bradley's concerns, but he needed the division to reinforce the Seventh Army as it supported the Third Army's offensive operations.

Although Sibert's interest in the Ardennes had increased, he was still far from convinced that the threat from the Germans in the area was as substantial as that posed by the German armour around Cologne, to where his focus thus returned. Sibert was also concerned by Dickson's latest report. Some of the assumptions made were sustained by naming units that were known to be on other fronts, and this suggested that Dickson's report was overly pessimistic. Sibert felt that a more measured assessment of the situation was required, and he set about producing a less dramatic intelligence summary. He was aware of criticism of the style of 12th Army Group's intelligence reports, which had been rather dull and dry in tone, and he asked Ingersoll to assist in the production of the final document. This was a sensible step, since Ingersoll was a journalist of some repute in civilian life. The resulting document, Summary Number 18, was certainly a good read, but Ingersoll's input only served to highlight the generally optimistic tone of the piece, which suggested that a German collapse on the western front was all but imminent.

Meanwhile, at SHAEF, General Strong shared the sense of optimism, tempered by the presence of Sixth Panzer Army somewhere behind the front. He suggested that it might be used to carry out what he called a 'relieving attack', and named the Ardennes as a possible location for this: however, he also suggested that Alsace might be the venue. As a result, although information pointing to the possibility of the Ardennes being the area chosen for a German offensive had been available since September, the intelligence staffs were unable to draw the clues together sufficiently.

DEFENDING VIII CORPS

Having noted that the front assigned to his divisions was longer than wascomfortable, Gen Middleton received a sympathetic hearing from Bradley when he visited VIII Corps. Although Middleton made his case well, he was unable to persuade Bradley that greater reinforcements were required for his supposedly quiet part of the line. The two men assessed the situation on the front fully at their meeting. Bradley argued that the Germans were most unlikely to attack, since it seemed doubtful that they could achieve the strategic success that such an operation would demand to justify it. After looking over an array of maps and situational reports, Bradley and Middleton came to the conclusion that an attack was unlikely. While Middleton was unable to remove nagging doubts from his mind, he agreed that, in the event of a German attack, he would be able to fall back on the Meuse, slowing the German advance while Bradley brought his forces to bear on the German flanks. Once again, though, the conclusion was that an attack was unlikely. And so, despite all the available evidence that appeared to suggest this, when the Germans launched their offensive it fell in the place that had been all but ruled out. Why had Allied intelligence failed?

INTELLIGENCE FAILURES

The Allies failed to appreciate that the Ardennes was the main focus for the German offensive for several reasons. Most of these resulted from a failure to look at the problem

Major General Troy Middleton commanded the US Army's VIII Corps, which bore the brunt of the German assault. Middleton had realized the risk of a counteroffensive in the Ardennes, but the demands from elsewhere on the front meant he was unable to reinforce his line.

properly, although the success of the German deception plan and the overall quality of their security also played a part. Much of the blame may be traced to a series of assumptions by the Allies that appeared to be perfectly logical, but which were flawed.

A prime reason for the failure was overconfidence. The general success of the Allied advance (albeit with some disappointments) meant that the intelligence staffs tended to agree that the Germans were on the brink of collapse. In such circumstances, it appeared most unlikely that they would be able to stage offensive operations on any major scale. This seemed a perfectly sensible supposition and was reinforced by the reappointment of von Rundstedt as the commander-in-chief on the western front. Von Rundstedt's style was well known to the Allies, and his reputation as a sensible, highly respected general suggested that he was unlikely to embark upon a deeply risky offensive when his forces were so clearly depleted. Had the information that Sixth Panzer Army was the OKW reserve and thus under Hitler's direct control been assimilated properly, such assumptions might have been tested a little more. While von Rundstedt might not have been prepared to risk an offensive, Hitler's record was such as to suggest that he might.

Having accepted the supposition that the Germans were not going to conduct major offensive operations, the Allies were able to explain away the increased rail and road traffic in the Eifel as being the natural consequence of the need for von Rundstedt to move his reserves back and forth along the front to meet the Allied attacks. The idea that the Germans were building up their forces did not fit the perception that they were unable to carry out offensive operations, and the possibility was almost completely ruled out. Intercepted signals talking about fuel shortages also convinced the Allies that no attack was imminent. Unfortunately, the intercepts were actually communications related to building up fuel stocks for the offensive, whether complaints from commanders who were being denied fuel because of the stockpiling or from those who wanted even more than was being made available to them.

The final failures of the Allied intelligence organization were the most profound. First, they failed to take account of Adolf Hitler. The adage that desperate times call for desperate measures was forgotten, and the possibility that

In front of a destroyed bakery in the French town of Tilly, two British soldiers pass a knocked-out Panther. Although not dating from the time of the offensive, this picture does indicate the ferocity of the fighting, even in small villages: not one building was left undamaged in Tilly.

General Courtney Hodges, the commander of the US First Army after Bradley's elevation to command of First Army Group. A quiet, self-effacing man, he was highly regarded by his soldiers but did not seek publicity, so he is not as widely known today as he deserves.

Hitler might have assessed that the time for those measures had arrived was ignored. The second failure was simply that of basing their assumptions on an assessment of how they would react in the same situation. Launching an offensive in the Ardennes was clearly not what the Allies would have done, so it was obvious that this was not what the Germans would do. Such complacency was shattered in the early morning of 16 December 1944 when the failure to work out the German plans was brought home in a massive artillery barrage.

THE ALLIED POSITIONS

By early December 1944, the Allies had closed on the German borders and were eagerly anticipating the end of the war, even if there were disagreements between them as to how best to conduct the remainder of the campaign. Their forces stretched from the North Sea to the Swiss border, which meant that even the huge number of men committed to the European theatre could not hold the line in strength everywhere. It was this factor that gave rise to Middleton's concerns about the frontage entrusted to VIII Corps: there were simply not enough men available to reduce the length of line held. This discomfiting position came about because of the deliberate decision by Gen Hodges to weaken his line in the Ardennes so that he would have enough strength to attack the Roer dams, preventing the Germans from flooding the ground over which the US First and Ninth Armies intended to advance into Germany itself.

In the northern sector of the Ardennes, Maj Gen Leonard Gerow's V Corps comprised four infantry divisions, two armoured combat commands and a cavalry group. Each combat command was about one-third the size of an armoured division, while the cavalry group acted as the reconnaissance element, and was equipped with light tanks and armoured cars. From Monschau to the small town of Buchholz, the 99th Infantry Division held the line in the southern part of the sector while two other divisions, the 2nd and the 78th, attacked the Roer dams through the 99th's positions and to their left.

Middleton's corps held the centre sector of the Ardennes, with the junction between the 106th Infantry Division and V Corps being held by the 14th Cavalry Group. This was the only force in a gap of more than 6km (4 miles) – the Losheim gap – between VIII and V Corps, and the divisional commander, Maj Gen Alan Jones, was not at all happy that his division covered 33km (21 miles) of front. To the south of the 106th, the 28th Infantry Division held positions along the Our river. To their right was the 4th Division, which had been heavily involved with the 28th in the battles in the Hürtgenwald. As their casualties had been heavy, they had been sent to the Ardennes to enable them to train the 9000 reinforcements required to make up their strength once more. Like Jones, the 28th's divisional commander, Maj Gen Norman Cota (of Omaha Beach fame), was more than a little disconcerted at the length of the line he had to hold. His men were spread over 36km (20 miles) from Lützkampen in the north to Wallendorf in the south. Cota had only one battalion in reserve, drawn from the 110th Infantry Regiment, which held the centre of the division's line.

This meant that four American infantry divisions, part of the 9th Armoured Division and the 14th Cavalry Group would be facing no fewer than 30 German divisions. By the second week in December, these German forces would be hidden in the woods opposite the four American divisions, ready to launch their assault. The failure of intelligence to note this location has been discussed above, but even as the day of the offensive neared, evidence was available that something unusual was taking place in the Ardennes. Both the 106th and 28th Divisions reported that the noise of tanks and other vehicles had been heard by their outposts, but this was put down to the regular movement of units in and out of the line. On 14 December, a Belgian woman made her way through the German lines to 28th Division headquarters to report that the woods near Bitburg were jammed full of German troops (a sign that Ralph Ingersoll's theory about the Germans building up in the area was accurate). She was then sent to VIII Corps headquarters and then on to First Army headquarters at Spa, but by the time she reached there on 16 December her information had been overtaken by events. A day after she had tried to tell her story, four German prisoners told their interrogators that a major attack was imminent, but their story was not given much credence. The story had been repeated on many occasions over the past month by German prisoners, who always talked of an attack taking place in the next 48 hours. There was no cause to treat

German infantry aboard what seems to be a Panther tank, heading for the front line. Soldiers did not ride into battle on the tank; they would have been vulnerable to enemy fire. Here, there are so many troops that the tank would be unable to traverse its turret or employ its armament.

An American tank crew makes final preparations while the driver has a coffee. The sandbags and other items strewn across the front of this M4 Sherman will be useful for building a defensive position, and act as a further (if not hugely effective) layer of protection against enemy fire.

the evidence provided on 15 December any differently. If the intelligence staffs had worked out that the Germans were planning something in the Ardennes, then the prisoners might have been believed, but since no attack was expected it was assumed that they were simply providing over-dramatic information.

OPPOSING ARMOUR

Both sides fought the Battle of the Bulge employing equipment with which they were very familiar, interspersed with some new items that had only recently reached the lines. The majority of American armoured units were equipped with versions of the M4 Sherman tank. A variety of M4 models were available to the Americans, with perhaps the most significant difference between any of the models being in the main armament. The earlier Shermans were equipped with a 75mm (2.95in) gun and experience had shown that this lacked the firepower necessary to tackle the latest German tanks. As a result, a 76mm gun had been substituted in the later Shermans. These started to arrive at the front in numbers from the middle of 1944 and were known to some crews as 'Jumbo' Shermans, owing to the new gun. Even this weapon, however, was not sufficient to tackle the frontal armour of some of the tanks in the German arsenal. The British had overcome this problem to some extent by managing to shoehorn a 17-pounder anti-tank gun into the Sherman's turret to produce a tank known as the Sherman

Firefly, but the American formations were forced to continue using the 75mm (2.95in) and 76mm guns despite their known deficiencies. Although recognized as a problem, the Sherman's armament was only modified after the war, by the Israeli Defence Force, which refitted them with 90mm guns and, in some instances, with the even larger 105mm gun.

The Americans could also call on a recently procured light tank, the M24 Chaffee. Although the Chaffee was described as a 'light' tank, it weighed just over 18,370kg (40,500lb) and was a robust and versatile machine. Like the early Shermans, it was equipped with a 75mm (2.95in) gun as its main armament and was equally unable to take on some of the German tanks head-on. Since light tanks were intended to be used for reconnaissance purposes, however, this was not such a disadvantage. The M24 entered service from July 1944 and was popular with crews, not least since it was relatively easy to maintain. Because the M24 remained in service with a number of armies for more than thirty years after World War II, it has been readily available for film producers and has appeared in numerous war films. Occasionally this has given the impression that it was in widespread service some months before it was actually accepted by the US Army (filmmakers have even painted M24s with iron crosses in the absence of any readily available German tanks, causing still more confusion).

> [The American soldier] is a very brave fighting man, and he has that tenacity in battle which stamps a first-class soldier. He is basically responsible for Rundstedt not doing what he wanted to do.
>
> *Field Marshal Montgomery, 7 January 1945*

GERMAN ARMOUR

The Germans, meanwhile, were equipped with a number of formidable tanks. This was a remarkable achievement, given the difficulties with tanks that the Germans had originally faced. They failed to produce a successful tank in World War I and were banned from developing them under the terms of the Versailles settlement. The army maintained an interest, however, since it saw the tank as a weapon of great potential. A number of German military thinkers proposed the use of armour as a means of avoiding the stalemate of World War I; when rearmament began in 1933, tanks were high on the list of priorities. The first Panzer division was formed in 1935, and as the army experimented with its new equipment it came to the conclusion that Panzer divisions should be used as an all-arms force, able to carry out operations without any external help. This enabled the development of the concept of *Blitzkrieg*, with the panzers at the head of the army, clearing the ground ahead of them. The new philosophy demanded equipment up to the task and the Germans undertook a great deal of design work, producing effective, fast and well-armed tanks. Speed and mobility were paramount, so protection was not the highest priority, although experience in Russia led to the development of heavier armour for later models. By 1944, the Germans had tanks that surpassed those of the western allies.

The oldest of the tanks was the Panzer Mark IV, the first versions of which had entered service in 1939. After some problems in the French and Russian campaigns, the design was updated, and from mid-1941 onwards the short-

The M24 Chaffee light tank was a robust and versatile machine that could pack a heavy punch with its 75mm (2.95in) gun. The M24 had a cross-country speed of 40km/h (25mph) – as fast as the maximum road speed of most of the heavy tanks of the period.

barrelled 7.5cm gun was replaced by a similar calibre weapon with a longer barrel. From 1943, a more powerful version of this weapon was fitted, and the Panzer IV was able to take on almost any tank it faced; by 1944 upgraded armour protection was fitted to the Mark IV as well, making it a formidable opponent.

Its successor, the Panzer Mark V, was better known as the 'Panther' and was even more formidable. The Panther was designed after the Germans encountered the Soviet T34. It was heavily armoured and equipped with a powerful 7.5cm (3in) gun that gave it the ability to stand off from Allied tanks and engage them almost at will with little risk of serious damage itself. The US Army came to the conclusion that five Shermans were needed to knock out a single Panther (by outmanoeuvring it and firing into the thinner side or rear armour). If the tank had a fault from an operational point of view, it was that the track bogies could freeze if they became clogged with snow. This was obviously more of a problem on the eastern front, but it should be remembered that the Ardennes in winter was not short of heavy snow and freezing temperatures.

If the Panther was not formidable enough, the Germans could also call upon the Panzer Mark VI, which is almost never referred to by that designation. As the Tiger it became by far the most famous German tank of World War II, even though relatively few of them were built. The Tiger's front armour was so heavy that the Allies were forced to develop

A Panzer Mk IV tank rolls forward, followed by an SdKfz 251 half-track carrying Panzergrenadiers. The terrain in the Ardennes made it difficult to advance across a broad front, since vehicles were confined to the few passable roads, which disrupted the German timetable.

A squad of M24 Chaffee light tanks prepares before moving off. The Chaffee entered service in mid-1944, and the Battle of the Bulge was the first action in which it participated in large numbers. As capable as larger vehicles, it remained in use with the US Army until the 1950s.

special tactics to deal with the Tiger, while it carried an 8.8cm (3.46in) gun (better known as the 88mm) that could deal with any tank it encountered. In the Normandy campaign, a single Tiger was responsible for knocking out no fewer than 25 Allied tanks before it was eventually overwhelmed. Although the Tiger was a formidable opponent, its weight made it less manoeuvrable and it proved too heavy for a number of bridges in Germany. Despite this, the Germans were not dissuaded from creating the Tiger II, also known as the *Königstiger* (literally 'King Tiger', but also known to the Americans as the 'Royal Tiger'). It was the heaviest, best protected and perhaps most powerfully armed tank of World War II (with a development of the 8.8cm gun [3.46in]), but was even less mobile than the Tiger I, making it an excellent tank for defensive purposes, but ill-suited to an offensive.

The Germans also enjoyed an advantage in tank destroyers and assault guns. The assault gun was not a type employed by

The Jagdpanzer 38(t) Hetzer was a small but powerful vehicle based on the chassis of the Panzer 38(t) light tank. Because of its size and manoeuverability, it was particularly effective in urban fighting.

the Allies, who used standard gun tanks to support the infantry in the advance. In 1935 the creation of *Sturmartillerie* units had been approved, using self-propelled guns to knock out enemy fortifications such as pill-boxes and to deal with machine-gun positions that were holding up the enemy advance. The assault guns were not fitted with movable turrets, and were thus far less costly and complex than tanks. This did not prevent them from being used effectively in the anti-tank role, however, since they were equipped with a sufficiently powerful main armament to stand at least a chance of fighting enemy armour on an equal basis.

By 1944 there were various assault guns in German service. Of these, the most common was the Sturmgeschütz (StuG) series armed with 75mm (2.95in) guns, although there were also a number of other types, including the Brummbär (incorrectly translated by the Allies as 'Grizzly Bear'), which had a 150mm (5.9in) gun for its main armament. The rigours of the war had taken their inevitable toll on the assault guns, however, and this meant that they were available in lesser numbers than the Germans would have liked.

TANK DESTROYERS

The assault guns were complemented by tank destroyers such as the Jagdpanther and the Jagdpanzer. To the untrained eye, these bear a close resemblance to the assault guns, and they were often used interchangeably in both roles when the situation demanded. For the Ardennes offensive, a new tank destroyer, known as the Jagdtiger, was to be brought into service, equipped with a huge 128mm (5in) gun. The Jagdtiger, however, was far too heavy for most roads and its fuel consumption was appalling: given the state of German fuel stocks at this time, it was hardly a sensible weapon.

The Americans also made use of tank destroyers. Unlike the German equivalents, the American vehicles were fitted

JAGDPANZER 38(T) HETZER

The Hetzer was one of the best of the German tank destroyers, since designers had learnt many lessons from some of their earlier efforts. It was clear that the early attempts had been clumsy vehicles. One of the grave disadvantages associated with these designs had been their height, which made them easy targets. The Hetzer was a considerable improvement in all regards. Based on a reliable chassis, the Hetzer was a small vehicle with a low profile, being just 1.8m (6ft) high. The vehicle was equipped with a 75mm (2.95in) gun, which, in common with most of the later German weapons of this calibre, could stop almost any Allied tank it encountered. With a good cross-country performance, the Hetzer proved immensely popular, not least when it became clear that its low profile meant that enemy gunners had difficulty in seeing it. Such was the success of the design, it was placed back in production after the war for the Swiss and Czech armies. The Hetzer was an economical and tremendously successful design. It was far more effective than some of the more extreme designs such as the Jagdtiger, and it is tempting to suggest that the Germans would have been far better to ignore such giants in favour of a clearly proven vehicle like the Hetzer.

with turrets, but these were open to the elements, in contrast to the turrets on tanks. This meant that the crew was vulnerable to small arms fire and shell fragments, while bad weather was also a problem. There were three main types of tank destroyer in use, the oldest of which was the M10. This was equipped with a 76mm (3in) gun, which had been derived from an anti-aircraft gun and could fire to a range of more than 14,600m (16,000 yds). The gun was rather outdated (its origins could be traced to 1918, if not before) and this prompted investigation of the 90mm (3.5in) anti-aircraft gun as an alternative. This could not be fitted into the M10's turret, so a new turret was designed to accommodate the gun; this was then fitted to the M10's hull to produce the M36 tank destroyer. The M36 entered service in July 1944

German tanks are marshalled away from their unloading point at a railhead. While the required number of tanks were moved to the battlefront before the offensive, it was impossible to build up the necessary reserves of fuel – a concern noted by the generals, but ignored by Hitler.

and was available in some numbers by the time of the Ardennes offensive, where it was the best-equipped vehicle for dealing with German tanks. The third tank destroyer in use was the M18 Hellcat, equipped with a 76mm (3in) gun and notable for its high road speed of 88km/h (55mph).

Overall, while the Germans enjoyed the advantage in terms of better tanks, they faced serious problems with fuel shortages. The Americans, on the other hand, had the advantage in numbers of tanks.

SMALL-ARMS FIREPOWER

In terms of personal weaponry both sides were well-equipped, although the Germans were by now beginning to experience some shortages of weapons. Both sides used effective standard rifles. The Germans used the 7.92mm (0.31in) Mauser Karabiner 98k, a shortened version of the Mauser Gewehr 98 rifle in service during World War I. A bolt-action weapon, the Kar 98k was reliable and generally well made (although the quality of the finish on some later

guns was not up to the usual standard). This contrasted with the American service rifle, the M1 Garand. The Garand was the first self-loading rifle to be adopted by any army, entering service in 1936. Its most peculiar feature was the method of loading via a clip of eight rounds. This ejected after the last shot had been fired, and the 'click' of the clip ejecting was loud enough to advertise that the gun was empty to anyone close enough to hear it. Despite this flaw, the Garand was an excellent weapon and continued to be made into the 1950s.

SUBMACHINE GUNS

While the two main service rifles were of comparable standard, the Germans perhaps enjoyed a slight advantage in terms of the amount of firepower that could be delivered by individual infantrymen. The sub-machine gun (SMG) was employed by both sides. The Americans employed two .45in weapons, the M1 Thompson and the M3, the famed 'Grease Gun'. The Thompson was an excellent weapon, although rather complicated to manufacture. It was well made, popular and fired a powerful round for the type of weapon. The M3 enjoyed similar advantages in terms of the round, but was a less popular gun for several reasons. It was not the most aesthetically pleasing weapon to see service (although the British Sten gun probably wins the prize for the ugliest-looking sub-machine gun of the war), and there were some

Soldiers from the 398th Infantry regiment head for a position where they can site the M1919 machine gun carried by the man second from the left. The third man from the left is carrying the tripod. All the men carry full personal kit, suggesting that they are intending to dig in.

A German StuG III assault gun passes a wrecked building, somewhere in Belgium. The vehicle has been camouflaged with foliage, indicating recent movement through countryside. That this has been applied only to the top suggests the crew is anxious about being seen from the air.

initial problems with reliability. Once these were overcome, it proved to be a more than adequate weapon, remaining in service for more than forty years. Nonetheless, given a choice between an M3 and the Thompson, the average GI would choose the latter weapon every time.

The Germans employed several sub-machine guns during the course of the war, including the MP18 Bergmann, the first of the genre, and its derivatives. The best-known and most widely used SMG on the German side, however, was the MP (Maschinenpistole) 38 and the follow-up MP40. For some reason, the popular name 'Schmeisser' was attributed to the gun, even though the designer Hugo Schmeisser was not actually responsible for its creation. The 9mm Parabellum round was less potent than the .45in bullet, but the MP40 was highly effective. It was particularly prized by British troops, who would discard their Sten guns if they captured an MP40, since it could use the same round as the unpopular British weapon. The only obstacle to this was the strange lack of magazines that seemed to be captured, but those British troops who were able to obtain both gun and a stock of magazines swore by the gun.

In addition to the SMG, though, the Germans had started to introduce semi- and fully automatic rifles to complement the Kar 98k. The first of these was the Walther Gewehr 43 (or Gew 43), a semi-automatic rifle firing the same round as the 98k. The next weapon of note – although not encountered in large numbers – was the *Fallschirmjägergewehr* 42 (literally 'Paratrooper's Rifle'). This was developed for the elite German parachute arm and was an absolutely outstanding weapon. Chambered for the standard 7.92mm rifle cartridge, it was a selective-fire weapon and provided the user with considerable firepower. Only 7000 were made, however, and the gun was never properly developed after the parachute arm declined in importance following the heavy losses sustained in Crete. The final weapon of note was rather different. This was a gun that had no fewer than three different names, although it was most commonly known as the MP43

Private (First Class) Robert Leigh shows off an array of captured German weapons. As well as his own rifle, he carries three MP40 machine pistols and two MG42 machine guns. The Americans were so impressed with the MG42 that it formed the basis for their own M60 machine gun, produced after the war.

or MP44. Whereas the MP designation suggests an SMG, the MP43 was what would now be termed an assault rifle and was developed from the first assault rifle to appear, the MKb42H (Maschinenkarabiner 42(H)), which used an 'intermediate' 7.92mm round. The MP43 first appeared in late 1943 and resembles the later AK-47 Kalashnikov. In April 1944, the designation was changed, for some undefined reason, to MP44 and then, at Hitler's behest, to *Sturmgewehr* (StG) 44. The StG44 thus provided a relatively lightweight fully automatic weapon, carrying a similar number of rounds in its magazine (30) as an SMG, but offering more firepower.

The Germans were also rather fond of an American weapon, the M1 Carbine, which had been developed as a light rifle to arm those who did not require the full-sized Garand. The Carbine used the .300 round, which was almost useless over any great distance, but this did not prevent its popularity. The light weight, reliability and easy handling the weapon enjoyed meant that it was in heavy demand. A fully automatic version, the M2, was developed, as well as the M1A1, which had afolding stock to let it be carried more easily by paratroopers. These qualities endeared it to the Germans, who made use of as many of these weapons as they could capture, to the extent that it even had its own German designation of SKb 455(a), with SKb standing for *Selbsladekarabiner* ('self-loading carbine') and the '(a)' derived from *amerikanisch*. Clearly, the Carbine was used in far greater numbers by American troops during the Battle of the Bulge, but it was certainly seen in the hands of more than a few German troops.

HEAVY MACHINE GUNS

The final weapons worthy of consideration are the machine-guns used by the two sides. There were three such weapons in American service. The first two were obvious machine-guns: the .30in Browning and the larger .5in Browning heavy machine-gun. Both were very effective weapons that had proved themselves time and time again. The third weapon was equally good, but whether it was a light machine-gun or a heavy automatic rifle has been the subject of some debate. This was the M1918 Browning Automatic Rifle, forever known as simply the 'BAR'. This fired the standard .30in round from its 20-round detachable box magazine. The small magazine meant that it required frequent reloading, particularly if it was fired on full automatic. Fired from the shoulder, it was also too light to be controlled easily when automatic fire was selected, but too heavy to be considered as a rifle; the weapon's bipod was thus rather useful. These caveats aside, however, it was a splendid weapon and very popular with the troops.

The Germans had introduced the first General Purpose Machine Gun (GMPG) into service with the MG34. This was a high-quality weapon, but was difficult to mass-produce and was replaced in production by the MG42, although the MG34 remained in service until the end of the war. Both the MG34 and the MG42 could be used either on a tripod to provide sustained fire or from a bipod, and the barrel could be changed easily to overcome the problem of barrel heating. The MG42 was a little inaccurate when fired from the bipod, owing to its high rate of fire, but the loss of accuracy was more than compensated for by the firepower it offered.

Thus, when it came to personal weapons, both sides were well equipped. The Germans had the edge in terms of the number of automatic weapons that were available to individual soldiers, but it would be easy to overstate this. More important for the first day of the assault was the benefit of surprise. When the German artillery opened fire in the darkness of the early morning of 16 December 1944, it is not unfair to say that they had achieved this key goal.

3-INCH GUN MOTOR CARRIAGE M10/90MM GUN MOTOR CARRIAGE M36 JACKSON

The 10 employed the chassis of the Sherman tank, upon which was a new hull and an open-topped turret. Although the armour was thin, its protective qualities were improved to some extent by sloping it. Production began in September 1942, and finished just three months later, by which point nearly 5000 had been built. The 76.2mm (0.3in) gun was a powerful weapon when first introduced, but as German armour protection for tanks increased, it became less effective. The British army solved this problem by replacing the main armament with a 17-pounder anti-tank gun.

The M10 was followed by the similar-looking M36, which carried a 90mm (3.5in) gun. This was capable of dealing with anything that the M36 was likely to encounter, but by the time that the vehicle entered service (just prior to the start of the Battle of the Bulge), it was more often used in the infantry support role than against tanks.

CHAPTER FOUR

SIXTH PANZER ARMY

The main thrust of the Ardennes offensive was carried out by the Sixth Panzer Army. It was the best-equipped of the three armies assigned to the assault, and its attack drove deep into the heart of the American positions. Despite achieving surprise, and notwithstanding their numerical superiority, the Sixth Panzer Army was met with fierce, uncompromising resistance. All along the line, small groups of GIs set about proving that Hitler's conviction that the Americans would fall back in panicked disorder was deeply flawed.

SIXTH PANZER ARMY'S ASSAULT commenced, in line with that of the other German forces taking part, at 05:30 on 16 December 1944. As it was entrusted with the main effort of the offensive, it was the strongest of the three armies, being made up of five parachute and *Volksgrenadier* infantry divisions, more than a thousand pieces of artillery and four SS panzer divisions. Sixth Panzer Army enjoyed some advantage over the others taking part in the offensive in that its men were generally well equipped and experienced; the replacements who had joined the formation had done so when the Army was not engaged in heavy fighting, so they had been able to receive some training. In addition, the replacements were generally younger (and arguably more enthusiastic) than those in other formations, which had been compelled to rely on a mix of former members of the *Luftwaffe* and 'overage' replacements. As the description suggests, the overage men would not have been considered for use at the front in less desperate times.

A squad of paratroopers aboard an SS Tiger II tank. This photograph not only shows the bulk of the Tiger II, but also gives an impression of the potency of the 88mm (3.46in) gun. A formidable tank, the Tiger II was hampered by its size and weight, which reduced battlefield mobility.

Sixth Panzer Army appeared to be best placed to lead the main effort of the offensive, but it still had problems to confront. While its artillery complement was far stronger than that of the other two Armies combined, it suffered from the disadvantage that it was of limited mobility owing to a lack of self-propelled guns. This was not the only area where shortages appeared. They extended also to the engineer companies needed to force the way through enemy obstacles, clear mines and undertake the seemingly endless array of tasks that fall to combat engineers once a battle is under way. A further significant problem was the paucity of assault guns that would support the infantry. These had been particularly effective in past battles, and the infantry had come to rely on substantial fire-power from the guns at crucial moments as they advanced. Only the 3rd Parachute Division (fighting as infantry) had its full complement of assault guns, and it was quite probable that the lack of the full number of guns would present difficulties for the other divisions as they attempted to advance. While Sixth Panzer Army had the benefit of surprise on its side, shortages in key areas meant that they were unlikely to have their own way if the Americans were able to organize anything approaching a coherent defence once the initial shock of the attack had been overcome.

An American NCO takes partial cover behind a tree log, as he scans the woodland ahead for possible enemy positions. His weapon is an M1 carbine, much-loved by the troops for its light weight and ease of handling.

> We had an official meeting and we were told that we are to be an elite troop. All of the armed forces are represented here: there are airmen, sailors, paratroopers and also civilians... Every offence can be punished with the death penalty... One of our comrades who had to leave camp to get some spare parts took letters with him which hadn't been censored and posted them outside the camp. This came to light in one of the inspections and he was shot as a result of this.
>
> *Unteroffizier Georges, 4./Panzerregiment 11*

The Sixth Panzer Army was tasked with attacking along the line southwest from Monschau to Krewinkel, 5km (3 miles) beyond Losheim. This was a narrower front than in the southern sector, owing to the difficult terrain: cross-country movement would be extremely difficult for the armoured units until the Hautes Fagnes was crossed, and this consideration dictated the narrowness of the front.

THE PLAN

The initial assault was to be conducted by the I SS Panzer Corps and the LXVII Corps. Despite their designation, these forces were not of similar size, since the I SS Panzer Corps had two armoured and three infantry divisions; its partner had only two infantry divisions. The planning phase had been marked by some dispute over whether the tanks or the infantry should lead the assault: Dietrich argued that the armour should have the responsibility, but was overruled by Model, who instructed that the three infantry divisions of I SS Panzer Corps would make the breakthrough, driving through American lines on either side of Udenbreth. Once a breach had been achieved, the infantry would swing round to enable it to act as a blocking force on the roads heading onto the route that the armour would take as it headed toward Liège. While this was done, LXVII Corps would attack either side of Monschau, cross the road that linked Mützenich and Elsenborn and then turn to both the north and west. In the process, they would move onto the high moorland of the Hautes Fagnes, and there join with von der Heydte's paratroopers. In conjunction with the paratroops and some of the formidable Jägdtiger assault guns, the infantry of LXVII Corps would then stop on the line Simmerat–Eupen–Limbourg so as to establish a flank. This plan meant that the five infantry divisions under Sixth Panzer Army's control would form a protective flank or 'shoulder', which would cover the advance of the two armoured divisions from I SS Panzer Corps. They would make their thrust around Krinkelt-Rocherath and through the northern sector of the Losheim Gap. As this armour rolled forward, it would be followed by the tanks of II SS Panzer Corps, which would serve as the second wave of armour to be committed to the fray. It was intended that the first 24 hours of combat would aim to penetrate the American lines, followed by a break-out. The second day would see the armoured units cross the Hautes Vagnes and strike out for the Meuse, which they would reach by the end of the third day. Once this had been achieved, the fourth day of action would conclude with the Meuse crossings being secured. This, at least, was the plan.

THE OPPOSITION

Sixth Panzer Army was faced directly by units of the US V Corps, and the southern sector of their front was occupied by Maj Gen Walter E Lauer's 99th Infantry Division, a relatively inexperienced formation that had arrived in Europe only in November. It had been assigned to its position in V Corps on the grounds that this would be a relatively quiet sector of the front; the soldiers would be able to gain experience here before being thrust into more testing conditions. The 99th was to gain rather more experience than it had anticipated. Its front extended from Monschau to Lanzerath (culminating at the line of the railroad to the north of the latter village), which meant that it was extended over 30km (19 miles). This was a notably long stretch of front for a brand new division to hold, but the reasoning behind this step appeared sensible. The commander of V Corps felt that the 99th Infantry could hold the line while his more experienced formations could be used in the operation to seize the Roer dams. Giving the 99th an extended front meant that the combat power of the experienced units would be enhanced, while the risk of an enemy attack appeared to be remote given the very awkward terrain and the apparently poor state of the German forces in the area. These assumptions were important, since the 99th's positions extended into the woodland of the Monschau Forest, which was a difficult area to hold, since the routes to the forward positions were little more than muddy, rutted logging trails. The density of the trees meant that it was difficult to establish fields of fire for defensive positions, and in some areas the terrain was so awkward that the 99th was forced to set up strong-points to cover the line of a possible advance. These strong-points left gaps in the line, and presented the danger that the enemy would be able to infiltrate through them, perhaps fatally unbalancing the defence.

The threat of an enemy attack was not foremost in the minds of American commanders, however. From 8 December, V Corps had been preparing for the attack against the Roer dams, which commenced on 13 December. Elements of the 2nd Division passed through the 99th Division's lines as they made their advance. The 99th was represented in the attack, since the 1st and 3rd Battalions from the 395th Infantry Regiment participated in the assault; other elements of the Division were responsible for creating diversions. The advance progressed well, but as the attacking forces reached German strong-points, the assault began to slow. Nevertheless, by 15 December it appeared that all was going well. There were some indications that the Germans had reinforced their lines, but this was thought to be an obvious step for them to take in the circumstances. American commanders anticipated that the enemy would launch a counterattack against positions held by the 99th. This meant that when the Battle of the Bulge opened on the morning of 16 December, the Americans were initially wrong-footed. They expected an attack, but one of limited scope only – hardly an apposite description of the events of 16 December.

OPENING MOVES

At 05:30 on 16 December, the German artillery opened up against American positions all along the front. The forward outposts of the 394th Infantry Regiment initially thought that the noise came from friendly guns firing out towards the German lines, rather than hostile action. This view was not held for long. Within a matter of minutes, it was clear that the fire was incoming. This did not accord with intelligence reports suggesting that the Germans had very little artillery opposite the 394th. The weight of incoming fire gave the lie to this, and the troops dived for cover. Fortunately, the 394th had not been idle during the relatively quiet period since its arrival and had constructed stout defences (making much use of the forest's timber for overhead cover), which kept casualties from the bombardment to a minimum. Shortly afterwards, German infantry were seen moving through the trees, but even this did not give credence to the notion that a major attack was under way. It must be recalled that the Americans expected some form of attack by the enemy, and this appeared to accord with their expectations, even if the amount of artillery fire was greater than anticipated. It did

German troops pass a battered American convoy near Poteau. This picture is part of a series that was photographed and filmed after the ambush that halted the convoy. The lead soldier carries the Mauser Kar98, while the man in the ditch has a StG 44 assault rifle.

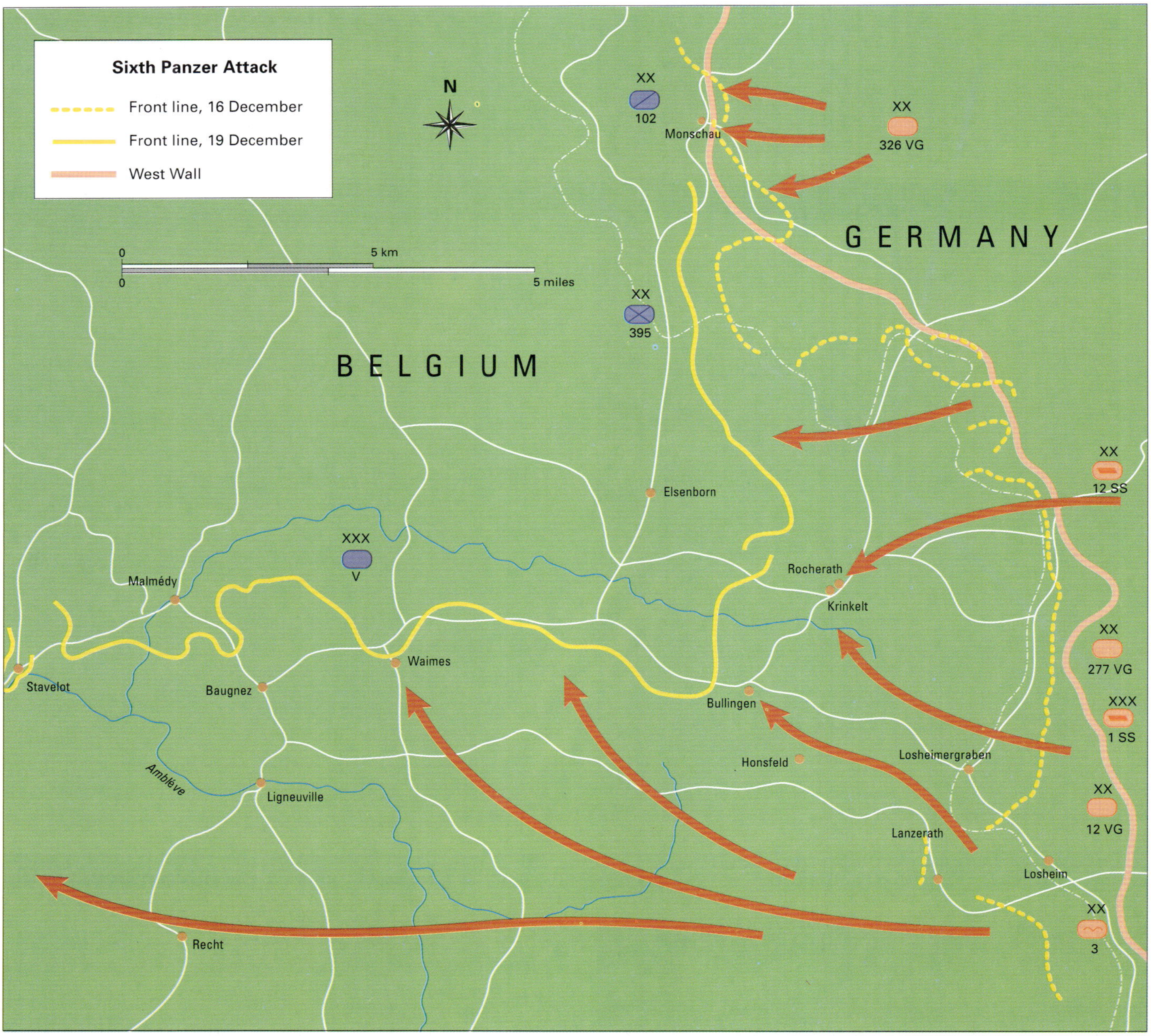

Some idea of the initial gains from the German assault is provided by this map. Despite bitter resistance, the assault succeeded in driving the Americans back all along the front. That said, the advance in the northern sector was not as spectacular as that in the south.

not take long for the inaccuracy of this assessment to become apparent. Reports were soon flooding in that all 30km (20 miles) of the 99th's frontage was under attack.

DEFENDING HÖFEN

In the northern sector of Sixth Panzer Army's area, the village of Höfen was an important target for the German offensive, since it overlooked the roads at Monschau. The side that held the village could control access to the road to Eupen, which served as the location for the headquarters of US V Corps. At Höfen itself, defence was in the hands of the 3rd Battalion of the 395th Infantry Regiment, which was woken by the enormous artillery barrage that caused considerable damage to the village. Buildings collapsed, and the streets were lit with an eerie glow from the flames and the watery artificial moonlight created by German searchlights being reflected off the low cloud. When the bombardment finished, the 3rd

Battalion's commanding officer, Lt Col McClernand Butler, found that his communications with the artillery had been cut. Although this was not ideal, the battalion had a number of compensating strengths for the forthcoming assault. The first was that they had been in Höfen since early November and had constructed substantial defences. The village itself was badly hit, but there were no casualties among the troops, who were safely ensconced in foxholes with good overhead cover. Höfen was also situated on a hill, with all of the advantages this gave to a well dug-in defending force; Butler had made sure that his men had sited their positions well, with good fields of fire. The battalion could also call on the anti-tank guns of the 612th Tank Destroyer Battalion, which, although part of 2nd Division, was in Höfen as a result of the movement of that division through the 99th Division's lines for the attack on the Roer dams.

Shortly after the artillery died away, the Americans were able to see the assault companies of the 326th Volksgrenadier Division advancing towards them. The approaching troops were later described as advancing in 'swarms', moving at a slow, methodical pace. The German forces were rather understrength. The attack was meant to be by both the 246th and the 326th Volksgrenadier Divisions, but the 246th Volksgrenadiers had been fixed in place by the recent American attacks and were unable to make it to the start line. The 326th Volksgrenadiers were missing some of their men as well. One battalion had been withdrawn to assist in defending against the attack on the Roer dams and, although it had been sent back to take part in the attack, it had not arrived in time. Another battalion had been pulled back to Wahlerscheid in an attempt to fend off an attack there by the US 2nd Division, and had left for the front only hours before the town fell. They too had not made it to the line of departure, which meant that the force attacking Höfen consisted of four battalions of infantry instead of the fourteen that were specified in the German plan.

The Germans marched up the steep hill in front of the village for some distance, until they were within 200m (656ft) of the American lines. At this point, every American gun opened fire, cutting swathes through the Germans. Appalling casualties were inflicted, but the determined Germans pressed

The commander of an M10 tank destroyer scans the horizon for the enemy. The M10 is making use of the terrain to lower its profile from observation. The fact that the turret is open-topped, leaving the crew exposed to shell fragments and the elements, can just be seen.

on – in some cases, the assault ended only when the Germans toppled into the defenders' foxholes. The weight of fire was such that the assaulting forces were unable to carry the American positions, and they had no choice but to fall back. About 30 Germans managed to get into some of the houses on the boundary between I and K companies, but after an hour they too were dislodged. Once they had gone, the 3rd Battalion checked for casualties: it had suffered four fatalities, while the *Volksgrenadiers* had lost more than a hundred men killed. This marked the end of German efforts at Höfen on the 16th. Just before the first 24 hours of the battle were over, they returned, supported by assault guns. Again, the defensive fire was murderous, and although some Germans were able to reach the village, they were then wiped out. Shortly after daybreak, a few determined Germans broke through, and it looked as though they might be in a position to take the battalion command post. Lt Col Butler, his links with the outside world re-established, called for artillery fire against his own position, but while this desperate measure was being arranged the anti-tank guns made their presence felt. The assault guns were forced back, and their accompanying infantry were unable to hold on without them. Once again the Germans fell back. They would not return.

Two American infantrymen take cover behind a tank while German artillery fire whistles overhead. Unable to move until the barrage stops, both men have chosen to smoke a cigarette. Note the man nearest the camera, who keeps a firm hold on his M1 Thompson sub-machine gun.

The attack on Höfen demonstrated that Hitler's view that American troops would be pushovers was not at all accurate. More than 500 his soldiers had died proving it, and Höfen remained very much in American hands.

MONSCHAU

The Germans had similar difficulties at Monschau, held by the 38th Cavalry Reconnaissance Squadron, which was under the command of Lt Col Robert E O'Brien. His troops were relatively few in number, but had 50 machine guns dismounted from their vehicles to bolster their defences. With the exception of the rocky terrain to the right flank of the squadron, which offered reasonable cover for any attackers, the defensive positions offered good fields of fire across the slopes leading to the town. Unlike Höfen, Monschau was spared an artillery barrage on the orders of Field Marshal Model, who appears to have wished to avoid destroying a German town.

The attacking troops from the German 752nd Regiment carried out the attack, beginning their move as the sounds of the artillery bombardment across the rest of the front died away. The cavalry squadron's outposts reported the sounds of troops approaching along the road that entered Monschau from the southeast. The Germans were allowed to reach the road-block on this road, whereupon the American mortars began firing illuminating rounds above them. The cavalrymen opened fire with every weapon they had, including the 37mm (1.45in) guns on their light tanks, which were firing canister rounds deadly to troop concentrations. The first assault was beaten off, and the Germans made one more attempt to take the town just after daybreak on 16 December. This was repulsed, and no further attempts against Monschau were made on the first day.

BUCHHOLZ STATION

Another of the first engagements of the battle took place at the small town of Buchholz. The 3rd Battalion of the 394th had been stationed here as the divisional reserve, so it was something of a surprise when they came into contact with the

A Panther tank pulls in to the side of the snow-covered road to allow a Kubelwagen utility car to pass by. The conditions are typical of those faced by both sides during the Battle of the Bulge.

> There was an intensive training phase at the end of November. We were confronted with American clothing, dollars and English pounds and of course we received the appropriate 'new' identity papers. We had to hand in all our personal effects and these were kept by the rear party.
>
> *Oberleutnant Dreier, Commanding Officer, 4./Panzerregiment 11*

enemy in the form of elements of the 12th Volksgrenadier Regiment. The Germans had good reason to attack Buchholz, since they needed to gain control of the railway. In the course of their autumn retreat, they had blown up the road bridge that crossed the railway – now they were on the offensive, the lack of this bridge (carrying the International Highway) was a serious problem. The heavy forest meant that tanks were confined to the roads, and if armoured units were to reach Losheimergraben to begin their dash for the Meuse they needed to use the now-demolished bridge. The only solution was to take the railroad track and to send engineers to reconstruct the bridge. Thus, the 12th Volksgrenadiers were given the task of evicting American units in the area to allow the engineers to go about their business.

A WELCOME BREAKFAST

L Company of the 394th's 3rd Battalion was at Buchholz station itself, and had already experienced an interesting morning. The bombardment had driven the men to take cover, and they had endured the artillery fire for about 90 minutes. They had suffered no casualties and, once the bombardment stopped, they left their shelter and began to line up for breakfast. L Company was particularly looking forward to this meal. The field kitchen had arrived the night before, and this would be the first hot meal for several days for any of the men. At about 07:45, while the hungry men were still forming into the queue for that much-welcomed breakfast, they began to make out figures marching down the railway line two abreast. It soon became clear that about fifty men were approaching, but the fog meant that it was difficult to work out exactly who these figures were. There was some speculation as to which members of the 394th they might be, and a consensus that it was probably the Weapons Platoon.

1st Sgt Elmer Krug, who was overseeing the distribution of breakfast, was not certain that this guess was correct. He peered into the mist a little more, and then the reality struck him: the approaching men were German. At about the same time, some men thought they heard voices, and they were not English. Krug did not need this confirmation, since he was raising his M1 Carbine to his shoulder. Shouting a warning to his men, he opened fire. The attractions of the hot breakfast were forgotten, and those L Company men who could see the Germans grabbed for their weapons and began shooting at the enemy. Breakfast – and the other meals of 16 December for that matter – would have to wait.

HIT AND MISS

The Germans broke for cover, either sheltering behind the boxcars outside the station or diving into ditches alongside the track. Once they had gained some form of protection, the Germans returned fire. L Company was supported by elements of the regimental Anti-Tank Company, and the gunners took the boxcars under fire with their 57mm (2.24in) guns. The gunners scored several hits, while Pte John Claypool endeavoured to engage the Germans with a bazooka. It was not Claypool's lucky day. To his frustration, he fired several rounds and missed with all of them: he did not miss by much, but he just could not manage to correct his aim sufficiently. His first bazooka rocket fell short, so he aimed higher. The second rocket sailed over the top of the boxcars. He adjusted his aim again – and this time the rocket hit the ground short of the boxcars, a little nearer than the first round that had fallen short. Claypool shifted his aim-point once more, and watched in irritation as the fourth rocket flew just over the top of the boxcars. At this point, Technician 5 George Bodnar joined Claypool after selflessly running out to cover a wounded German with the shelter half of a tent, in the hope that it would give the man some protection. As he dropped down by Claypool, Bodnar asked, by way of greeting, how Claypool was faring with the bazooka. Claypool reported on his bad luck, and agreed to let Bodnar have a go with the weapon. It is perhaps fair to observe that Claypool was forced to load, aim and fire the bazooka by himself while under heavy fire, which may have distracted him a little. Bodnar had the advantage of being able to concentrate on his target as Claypool pushed a rocket into the weapon; then he opened fire. Bodnar's initial attempt missed by a few yards, but the second rocket penetrated the first boxcar. Germans jumped out and ran for cover as Claypool reloaded. The

Weary members of B Company of the 101st Engineer Battalion emerge from the frozen woods around Wiltz after a night in forward positions. The two men in the foreground carry Bazookas, while the rearmost figure pauses for the camera with his load of ammunition boxes.

third rocket slammed into the roof of the boxcar, and the rocket hits, combined with the fire from the anti-tank guns, set the cars ablaze. The surviving Germans wisely abandoned their position and ran for safety, pursued by small arms fire kicking up the dirt around them.

At this point German artillery rounds started landing around the station, but after a few minutes the fire slackened, then stopped. The Americans realized that the Germans were withdrawing, and the NCOs started to yell orders for their men to cease firing and conserve their ammunition. GIs began to approach the boxcars, demanding that the surviving Germans surrender and rounding up more than 30 prisoners who were taken back to the station area.

TRAVALINI CRAWLS FORWARD

Maj Norman Moore, L Company's commanding officer, was not fooled into thinking that the Germans had given up for the day. He sent a runner to the nearby K Company, with orders for their commander, Capt Wesley Simmons, to move up in support. Moore then sent instructions to the mortar platoon from M Company to provide fire support when it was next needed. As he was doing this, a German patrol ran straight into K Company and was driven back after a short yet fierce exchange of fire. K Company then dug in, certain that they would be seeing more action before too long. At 10:50, movement was detected to the front of K Company; within moments a German patrol was spotted and taken under fire. The American fire was sporadic, and the patrol withdrew swiftly, having achieved the aim of locating K Company's positions. Ten minutes later, the Germans attacked again, beginning with a mortar barrage against Buchholz station. Two companies of Germans charged in against K Company, and another fierce exchange of fire occurred, neither side giving way.

The new assault brought the men of the anti-tank platoon

To enable them to engage enemy snipers, two soldiers have taken up position on top of a small building. They are loading their M1 Garand rifles; probably no German marksmen are nearby at this point, since both men are sitting in a way that makes them ideal targets.

THE STURMGESCHÜTZ

When reviewing the lessons learned from World War I, the German army reached the conclusion that a mobile gun able to follow infantry attacks and provide fire support was needed. Development began shortly after Hitler took power and began the process of rearming Germany, and a mobile gun based on the chassis and running gear of the Panzer Mark III was developed under the title of Gepanzerte Selbstfahrlafette für Sturmgeschütz 7.5-cm Kanone SdKfz 142 – which was always reduced to Sturmgeschütz III (assault gun model III), and often yet further to just StuG III. It was intended that the StuG III would be employed in assault gun battalions with eighteen to twenty-four vehicles apiece, these battalions being assigned to support Panzergrenadier divisions. Their powerful gun meant that they were often used in the anti-tank role as well. As early as 1941, it was clear that German industry would not be able to produce the number of tanks required for panzer divisions, and the StuG was impressed into service alongside turreted tanks to give the panzer units the strength they required. The StuG was not the best answer, since its lack of a turret meant that it did not have the flexibility of a true tank – nonetheless, it was much better than nothing.

under fire as the Germans advanced towards a small roundhouse on a nearby farm. Sgt Savino Travalini, the anti-tank platoon's leader, was directly opposite the roundhouse and was able to observe as the Germans set up a machine gun position just outside the building. The MG42 machine gun crackled into life with its familiar firing signature that sounded like ripping calico, and Travalini soon appreciated that the machine-gunners were in a position to influence the battle: if they managed to pin down the men of the 3rd Platoon (with whom the anti-tank platoon was located), they would be able to put K Company's flank under heavy pressure, with the possibility of surrounding the whole Battalion. Travalini gathered grenades from one of his men, and stuffed them into his jacket. He crawled forward, pausing occasionally to put a few rounds from his M1 Carbine in the direction of the Germans. When he judged that he was in range, Travalini jumped to his feet and hurled the grenades at the Germans. As the grenades sailed through the air, he dived for cover. The grenades exploded, killing the machine-gunners, and Travalini ran back to his position.

Although the MG42 had been knocked out, the Germans in the roundhouse were still putting down a considerable amount of fire. Travalini gestured to one of his men for a bazooka, which was pushed forward to him with a couple of rounds. Travalini loaded the bazooka and sighted it on the roundhouse; then he fired. The rocket struck the centre of the building, and traces of smoke came from the entrance hole. Two dazed Germans left the roundhouse and staggered away: Travalini shot both of them. The Germans appeared to lose heart at this point, and the assaults petered out.

In the heat of battle, Capt Simmonds had been unable to see how many of his men had been hit. Once the Germans had withdrawn and the firing had died down, he was astonished and relieved to learn that just one man had died and another two were wounded. Given the intensity of the fighting, he feared that his casualties would have been much higher.

LANZERATH

Although the attacks on the right flank of the 394th were driven back, it was alarmingly obvious that the 99th Division had lost contact with the 14th Cavalry Group and that its southern flank was exposed. At 1140, news reached the 99th command post that the cavalry was withdrawing from Lanzerath. This left one small unit, the 394th's Intelligence and Reconnaissance (I&R) Platoon under the command of Lt Lyle J Bouck jr, dug in on a hill just to the north-west of Lanzerath.

Even though Lyle Bouck was just 20 years old, and the second youngest man in his platoon, he already had considerable military experience. His father, who had served as an NCO in the National Guard, persuaded him to go to the St Louis National Guard summer camp in 1938. His father also used his contacts to persuade the Guard unit to be flexible on the age rules for joining, and Bouck had signed up just before his fifteenth birthday. He enjoyed the summer camp, and the fact that he was able to earn some money for his trouble. As the youngest member of the formation, he was assigned to duties in the storeroom as part of the 138th Infantry Regiment, 35th Infantry Division. Just before Christmas 1940, the regiment was activated and sent to Little Rock, Arkansas. Bouck went with them, even though he was still only 17. He proved competent at his job in the stores and was promoted to Sergeant. The activation of the regiment was supposed to be for just one year, but as this period was coming to a close the Japanese attacked Pearl Harbor. As his eighteenth birthday approached (on 17 December 1941) Bouck was encouraged to apply for Officer Candidate School, was accepted, and graduated as a Second Lieutenant in August 1942. He was clearly regarded well enough to be retained on the staff of the School, working as an instructor for two years. He was then sent on the officer advanced course, where he was the most junior student by a long way. Once he had completed the course, Bouck was sent to Fort Hood, Texas, as a company commander at a training centre. The commanding officer was not to Bouck's liking, and he looked for a way out. He applied for a vacancy in the 99th Division and was posted to the 394th as the weapons platoon leader and then the executive officer in Company C. He was not to be there for long. During divisional training exercises, the 394th's I&R platoon had performed so badly that the divisional commander removed the platoon leader and the regimental commander. The new regimental commander then removed the regimental intelligence officer, replacing him with Maj Robert L Kriz. Kriz was told to disband the I&R platoon and start again. Kriz looked at the material he had already, decided that he did not like what he saw, and reassigned all but four of the men. As Kriz was searching for a commander for the I&R platoon, he happened to observe Bouck conducting training on the machine-gun range, and was impressed enough to ask Bouck to take command of the I&R platoon. Between them, Kriz and Bouck selected 32 men

> I regret to say that it seemed to me that parts of this offensive could hardly be described as well-planned and well-organized. Before 16 December the concept of the planned offensive that we were given was far too optimistic and once the offensive was under way there were a lot of disappointments and problems.
>
> *Hauptmann Scherf, Commanding Officer Kampfgruppe Y (II./150)*

American soldiers 'somewhere in Belgium'. The men have dug into an earth bank to offer some overhead protection against enemy fire and the weather. The importance of building good defensive positions was demonstrated on countless occasions during the Ardennes campaign.

A German mortar crew prepare to engage the enemy. The photograph demonstrates how German forces were stripped from other areas for the offensive. This film was captured in Belgium – but shows the men engaging Russian positions.

and rebuilt the platoon. It became an efficient body, but by 16 December the I&R platoon was down to 24 men. Of these, six were carrying out duties away from the platoon. Bouck had eighteen men with which to defend his position against the main thrust of the German attack.

SOMETHING SERIOUSLY WRONG

Bouck, of course, did not know that an attack was planned. At 05:30 on 16 December, he heard the start of the German bombardment and ordered his men into their foxholes. The artillery was landing well to the west and presented no immediate danger to the platoon, but it was a sensible precaution. Bouck and his men watched the bombardment light the dawn sky for more than 90 minutes, before the unmistakable sound of incoming shells was heard. The men of the I&R platoon dived for cover, and the ground shook as the first rounds landed. Bouck radioed the regiment and was told that the whole division was being bombarded. A few minutes later, when the shelling stopped, Bouck and his men left their foxholes to assess the damage. To his relief, he learned that none of his men had been injured. He raised his binoculars and started scanning the terrain to the south, correctly assuming that the Germans would not have fired so much artillery without following it up. At 08:30, the sound of small arms fire and explosions could be heard coming from

Losheimergraben, and Bouck turned towards the north to see if he could spot anything. Four half-tracks, towing anti-tank guns, were leaving the town. These were the guns of Company A of the 820th Tank Destroyer Battalion. Bouck was surprised. Although the I&R platoon and the tank destroyer unit were not from the same formation (the I&R platoon was operating just beyond the V Corps boundary) he had established communications with the anti-tank gunners, and it seemed a little strange that they had left in such a hurry without sending some indication as to why.

Bouck's platoon sergeant, Tech Sgt Bill Slape, suggested the only conclusion to be drawn was that something was very seriously wrong. Bouck returned to his foxhole, and took the radio handset from his radio operator, Pte William James Tsakanikas. Bouck called regimental headquarters, and managed to speak to Maj Kriz. Bouck explained that the tank destroyer unit had left and requested instructions. He was told to set up an observation post (OP) in the town and report back. Bouck decided that a two-man OP would be appropriate, although four men would be required to establish it. He decided that he would lead the patrol into the town, taking Slape, Tsakanikas and Pte John Cregar. As the patrol headed towards the town, a four-man OP from the 371st Field Artillery was looking out from its position in a house, attempting to discern anything in the early morning mist. The OP's commander, Lt Warren Springer, was on watch and peering intently through his binoculars. His second-in-command, Sgt Peter Gachi, asked if he could see anything, but did not receive an instant reply: Springer carried on looking out the window. After a moment, he gave the answer. Through the mist he could see large numbers of Germans approaching the town. He instantly called for artillery fire, but was informed that the batteries were under small arms fire and the guns would not be able to respond. It is, in fact, unlikely that the artillery positions were under small arms fire from attacking infantry, but in the confusion surrounding the opening of the offensive such mistakes are comprehensible. This did not help Springer, of course, who decided that the only course of action was to pull out and head for a nearby hill, from where he could maintain observation and try to call in fire when it was required.

FORCED TO RETREAT

Just as Springer's team made their exit from Lanzerath in their jeep, Bouck's small patrol arrived. They had advanced down a small ravine for cover, and emerged near a house that Bouck thought would be the ideal location for their OP. They entered the building and Tsakanikas went to check the top floor, followed by Bouck. In the first room they discovered an elderly man, deep in conversation on the telephone. This appeared most suspicious, not least since the man was talking in German. Tsakanikas snatched the handset from the man and levelled his rifle at him, convinced he was a spy. Bouck agreed with the assessment, but pointed out to Tsakanikas – who may have felt like shooting the man, but who was not going to – that they could not take the man prisoner. The old man fled the building, passing a surprised Sgt Slape on the way out.

Bouck told Slape to site the OP upstairs. He and Tsakanikas would return to the platoon, taking with them the communications wire needed to link the OP with the platoon. As he was giving these instructions, Tsakanikas declared that he could hear a jeep. He went to look outside, followed by Bouck, and saw columns of troops approaching the town. Bouck studied them carefully and realized from the shape of some of their helmets that these were German paratroopers, who were heading straight for the house. Slape urged Bouck to go immediately, and the lieutenant and Tsakanikas left hurriedly, heading back to the platoon's position the way they had come. Slape and Cregar were

PANZERKAMPFWAGEN V PANTHER HEAVY TANK

The Panther originated as a counter to the formidable Soviet T34, which came as a rude shock to German armour when it was first encountered in late 1941. The German response was to call for a tank armed with a long-barrelled 75mm (2.95in) gun and with sloped armour to improve the levels of protection offered to the vehicle and its crew. The first models of the Panther appeared in September 1942, and were rushed into service without proper field trials. This meant that many of the first Panthers broke down far too easily, and more were lost to mechanical failure than to enemy action. Once these problems had been overcome, confidence in the tank increased, and it was intended that the Panthers would totally replace the Mark IV. The factories were unable to meet this demand, and the maximum intended output of 600 Panthers per month was never achieved: the maximum number ever produced was 330 in a month. The Panther was probably the best all-round German tank of the war, and some were pressed into use by the French Army while it awaited re-equipment after the war.

instructed to send reports for as long as they could, but as soon as the Germans came close they were to leave and make their way back to the platoon.

DISBELIEF

The Germans were moving forward with caution, and this gave Bouck and Tsakanikas time to escape: it was likely that their slow rate of advance would give a similar opportunity to Slape and Cregar. Their lack of dynamism stemmed from the inexperience of the vast majority of the paratroops. While there were one or two veterans, most of the men had been drawn from other parts of the *Luftwaffe*. This even applied to the commander of the unit, Oberst Helmut von Hofmann, who had been performing desk duties in Berlin until a few weeks before. He did not wish to make any mistakes or encounter any nasty surprises, and decided that one way of reducing the risk of this was to proceed slowly and carefully. This meant that the Germans were not in a position to see the two American soldiers leaving a house and running for the ravine. Within minutes of leaving the house, Bouck and Tsakanikas had reached the platoon's position and connected the communications wire to enable them to talk with the exposed OP. Bouck ordered his men to prepare to engage the Germans, even though the odds facing them appeared to be hopeless. He took the opportunity to radio regimental headquarters and was answered by an officer he did not know. Bouck reported that at least one German battalion had entered Lanzerath and that he needed artillery fire. The officer was incredulous and told Bouck that he was imagining things. He made no reference to artillery support, and gave the rather crass order to hold the town at all costs. Bouck threw the radio handset down in disgust and returned to observing the German advance.

Bouck was distracted by the arrival of four men in a jeep, which had made its way down one of the tracks leading to the I&R platoon's position. One of the men moved from foxhole to foxhole, asking for the location of the platoon

German NCOs look up from work ing out their position on a map . The original US army caption for this photograph says that the men are sheltering from artillery fire, although their relaxed demeanour suggests they are not directly threatened by incoming rounds.

> The loader was a 'speaker'... His job included operating a medium-wave radio with an umbrella aerial on the turret. The deployment of 'speakers' in panzer crews was controversial as they hadn't had any specialist panzer-crew training. We were afraid they would weaken our combat strength by making operational mistakes. In addition, our 'speaker' didn't know the first thing about how the duties in a panzer are divided up between the individual members of a panzer crew. Leutnant Gertesnschläger was keen to get rid of him at the first opportunity.
>
> *Obergefreiter Gries, radio operator, Kampfgruppe Z (III.150)*

leader. He reached Bouck and introduced himself as Warren Springer. Bouck was relieved to learn that Springer was an artilleryman, not least since he offered to call in artillery fire when it was needed. Given the disparity in strength between the Germans and the defending American troops, Bouck considered that he would need this support fairly rapidly once any fighting started. Springer went off to set up his radio, while Bouck was called to speak to Slape, reporting from the house in the town.

The Germans had not only reached the house, but had even entered the ground floor. Bouck ordered Slape and Cregar to leave the house as soon as it was safe to do so, and said that he would send some help. Slape and Cregar waited until they were sure that the Germans had left the house, then raced downstairs and outside, heading for a nearby barn, where they waited to make certain there were no Germans in a position to observe them. Meanwhile, Bouck detailed Cpl Aubrey McGehee, Pte James Silvola and Pte 'Pop' Robinson to assist Slape and Cregar as they left the town. They set off towards the town, hoping to find their

A German soldier advances cautiously (although certainly aware of the camera's presence) through scrubland recently vacated by American troops. Interestingly, he appears to be carrying a captured M1 Carbine rather than a German weapon.

A German foot patrol passes an abandoned American M8 armoured car. The historian Jean Paul Pallud was able to establish that the 'advancing' Germans were actually withdrawing towards their own lines; presumably this position gave the cameraman a better shot.

colleagues quickly. Once Slape and Cregar were satisfied that there were no Germans around, they left the barn and dashed into the woods. As they made their way across the road in the middle of the woods, their luck ran out. They were spotted by two paratroopers, one of whom was armed with an MG42 machine gun. The Germans opened fire. Cregar made it across the road and back into the wood safely, but Slape was less fortunate. A round passed straight through the heel of his boot, knocking it off. This caused Slape to fall, and he landed heavily on the roadway, breaking a rib and his chestbone. Despite this, he picked himself up and dived for cover, pursued by a fusillade of shots.

As they moved through the woods to the I&R platoon's position, they were surprised to bump into Bouck and Cpl Risto Milosevich: Bouck had grown impatient and had gone out to look for the two men himself. In fact, they had missed McGehee, Silvola and Robinson by a matter of yards, passing each other in the trees. McGehee and his companions had made their way into the town and reached the barn in which Slape and Cregar had hidden, only to find that they were cut off by a machine gun. In order to make their way back to the woods it was necessary for the machine-gunner to move: it looked as though they might be in for a long wait.

FIRST ATTACK

Bouck returned to the platoon position just in time. Some Germans were now approaching, but they appeared to be a little lost. It seemed that the party in front of the platoon was made up of officers who were discussing the situation. The platoon prepared to open fire but, just as they were about to do so, a girl ran into the road. The Americans held their fire, and the Germans dived for cover as the girl gestured in the direction of Bouck's position for reasons that were not altogether clear. Other elements of the German force opened fire on the I&R platoon, but their fire was wild and high. Bouck yelled to Springer to call for artillery support, and then joined his men in returning fire. Those Germans still in the open were cut down. To Bouck's astonishment, the remaining Germans attacked straight up the hill, without any attempt to outflank the I&R platoon. Since they had very little cover, the Americans were able to inflict serious casualties. After several attempts, Springer managed to obtain some artillery support and a few rounds landed among the Germans, causing even more casualties. To Springer's intense irritation, the artillery fire stopped almost at once. He was informed that the demand for artillery support was so intense that the guns were only able to provide a few shells before they had to switch targets. With the benefit of hindsight, this appears to be a perfectly reasonable attempt by the artillery to support as many units as they could – but it is easy to comprehend Springer's annoyance at what seemed to show a lack of understanding of the desperate situation in which the I&R platoon found itself. The Germans continued to attack, getting within 150m of the platoon's position before they fell back.

A line of American POWs trudges past a German tank. The Germans were keen to photograph the lines of prisoners in a bid to maintain the morale of the population at home, but it is difficult to assess how effective this strategy was by this stage of the war.

STRUGGLING TO HOLD

As the battle progressed, McGehee and his two companions realized that the machine gun blocking their line of withdrawal had gone. They moved off, intending to head towards the rail line that led to Buchholz station, hoping to move along it and join with the companies located there (they correctly judged that it was now impossible to return to the I&R platoon's location). As they moved through the woods, they were spotted by men from the German 27th Fusilier Regiment. The three Americans knew they had no option but to open fire, even though they were hopelessly

A despatch rider takes a cigarette from the men on the rear decking of a Tiger II tank. The men on the tank are carrying an interesting variety of weapons, not least the man standing nearest the camera, who is holding a captured British Sten Gun.

outnumbered. Several Germans succumbed to their fire, but their comrades responded. Saviola was hit in the shoulder and Robinson was wounded in the right leg. By great fortune McGehee was not hit, but he had run out of ammunition. Since there was little point in resisting, he reluctantly raised his hands. The Germans took the three Americans prisoner, leading McGehee away while the medics treated Saviola and Robinson alongside their own casualties.

After the Germans had withdrawn, Bouck made a quick assessment of the position and ordered the redistribution of ammunition among the platoon members, anticipating another attack. He then sent a situation report to headquarters. There was little that headquarters could say, other than to acknowledge his report and encourage him to try to hold on. This convinced Bouck that regimental headquarters had not yet grasped the scale of the attack at Lanzerath. There was nothing more to do beyond encouraging his men and wait for the next attack, which must surely come.

At 11:00, the Germans reappeared and put in their second assault. Bouck was dumbfounded by their tactics, which were an exact replica of those employed in the first attack. The Germans approached up the hill and were swept with a wave of fire from the I&R platoon. Once again, many casualties were caused and, as the Germans fell back again, the ground in front of the American position was covered with the dead and wounded. At about 11:45, the Germans asked Bouck to permit their medics to remove the wounded from the field. Bouck agreed, and for the next hour or so the Americans watched as the medics made a series of journeys to and from the battlefield, giving first aid to the wounded before carrying them away. Bouck was not idle during this period, as he was attempting to secure reinforcements and artillery support from headquarters; he was unsuccessful, as was Springer, who found it difficult to convince the artillery that he was faced with an attack by very substantial forces. These attempts over, all the Americans could do was wait.

THIRD WAVE

At 14:00, the German paratroopers launched their third assault. By this time, Bouck was beginning to have serious doubts about the German commanders, since this was yet another frontal assault. Once again, the vastly outnumbered I&R Platoon inflicted serious casualties, but the weight of the

The Tiger II was a further development of the Tiger I, with the intention of producing an even more powerful tank that would counter any future Soviet heavy tank. It was hard to manoeuvre on the battlefield, which limited the design's effectiveness.

German attacks began to tell. The I&R men were now taking casualties, and Bouck's radio handset had been hit by a bullet: he was now unable to communicate with anyone outside Lanzerath. Two members of the platoon were instructed to try to reach either the 3rd Battalion of the 394th or regimental headquarters. They set off, but were unable to break through; after three days hiding in a barn, they were found by the Germans and taken prisoner.

AN ORDER TO LEAVE

Once the third assault was over, Bouck assessed the position once again. The I&R platoon was now in a desperate situation: there were only twelve men, including Bouck, and the platoon's two machine guns were out of action. The .30-calibre machine gun had stopped firing after the barrel had overheated, and was visibly drooping. The .5-inch machine gun mounted on one of the platoon's jeeps had taken hits from rifle fire, and was also out of action. On top of this, there was very little ammunition remaining. Bouck decided that there was no option but to withdraw. He ordered his men to prepare for the signal (three blasts on a whistle). While the men made preparations to depart, Bouck resolved to stay and defend the position: after all, this was his task. Fortunately, Tsakanikas walked past Bouck on his way back from disabling the jeeps. Realizing something was wrong, and asking his officer what it was, Bouck told him that he was going to stay. Tsakanikas's vehement reaction was to tell Bouck in no uncertain terms that, if he were going to stay, the rest of the platoon would stay as well. Bouck gave in and agreed to go with the men, but just as he was preparing to give the signal there was a shout from one of his men – the Germans were

American prisoners captured as a result of the German advance. The variety of uniforms indicates that they come from different units. POWs faced an arduous trek to prison camps, liable to air attack and with little food. Some took the opportunity to escape, but few succeeded.

PANZERKAMPFWAGEN VI TIGER AND TIGER II HEAVY TANKS

Like the Panther, the Tiger had its origins in the recognition even before the war that that the Mark IV would need to be replaced in production (which, of course, it never was). The first orders were placed in 1941, and the tank entered service in September 1942. It was an excellent tank for its day, and caused great alarm amongst Allied tank crews from its first service action in the Tunisian campaign until the end of the war. Its frontal armour was virtually impervious to Allied tank guns, and its 88mm main gun could defeat any Allied tank. Even though the Tiger was a formidable weapon, plans for a replacement were in hand even as it entered production, and the result was the Tiger II or Königstiger (King Tiger). The King Tiger was disadvantaged by its low power-to-weight ratio, which made it rather less manoeuvrable than was desirable. It was also unreliable and difficult to move around the battlefield, a disadvantage that became obvious during the Battle of the Bulge. Like the earlier Tiger, the King Tiger's armour gave it almost total protection against Allied tank guns, while its 88mm main armament could destroy any British or American tank at considerable range. The King Tiger's weight and lack of numbers combined with crippling shortages of petrol during the latter stages of the war to make it a far less formidable weapon than it might otherwise have been.

attacking on the left flank. This was followed by another shout. German troops were approaching on the right as well.

This change in tactics had come about through a rather unusual planning process. As the paratroop officers were debating the next move to take, they were approached by one of their NCOs. Feldwebel Vincent Kuhlbach was one of the few experienced men in the entire parachute regiment, and had become increasingly exasperated with the way in which the officers had sent in their attacks. He bluntly informed the officers that their approach had been frankly ridiculous, and explained that the Americans could be dislodged if the near-suicidal frontal assaults were abandoned in favour of an assault from the flanks. The officers seemed glad to have received a new suggestion: before they could say anything, Kuhlbach stalked off and briefed his men as to the tactics for the new attack.

This one worked. The I&R platoon was now in a hopeless position, and the Germans were soon on top of them. Bouck

shot two Germans, but within moments two more soldiers ripped the cover off the foxhole in which Bouck and Tsakanikas were sheltering. Tsakanikas instinctively pointed his Garand at the soldiers, but one of the Germans fired a burst from his MP40 sub-machine gun at near point-blank range. The shots wounded Bouck in the legs, but inflicted massive damage on Tsakanikas: as the Germans pulled him from the foxhole, one of the Germans turned away in horror at the sight. The right side of Tsakanikas's face had been destroyed, and his eyeball was left hanging out of its socket. Incredibly, these wounds did not kill Tsakanikas, and German medics were soon trying to save him. Bouck was approached by a German NCO, who recognized him from his insignia as an officer. Bouck had no need to surrender the position, since it had fallen. The Germans rounded up the members of the I&R platoon or milled about trying to find their companions. Bouck and Tsakanikas were taken down to the local café, where Oberst von Hofmann had set up his headquarters. The I&R platoon's epic battle to defend Lanzerath was over.

THE 394TH

While Bouck's platoon made its last stand, the rest of the 394th was still holding on. Maj Moore had not faced any further attacks at Buchholz station, and he took the time to consider the position confronting his men. By 14:30, he had consulted with his Executive Officer and Operations Officer, and together they concluded that their present location was untenable. Moore therefore decided to withdraw his forces to a more secure location. They would move north and position themselves across the road that linked Losheimergraben and Büllingen (6km [4 miles] to the northwest). L Company moved out first, leaving K Company to hold the position at Buchholz. Capt Simmons decided that it would be useful to send out a patrol at dusk to gain an appreciation of the situation facing the company. The patrol saw nothing, but they heard a great deal of movement by tanks and vehicles on the Losheimergraben–Lanzerath road before they returned to the lines at 1800. Simmons passed on the information about road movements to Moore, who then forwarded this to headquarters. Before Moore was able to issue orders for K Company to fall back on the new position, Col Don Riley, the 394th Infantry Regiment's commanding officer, sent him new orders for K Company to leave two platoons at Buchholz station as a security force. Moore was not happy with these orders, and tried to persuade Riley to change his mind, but to no avail. He therefore passed the new instructions on to Simmons, who was faced with the unenviable task of implementing them. Detailing Lt Joseph P Rose to command the two platoons left behind, he moved out with the remnants of the company. All was quiet, since the Germans had not followed up their attacks. The calm would not last for long.

A German half-track makes its way over difficult terrain as it passes a knocked-out M10 tank destroyer. While the Germans made great use of half-tracks, large sections of the army remained dependent upon horse-drawn transport until the end of the war.

Malmedy 13 km
St. Vith 8

CHAPTER FIVE

THE SIXTH PANZER ARMY DELAYED

The fierce resistance encountered by the Sixth Panzer Army imposed an increasing delay upon the German advance. While the tanks and infantry fought to break through, a combination of bad luck, over optimism and the delays caused by the Americans ensured that two of the most audacious elements of Hitler's plan were on the brink of failure almost before they could be enacted.

LYLE BOUCK SAT IN THE CAFÉ at Lanzerath, looking around in some puzzlement. It was filled with Germans resting after the fierce battles of the afternoon and he could not help wondering why the Germans had stopped in the town when they could easily have pressed on. He was disturbed from his thoughts by movement outside the café. The door swung open and a man dressed all in black strode in, demanding to know who was in charge. The long-suffering Oberst von Hofmann stood up and confirmed that he was the commander of the assorted troops around the town and resting in the café.

The new arrival was clearly agitated, and with good reason. He was one of the most relentless, dynamic and ruthless soldiers produced by the Third Reich and, to his mind, things in Lanzerath were not as they should be. He

In this famous photograph, the man in the Scwhimwagen's front passenger seat is often misidentified as Joachim Peiper. Yet it is known that Peiper never went past this spot. The rifle hanging off the sign was actually placed there to hold the sign in position by the photographer.

walked straight up to Oberst von Hofmann, stood within inches of him and announced that he was SS-Obersturmbannführer Joachim Peiper. He had not had a good day, and his temper was not improved by his discussion with von Hofmann. Although Peiper was a rank junior to von Hofmann, it became quite obvious that this was of no concern to him: he was going to take charge.

Peiper demanded to know why von Hofmann had stopped advancing. Von Hofmann wearily explained that American resistance had been strong. He thought that there was at least one American battalion ahead of them and he was concerned that the road might have been mined. He produced a map to make his points to Peiper. Peiper was unimpressed. He could not see the map properly in the dim light, and made the dramatic gesture of pinning it to the café wall with a dagger. He asked von Hofmann if he had sent patrols out to probe the American positions, but von Hofmann admitted that he had not, since he thought it had become too dark. As Peiper scrutinized the map, his irritation rose. Von Hofmann attempted to assist, but Peiper rounded on him, shouting that there were no Americans in front of the parachutists, and that von Hofmann hadn't even bothered to send out anyone to check. He demanded that von Hofmann turn over one of the parachute battalions to him, adding that he would begin preparations for an attack at 04:00 the next morning. With that, he turned on his heel and stalked out.

JOACHIM PEIPER

Joachim Peiper was commissioned by the SS in 1936. He began the war as a staff officer, but then transferred to the Leibstandarte Adolf Hitler. He won decorations for gallantry in both the French and Yugoslavian campaigns, and the Knight's Cross for his actions in Russia, and by the time of the Ardennes offensive, had been promoted to full Colonel.. The massacres carried out by Kampfgruppe Peiper as it advanced led to Peiper's indictment for War Crimes. He was sentenced to death, but this was commuted to life imprisonment in 1951, and he was released in January 1957. He retired to France, but the revelation of his address in a local newspaper led to death threats. He sent his family back to Germany, but before he could join them, his house was firebombed on Bastille Day, 1976. Peiper's body was found in the ruins, a rifle and pistol at his side: it was clear that he died fighting.

SS-Obersturmbannführer Joachim Peiper, commander of the 1st SS Panzer Regiment Leibstandarte Adolf Hitler *in the Ardennes. Here, Peiper is wearing his Knight's Cross with Oak Leaves, awarded for actions on the Russian Front.*

Lyle Bouck witnessed this odd scene, but thought no further of the matter. He was distracted by the sound of the clock striking midnight. It was 17 December 1944, and Lyle Bouck was now 21 years of age. He had not quite expected to be spending the first hours of his birthday in a small café, a prisoner of the German army. His last day as a 20-year-old had been significant, though, and not just for Bouck. Although they were not to know this, the I&R platoon, alongside their companions from the 394th Infantry Regiment, had played a major part in disrupting the entire German offensive. Hence Peiper's irritation with von Hofmann, since his soldiers were meant to play a special part in the advance, forming part of the spearhead driving towards the Meuse and working alongside some of the troops from a specially formed unit called Panzerbrigade 150. The delaying action by the 394th had seriously impinged upon Peiper's advance, wrecking the already shaky plans for Panzerbrigade 150 before they had even been put into practice.

KAMPFGRUPPE PEIPER

When the plan for *Wacht am Rhein* had been presented to the Sixth Panzer Army on 6 December 1944, the role of the Army had been discussed. As noted earlier, the panzer divisions were not to be used for the initial assault, since this would be conducted by the infantry. It was quite clear, however, that some form of armoured assault would be required to ensure rapid progress to the Meuse crossings. This led to the decision to employ special task groups from I SS-Panzerkorps to achieve this goal. The Sixth Panzer Army staff were not happy with the sector assigned to them for the attack, since the terrain was most unfavourable to tanks: it was wooded and the roads were poor. A request to move the attack further to the south where better roads might be found was rejected, and this had led to the decision to employ the special task groups. One of these was placed under the command of SS-Sturmbannführer Herbert Kühlman, while the other was to be commanded by Joachim Peiper.

Peiper was from a distinguished military family, and had reached the SS rank equivalent to Lieutenant-Colonel at the age of 29. His choice as a task group commander was almost inevitable. Dietrich knew him well, having been immensely impressed by Peiper's performance on the Eastern front

Panther tanks advance along a snow-covered road as the offensive begins. Although German tanks were generally superior to those of the Allies, there were not enough of them, and the quantity of the available tanks, rather than the quality, made the difference in the end.

when Dietrich had commanded the SS *Leibstandarte* Panzer Division. At one point during the bitter fighting, Dietrich had been asked to assist the 302nd Infantry Division, which was attempting to withdraw in the teeth of a Soviet attack. Dietrich selected a Panzergrenadier battalion commanded by Peiper and sent it to aid the infantry. Peiper crossed the Donets river against fierce resistance, and had driven back a series of counter-attacks as he advanced towards the 302nd Infantry. He joined the hard-pressed infantry unit, and they withdrew to the Donets. The infantry division successfully crossed the frozen river, but Peiper was in trouble: the ice was too thin to take the weight of his vehicles. Peiper did not panic, but turned his unit round and fought his way through the Red Army units in front of him, cutting neatly through them until the Panzergrenadiers reached a bridge. The Panzergrenadiers crossed the bridge, then headed back for their parent unit. Peiper was awarded Germany's highest award for gallantry, the Knight's Cross. His unit went on to earn a reputation for its performance in combat, but also acquired some notoriety for its commander's willingness to burn Russian villages at the slightest provocation. By 1944, Peiper's fame had increased his already large pool of self-confidence, and he was not afraid to contradict general

JAGDPANZER IV

The first Jagdpanzer IV entered service in 1943, and soon became extremely popular with crews. Armed with a powerful 75mm (2.95in) gun and well armoured, the majority were employed on the Eastern Front, but those used in the western Europe proved formidable advesaries.

> Soldiers on the Western Front!
> Your hour has come! Powerful assault armies have gone into combat against the Anglo Americans today.
> I do not need to tell you any more. You can all feel it. It's all or nothing now.
> Bear with you the holy duty to give all and accomplish the super-human for our fatherland and the Führer!
>
> *Feldmarschall Gerhard von Rundstedt, Order of the Day 16.12.44 Oberbefehlshaber West*

officers if he thought that their ideas were wrong – with the patronage of Dietrich (an old friend of Hitler's, it must be recalled) he was able to do this without facing the threat of disciplinary action from the frustrated generals. This, of course, meant that the inexperienced von Hofmann (a mere one rank above the self-confident Peiper) was always going to find himself bossed around by his junior.

QUESTIONING ORDERS

This blend of arrogance, competence and sheer ruthlessness meant that it was not hard to decide that Peiper would head one of the key battle groups for the Ardennes offensive. Despite his high standing, Peiper was not brought into the planning process for the assault immediately, although he had an idea that something important was in the offing when he was approached by the chief of staff to the Sixth Panzer Army, SS-Brigadeführer Fritz Krämer. Krämer asked three intriguing questions. The first was what Peiper thought about the notion of an attack in the Eifel region. The next was how long did he think it would take a panzer regiment to advance 80km (50 miles)? And finally, could this be done in one night? Peiper had no idea and, guessing that the first question depended on the answers to the next two questions, that he would take a more practical step than just consulting a map: he took a Panther tank for a night-time drive of the required distance. He returned to Krämer with the information that it was possible for a single tank, driving down a clear route, to cover the required distance in a night. Krämer was happy, and returned to report this to the rest of the Panzer Army's staff. Peiper's suspicions that the issue was important were confirmed when he was given his instructions for the offensive on 13 December.

Peiper was not entirely impressed with his orders. The route that he was assigned was a secondary road and he protested that this was not suitable for tanks. He was cut short by being told that Hitler himself had selected the routes, and that they simply could not be changed, no matter how impractical those tasked with putting the orders into practice knew them to be. He was also unhappy to learn that much of the fuel that was supposed to have reached his unit was still in the assembly area, and that he might well be compelled to rely upon captured fuel instead.

Kampfgruppe Peiper, in keeping with most German armoured units, was made up of a variety of tanks and self-propelled Wirbelwind anti-aircraft guns (which carried four 20mm [0.8in] cannon). Two of the group's companies were equipped with Panther tanks, and another two with the older, but still highly effective, Panzer IV. In addition to these units, Peiper's forces included a number of the formidable and much-feared Tiger II tanks. The armour was completed by assault guns (StuGs) and a few Jagdpanther tank destroyers. Peiper intended to employ the two Panzer IV companies in the vanguard, followed by the Panthers. The Panthers would be accompanied by the half-tracks conveying the Panzergrenadiers, with the engineer and artillery units behind them. The Tigers were to bring up the rear: although they were formidable weapons, the Tigers were heavy and lacked mobility. Peiper concluded that these were not altogether suited to the rapid advance he was supposed to

The Jagdpanzer IV was a tank hunter built on the chassis of the Panzer IV with a new low-profile welded super-structure. This made it very suitable for ambush tactics.

make, hence his decision to leave them at the rear of the formation. When the offensive began, Peiper was not with his command, but at the command post of 12th Volksgrenadier Division, monitoring the progress of the infantry. Once the infantry had forced a breach in the American lines, he would join his Kampfgruppe and advance. It soon became clear, however, that the infantry were in difficulties; by 1400 Peiper had decided to leave for his command.

MOVING FORWARD

Kampfgruppe Peiper had begun to move out of its assembly area, but had run into a massive traffic jam and was now stuck. When Peiper arrived, he was furious at the lack of organization that had left his units embroiled in such chaos, and issued instructions that his column was to move forward regardless. If anything got in its way, it would be pushed off the road. As Peiper's troops moved further along the road, they saw the problem: the bridge over a railway cutting some 2km (1 mile) east of Losheimergraben had been blow up during the course of the German retreat, and had not been rebuilt. Traffic had built up while waiting for German engineers to appear to bridge the gap. Peiper spent some time attempting to inject some organization into the proceedings, as well as trying to work out how his men were going to move one. It soon became obvious that part of the cutting, within 50m (164ft) of the blown bridge, was passable with care. Peiper ordered his tanks to make their way carefully down the slope, which they did successfully. The tanks then traced their way up the bank on the opposite side and were on their way again. By the evening Peiper had arrived just outside Losheim, and by 22:00 hours even the unmanoeuvrable Tigers had caught up. The column was further delayed just outside Losheim, since the Americans had sown a large number of mines that made movement

American prisoners make their way into captivity as a result of the German advance. The variety of uniforms here demonstrates that the men are from a number of different units. The POWs faced a long and arduous trek to prison camps, liable to air attack and with little food.

almost impossible. Peiper waited for the engineers to arrive with mine detectors, but when he learned that they were still some kilometres away, he ordered his men to continue despite the risk. A few tanks were destroyed or damaged, but the majority made it through: this saved hours, but the traffic jams and the lack of progress by the infantry had already delayed what was meant to be a rapid advance – and it would transpire that this delay was a fatal blow to the already faint chances of crossing the Meuse and driving on to Antwerp. This was bad enough for Peiper, but for the units of Panzerbrigade 150 the situation was even worse.

THE GREIF COMMANDOS

Hitler may have been totally disconnected from the reality of the strength and combat potential of his forces, but he did comprehend some of the basic issues that would have affected a force that was actually able to drive towards Antwerp. He fully appreciated the vital importance of the Meuse crossings, and knew that even special battle groups would not be able to gain sufficient surprise to guarantee their capture intact. If the Allies understood what was happening, there was a considerable danger that they would destroy the bridges and bring the offensive to a crashing halt. Without the Meuse bridges, Antwerp would be nothing more than a distant dream (in reality, of course, without the Meuse crossings, capturing the port would have been an even greater impossibility than it already was). As always, though, Hitler knew the answer.

On 21 October, the man who was probably Hitler's favourite commando, Otto Skorzeny, responded to a summons to visit the Wolf's Lair headquarters. Skorzeny had made his name with a daring raid to rescue Mussolini from captivity in Italy and had since maintained his reputation for daring. At the meeting, Hitler congratulated him on his recent exploits, which included kidnapping the Hungarian regent's son and seizing the seat of government in Budapest. After Skorzeny had presented his report, Hitler told him that he was being promoted to SS-Obersturmbannführer. Skorzeny thought this was the end of the audience, but Hitler told him to remain behind and then proceeded to brief him about the forthcoming offensive (meaning that Skorzeny was perhaps the first field commander to learn of the plan). He explained that the Meuse bridges were crucial to the offensive and directed Skorzeny to set up a special unit to secure the crossings. Since there was no chance of this unit achieving this task overtly, they would wear American uniforms in order to advance behind enemy lines towards the bridges. Once the offensive began, they would discard the American uniform for their normal combat dress, with the exception of a small group who would remain disguised so as to permit movement behind enemy lines. Those who had resumed wearing German uniform would secure the crossings until the leading elements of the advance relieved them, while the group remaining undercover would be used to spread confusion among the enemy, through sabotage and spreading disinformation.

PROBLEMS

Skorzeny left the meeting aware that he had very little time in which to set up the special unit, whose mission went under the codename Operation Greif. Skorzeny soon found that the task was even more difficult than he had first thought. Since the mission was so important, a high level of secrecy was attached to it. This presented the first set of difficulties. Skorzeny needed to obtain large amounts of captured American equipment and, equally importantly, men who could speak English well enough to pass themselves off as Americans. The only way of finding the necessary personnel in such a short space of time was to send out an order for English-speakers to volunteer. Unfortunately, the way in which this was done went against all the basic tenets of operational security. On 25 October, the OKW issued an order to all commands, which plainly stated that there was a requirement for recruits who had knowledge of English and especially the American dialect. Skorzeny was outraged and immediately expressed his displeasure by drafting a signal direct to Hitler. He argued that the operation was fatally compromised and should be postponed. This, however, was not to happen. It appears that no one could quite bring himself to take the signal to Hitler, revealing the mistake. Hitler's inevitable fury at learning that the error had led to the cancellation of what he considered to be one of the most vital parts (if not *the* most vital part) of the offensive was best left to the imagination. The OKW sympathized with Skorzeny, made soothing noises and told him to get on with it.

YANKEE GERMANS

This was not Skorzeny's only problem. He expressed deep misgivings at the use of Allied uniforms, which appeared to break the laws of war. General Westphal was particularly concerned about this issue, since it was obvious to him that the only way to obtain the uniforms quickly would be to remove them from prisoners of war. This was of dubious legality (although, of course, such issues did not concern all German leaders during the war), especially as it was winter. Westphal thus vetoed this means of obtaining the uniforms, also noting that to obtain them in this fashion might have

Otto Skorzeny, one of the most famous commando leaders of World War II, and a favourite of Hitler. Skorzeny was chosen by the Führer to lead Operation Greif, the daring attempt to seize the Meuse river crossings by disguised commandos, but soon realized his task was impossible.

adverse repercussions for German PoWs. This matter was insignificant compared with the strength of the unit to be formed. Skorzeny had planned on the assumption that, since his unit was designated Panzerbrigade 150, it would have the same strength as a regular brigade formation – but it became increasingly obvious that he would not be able to obtain enough men. An assessment of the task also made it plain that he would need armoured support if he were to hold the Meuse crossings until support arrived. This was a profoundly difficult problem, since the armour would need to be American in origin: and the Germans simply did not have anything like enough captured American tanks. On further investigation, Skorzeny discovered that there were only enough captured Sherman tanks to equip a section rather than a brigade. This meant that he had to modify his plans, reorganizing the planned establishment of Panzerbrigade 150 so that it had two tank companies, each with ten tanks (although what these tanks would be was difficult to work out), three armoured reconnaissance companies with ten armoured cars each, and the balance made up of infantry, anti-aircraft and anti-tank units.

While Skorzeny was grappling with this issue, it became clear that the planning would remain theoretical if he could not recruit more men. It was obvious that the brigade, 3300 strong, would not all be able to speak English, and the lack of success in obtaining men initially meant that it appeared that Skorzeny would be able to form only two combat groups instead of the three he had intended.

By 28 October Skorzeny was increasingly pessimistic about his prospects of success. There were just ten new recruits who could speak English fluently and do so in a manner that would enable them to pass themselves off as American troops. About the same number of men could speak fluent English, but their accents were not sufficiently American; they also spoke using British idioms rather than American. A third category, 120 in number, spoke passable English, but would never be confused for Americans, while the fourth and largest group of 200 men could just about manage 'yes' and 'no'. Skorzeny was forced to adapt his plans – the majority of the men would just have to advance in sullen silence and avoid situations in which they were required to speak.

SHORT OF MEN

The men were assembled at Panzerbrigade 150's training area at Grafenwöhr and subjected to strict security measures as their training began. Many of the volunteers came from the non-combatant arms of the army, or even from the *Luftwaffe*, and had no experience of infantry combat. Skorzeny soon realized that moulding these men alone into an effective fighting force would be impossible, so he asked for some established units to support them. He was assigned two parachute battalions, a panzer company and a signals unit. Two reinforced companies of Skorzeny's own command, Fallschirmjägerbataillon 600, completed the line up. He was now marginally happier, but was still 800 men short of his originally intended total, even if he was finally able to have the three battle groups that he had planned upon. He was also drastically short of uniforms and equipment.

The difficulties with the provision of both uniforms and equipment were varied. First, as with the armour, some items were simply not available in sufficient numbers. Another difficulty was posed by the fact that the order for units to surrender captured equipment did not stress that this was important. Many units had captured American uniforms, weapons and vehicles, but turned a blind eye to the signal. They had good reason for doing so – short of their own equipment, they had made good use of any they had captured and were most reluctant to surrender it. Other units were confused by the vague terms in which the order was worded, and sent Soviet equipment instead.

SHORT OF EQUIPMENT

Finally Skorzeny was forced to ask Westphal for assistance: on 9 November an order was issued for the provision of ten tanks, twenty armoured cars, a similar number of self-propelled guns and more than a hundred jeeps to Skorzeny, alongside trucks and British and American uniforms. This helped a little, but some of the equipment that arrived was of dubious quality. Much of it was damaged, and although the

Two M4 Sherman tanks pause in a recently liberated and badly damaged Belgian town, on their way to the frontline. The camouflage applied to their front and sides is notable. Both tanks are equipped with the standard M2 Browning heavy machine gun.

supply of American weapons improved, there was not enough ammunition to go around. Had the Americans used the 9mm (0.35in) round for their sub-machine guns the situation might have been slightly better, since German stocks could have been raided: even this slight possibility, however, was crushed, as every American service weapon employed different calibre ammunition to German weapons, and the captured stocks were all that were available.

A further search located captured equipment that had been forgotten in a number of depots in Germany, but this still added only one or two items to what was a long list of requirements. Finally Skorzeny admitted defeat and requested the supply of Panther tanks that were disguised to provide a passing resemblance to American M10 tank destroyers. The disguise would not stand close scrutiny, but it was better than nothing. As the date of the offensive approached, it became clear to Skorzeny that he had created a rather different unit to the one that he had set out to build. Instead of a fully covert brigade, he had a mixed formation made up of what were effectively conventional infantry and a few men who could pretend to be Americans, thus enabling them either to cause confusion behind enemy lines by spreading misinformation and bad news, or to reach the river crossings without being identified as the German soldiers that they were.

START OF OPERATIONS

Following all the difficulties in assembling and equipping Panzerbrigade 150, it was perhaps not altogether ironic that only a small number of Skorzeny's men actually operated in the intended fashion. At the end of November, Skorzeny briefed his formation commanders about their task. The two combat groups would move forward with the battle groups heading for the Meuse crossings. Once the Americans had begun to fall back, the commandos would pass through the

American soldiers look down at a dead German soldier in US issue clothing. It was not always easy to tell whether Germans with American equipment were Greif commandos or not, since many rank-and-file soldiers wore the uniform to keep out the cold.

German tanks advance across open ground. The Ardennes terrain was hard for tanks, and the Germans had to rely upon a limited number of routes. Some were barely adequate for the task, which led to numerous traffic jams, and badly affected progress on the first day of the assault.

German front line and mingle with the enemy. Once they had reached the Meuse crossings, they would secure them and wait for the first armoured units to relieve them. The plan was daring, but appeared simple. When the offensive started on 16 December, however, the slow pace of the advance meant that the plans began to fall apart. Panzerbrigade 150 spent the day waiting for the anticipated breakthrough to occur, but instead was forced to endure the huge traffic jam. Rather than heading towards the Meuse bridges, the men of Panzerbrigade 150 were largely sitting around waiting. A few of them had penetrated American lines and were attempting to cause confusion, but they were out of contact. Without some dramatic improvement in the situation, the Greif commandos were in danger of not even joining the fight.

LAST STAND AT BUCHHOLZ STATION

Just before 04:00, Peiper's men roused the paratroopers from von Hofmann's 1st Battalion. The paratroopers clambered to their feet and began to climb onto Peiper's tanks, which would carry them into battle against the Americans at Buchholz station. Once they were all assembled, Peiper's half-track moved to the front of the column and it set off.

At the station, Lt Rose began to receive reports from his platoon leaders that they could hear the sound of enemy vehicles, including tanks, moving towards them. These reports were soon followed by other brief transmissions stating that voices could now be heard, and that these were definitely German. Rose acknowledged these reports and gave instructions that his men should not open fire until he gave the order, no matter how tempted they might be to initiate contact: if the German force was impossibly large, it might be possible for the American troops to fall back. The lack of firing from the American positions had a secondary benefit, in that it began to unnerve some of the less experienced German soldiers, who made anxious comments as they advanced without meeting opposition. Eventually, however, Rose knew that he had no option but to order his men to fire. The enemy were all around his positions and there was little point in staying silent any longer. The order was given, and the early morning was shattered by a fusillade of shots interspersed with bazooka rounds. The paratroopers scattered as the American fire reached them, but Peiper's group held all the advantages. One of the Wirbelwind anti-aircraft tanks was sent forward and started engaging the Americans with rapid cannon fire, against which they had no response. The weight of fire from the Wirbelwind was such that the Americans were forced to keep their heads down,

An M10 Tank destroyer and an M4 Sherman. The M10 is camouflaged with foliage, and the machine gun is covered on the rear of the turret. Note the extended exhaust trunking on the rear decking of the Sherman, suggesting it may have been modified to allow it to 'swim'.

enabling the paratroopers to rush into K Company's positions. Desperate hand-to-hand fighting broke out, and the defensive positions began to fall apart despite the effort being put in by the Americans. Peiper sent his tanks forward now, and then began to fire their machine-guns and their main armament. Shells started to rain into the station building, and it was evident that the end was near. At the 3rd Battalion's command post, Maj Norman Moore listened in frustration to the reports being sent back from Buchholz

"0530 hours: Short commands are given along the entire area of the assault front. The company lines up in an open formation looking westward. We are shivering with excitement. Watches have long since been synchronized...20 seconds...10 seconds,... 5,...4,...3,...2,...1,... Fire! The muzzles of several thousand guns, howitzers and launchers roar together almost as if they were just a single detonation.
The muzzle flashes light up the sky to the east behind the paratroopers so that it is almost as bright as day...
...0600 hours: All at once this hell of a noise stops!
Then the command is given: 'Charge!'
We start running forward!"

Paratrooper Rudi Frühbeisser, 1. Kompanie, Fallschrimjägerregiment 9

station. Then Rose's radio operator, Sgt Alvin Rausch, calmly reported that the Germans had entered the command post and taken Rose prisoner. He continued in the same tone, asking for immediate artillery fire on the position, then announced his intention to destroy the radio so that it would not fall into German hands. He signed off and radio contact ceased. Buchholz station had fallen at last, nearly 24 hours after it was meant to have been taken by the Germans.

SITUATION HOPELESS

Rausch's dramatic radio messages were also being listened to by Lt Col Robert Douglas in the 1st Battalion's command post; from here he could also hear the noise of the battle, which was less than a kilometre away. Douglas knew that the Germans would soon be heading for his position, on and around the crucial Losheimergraben crossroads. His battalion was down to about half strength. Acting on the reports he received from the patrols he sent out, some of whom had not returned, he had decided to move his command post to the customs houses by the road, in order to have a better view of the battlefield. At 06:40, shortly after Douglas had completed the move, the men of Oberstleutnant Osthold's 48th Grenadier Regiment followed their commander into the fray against the remaining elements of Douglas's battalion.

The attack made some progress, but, just as it appeared to be on the point of success, the assault guns he was expecting failed to appear. The German advance stalled and, to compound Osthold's difficulties, the artillery stopped firing several minutes before the supporting barrage was scheduled

THE TANK DESTROYER

The basic concept of the tank destroyer as a vehicle discrete from the tank itself stems from two complementary philosophies which had their basis in a mixture of doctrine and expediency. The first philosophy held that the specialized tank destroyer would be used against enemy tanks only, while tanks could be employed for infantry support duties as well as dealing with any enemy armour they encountered. The idea of specific anti-armour vehicles owed much to American thinking in the inter-war period, which believed the tank destroyer, equipped with a high-velocity gun and blessed with good manoeuvrability, to be a means of overcoming massed, fast-moving formations of enemy armour. Experience in the Second World War demonstrated that normal tanks were just as effective in the anti-tank role as their specialized brethren. The second concept was based upon expediency. The demand for tanks with greater main armament could not be matched by supply, since fitting larger weapons to tanks was limited by the turret ring. If the turret ring on a tank was unable to bear a heavier weapon, a new design was required. Designing a completely new tank in the midst of a war was impracticable, so one solution was to convert existing chassis to take a fixed superstructure into which a larger calibre gun could be fixed. For Nazi Germany, this was an appealing concept as the war went on. Initial 'lash-up' designs were superseded by dedicated tank destroyers, which could be built much more expeditiously than a turreted tank on the same chassis. This gave the Germans the ability to put more armour in the field than would otherwise have been the case: by 1944, this was a vital consideration.

American tank destroyers did not follow the same route of using turret-less designs, but a swift appreciation of the superiority of using tanks themselves as a counter to enemy tanks meant that their tank destroyers were employed not as specialized anti-armour weapons, but in the conventional armoured role.

to end. While Osthold's men were coming to a halt, Oberstleutnant Heinz-Georg Lemm's 27th Fusilier Regiment attacked B Company, who put up fierce resistance. The Germans paused at a line of foxholes, waiting for the opportunity to continue their advance. Despite the desperate resistance, Douglas realized that his situation was hopeless: he radioed to Col Riley asking for permission to withdraw to the west, where a better defensive position could be set up. Riley pondered the request for a few moments before giving his approval. Douglas set about informing his battalion that they would move out, but this was made more difficult since contact had been lost between the battalion command post and some of the unit. His instructions were sent out using messengers, and the men of the 1st Battalion began to slip away as quietly as they could.

HONOURABLE SURRENDER

The German attacks restarted, but despite the withdrawal of many of their opponents Osterhold's men were confronted by vigorous resistance from a group of Americans who were still holding out in positions near the customs houses: Douglas's message had not reached them. The attack began to falter and Osterhold ran forward to see why. Once again, the lack of assault guns proved to be the problem. The guns had started to move against the American positions, but had taken heavy bazooka fire. The assault guns' commander was lying in a ditch by the side of the road receiving treatment for his wounds, and it soon became obvious that the guns would not be able to provide support for this part of the assault. Osterhold thought about how to overcome the problem and recalled that his men had captured a number of American mines. He gave orders for these to be brought forward along with some German time fuses; he planned to attach the time fuses to the mines and use them as what would effectively be large, improvised hand grenades against the customs houses. Men ran back and obtained the necessary items. As the mines were being prepared, Osterhold secured the services of two NCOs who would make the attack on the customs houses with him. They picked up their mines and dashed across the road. Osterhold prepared to throw his mines into the building, but something made him stop. He could see that his men were now in control of the crossroads, and it seemed pointless to kill the Americans when the Grenadiers had already achieved their objective. He put his mines down and called out to the Americans, grateful that he spoke good English. A few calls of abuse confirmed that the men in the building's cellar could hear him, so he continued. Since the Germans had control of the entire area, and the Americans were now in a hopeless position, there was no disgrace in surrender. If they did not accept his offer, he would throw the mines into the building and it would inevitably collapse. He did not want to do that, so would the Americans please give up?

SCRAMBLING FOR PINS

The American troops in the cellar realized that Osterhold's offer made sense. A white flag was fashioned and one of the men went out to meet the German commander. Osterhold followed him back to take the surrender. Once he reached the cellar, there was a moment of almost deadly farce. It became apparent that several of the Americans had been about to throw hand grenades just as Osterhold had shouted his plea for them to surrender. They had not thrown them but, not expecting to need them again, they had dropped the safety pins. Osterhold realized that he was standing among a group equipped with armed grenades. One of the Americans helpfully suggested that they should throw them out of the windows, but Osterhold sensibly noted that this was only likely to convince his men that their commander had been ambushed and prompt them to attack. There was only one option: Osterhold pulled out his flashlight and, in the dim lighting of the cellar, a group of American prisoners and a German lieutenant colonel scrambled around on the floor, looking for the grenade safety pins. After the grenades had been made safe, Osterhold led the Americans out of their position and let his men take them captive. He yelled at one or two of his soldiers for trying to take cigarettes from the Americans, having already made it clear that anyone

A German soldier passes the remains of an American convoy. The debris on the ground suggests that the supplies have been rifled for anything useful. The parlous supply situation faced by the Germans meant they were eager to use any enemy supplies they could obtain.

Above: German paratroopers leaving their Ju 52 transport aircraft. Note the first parachute, which carries a stores container. At the Battle of the Bulge, many of these troops were inexperienced to the point of never having exited an aircraft in flight. No wonder the mission failed.

Right: The size of a Tiger II is amply illustrated by the number of men on the rear decking. The man about to throw a packet of cigarettes has an MG42 machine gun. One of the best designs in history, it was modified for 7.62mm (0.3in) ammunition and is still used by the German army.

attempting to relieve the captives of personal possessions would find themselves answering to a very irate battalion commander. As the Americans were marched away, Osterhold looked around Buchholz station, reflecting on the hard fight it had taken to dislodge the enemy. It was now 15:00 on 17 December and the Sixth Panzer Army was way behind schedule. Although they did not know it at the time, determined fighting by the Americans in the path of the Sixth Panzer Army (and, it cannot be overstressed, not just by the elements of the 394th Infantry Regiment concentrated upon here) had almost guaranteed that the plans to seize crossings over the Meuse would never be realized.

FAILURE OF THE PARATROOPS

While the 394th Infantry Regiment had bought the Allied troops valuable time in delaying the Germans, some elements of the attacking force had not been able to make any contribution. As has been recounted, most of Panzerbrigade 150 was sitting in a traffic jam for much of the first day of the offensive, with its leader becoming ever more convinced that his troops would not be able to carry out their mission. For the paratroops commanded by Lt Col von der Heydte, the situation was even worse. On the journey to the airfield from which their transports would depart, some of the vehicles carrying the paratroops broke down through lack of fuel. By 22:00 on 15 December, only a third of the 1200 men scheduled to make the parachute drop had arrived. The drop would have to be delayed. While he was waiting, von der Heydte found out about the squadron of Junkers Ju 52 transport aircraft that would be carrying them. The unit had a good reputation, since it had supported the besieged Germans at Stalingrad, but this was built on past glories. The only member of the squadron who had flown on these missions was the commander. None of his men had dropped paratroops in combat before, or, for that matter, flown on a combat mission. To round off this sorry tale, the squadron commander revealed that he was the only one who had even flown his aircraft at night. Von der Heydte was

horrified, and hoped that the operation would be cancelled. He was not to have his wish. Sixth Army headquarters sent an officer to investigate why the mission had not started, and General Krämer gave orders that the drop was to take place on the night of 16/17 December. Shortly before midnight, an armada of Ju 52s left the runways of two airfields and headed for their drop zone. In the lead aircraft, von der Heydte became more confident as everything appeared to be progressing smoothly. At the drop zone he was the first man out, as tradition demanded.

Von der Heydte was disadvantaged by the fact that his right arm was in a splint, making it difficult to control his parachute. As he neared the ground, a gust of wind hit his canopy and he landed with great force. The impact was enough to knock him out and he lay on the ground for some time, oblivious to what was happening. Eventually, he came round and discovered he was utterly alone. Not panicked by his solitude, he took out a compass and calculated in which direction the rendezvous was. He walked purposefully toward it, knowing that his men would be waiting for him. When he reached the road junction designated as the meeting place, he saw a small group of men. He closed on them and found 20 of his troops waiting for him. They were all that he had. Out of 1200 men, the 21 standing at the Belle Croix road junction were the only ones who had landed roughly where they should have done. While the pilots had done their best, their formation had been broken by strong cross-winds, and they had disgorged their cargoes over a wide area. A few more men arrived, and then a few more. Von der Heydte sent out small search parties to hunt for any of their colleagues who had come down in the surrounding woods. They found more, but once the search parties returned it became clear that nobody else was likely to appear. Another head count revealed that there were now 350 men. It would be utterly impossible for the paratroops to

A column of German prisoners is marched to the rear, passing through a destroyed Belgian village. Both the guards and the prisoners are tired and dishevelled after hard fighting. As the Battle of the Bulge wore on, such scenes were often repeated, the columns of Germans lengthening.

The Supreme Commander, General Dwight D Eisenhower (seen here preparing for the Normandy landings) directed Allied operations in Western Europe. He insisted that his commanders regard the Ardennes offensive as an opportunity rather than a setback.

carry out their original mission. To make their situation even worse, the signals platoon had disappeared completely and von der Heydte's personal radio had been destroyed in the descent. As well as missing more than two-thirds of their manpower, the paratroopers were virtually cut off from the outside world. Von der Heydte determined that he would do as much as he could with his small force, adopting hit and run tactics against any small American units they encountered, so as to give the impression of being a much larger body of men than they actually were. Von der Heydte had little idea that, while he was planning to make the best of a bad job, the Americans had reached a rather different conclusion as to the effectiveness of his forces.

CONFUSION

The failure of the parachute drop as a result of the wide dispersion of the paratroops proved to be a bonus for the Germans in that it confused the Americans as to what exactly had happened. They spent much of the morning of 17 December (and some time afterwards) rounding up stray paratroops from all across the front. This confused the American high command. The desperate fighting meant that they did not have a full picture of the situation on the ground, only an incomplete picture based on reports of numerous local actions involving large numbers of their units: of small groups of Americans fighting to the last man; of retreating soldiers and civilians clogging the roads; and worrying hints that Germans wearing American uniforms were acting as saboteurs. Additionally, they were confronted with reports of paratroopers all along the front. The logical explanation was that the Germans had dropped sizeable numbers of men: the thought that this was actually a small number of men dropped all along the front thanks to a mixture of bad planning, bad weather and bad luck simply did not occur. As it was, one of the combat commands from a reinforcing battalion spent a week in the anti-paratrooper role, seeing nothing and missing the fighting where they would have been of far greater use.

EINHEIT STIELAU

The reports of Germans wearing American uniforms also contributed to the confusion. Of course, the majority of Panzerbrigade 150 had spent much of 16 December sitting in a traffic jam; on the following day Skorzeny decided that his men stood no chance of carrying out their original task – if they were to succeed in reaching the Meuse, they needed to mingle with an almost-routed army. Although the Americans were falling back, the stiff resistance that had encountered the attack meant that the commandos were likely to be spotted. On the afternoon of the 17th, Skorzeny suggested that his operation be called off and that his men be employed as conventional troops. This was accepted and Operation Greif ended before it had really begun. One part of the mission had some success, however, in the form of the small groups who operated as intended. These were the members of Einheit Stielau, the only element of Panzerbrigade that was to operate undercover. They comprised the men who had demonstrated the greatest proficiency in English and who had been provided with American clothing, weapons and jeeps. Without prior experience of covert operations, they were at a profound disadvantage in that they had not had time to develop the necessary sense of when a move that appeared to be a good idea was simply too risky to implement. They also had inadequate time to study the Americans in depth and were in serious danger of making basic mistakes that would demonstrate that they were not, in fact, who they appeared to be.

JAGDTIGER

The Jagdtiger represented the ultimate in tank destroyers as far as size and armament were concerned, but it was otherwise an inferior combat vehicle to the Jagdpanther. Based upon the King Tiger's chassis, it was incredibly heavy and utterly unsuited to mobile warfare. The Jagdtiger's 128mm (5in) gun was the largest anti-tank gun fitted to a combat vehicle during the war. Although they were the best armed and best protected tanks of their era, they were underpowered. This lack of mobility made then of little use during the Ardennes offensive. They were assigned to provide support to Colonel von der Heydte's paratroopers, and even had the parachute drop been successful, there must be some doubt as to whether the Jagdtigers would have been able to make it through, given the difficult terrain to which they were far from suited.

GETTING THE RIGHT ANSWERS

Nearly sixty years after the event, it is difficult to know exactly how many of the Einheit Stielau managed to succeed in their tasks, since the Americans became almost paranoid about the threat posed by what was, in reality, a very small group of men. The problem was compounded by the many ordinary German soldiers who, during the Battle of the Bulge, made use of looted American clothing simply to keep themselves warm – they were frequently mistaken for Greif commandos when they were no such thing. Various incidents have been attributed to Skorzeny's men, including moving signposts to send American reinforcements in the wrong direction, posing as retreating men and giving dire warnings of approaching German forces to small groups of Americans and interfering with demolition charges.

One captured Greif team leader added to the chaos by claiming that the commandos were on a mission to kidnap Eisenhower, and that he was confined to a hotel for his own safety. The American troops began to implement their own security measures – rather than just requiring a password, they demanded the answers to questions that only Americans would know. Gen Bruce Clarke was briefly imprisoned by a guard when he failed to answer a question about which league the Chicago Cubs played in, while Omar Bradley himself was asked questions about state capitals and football. He failed to identify Betty Grable's husband (the bandleader Harry James), but the guard let him through anyway – probably realizing that the Germans were unlikely to send an impostor dressed as Gen Bradley. There is a story – which, sadly, is probably untrue – that some units were told to ask for the words to the third verse of the *Star Spangled Banner* on the grounds that, if the respondent knew them, it was most unlikely that he was American. The fate for those captured was a firing squad, and the presence of the commandos behind the American lines had an unfortunate

The enormous Jagdtiger was the ultimate expression of Hitler's obsession with heavy tanks. Although armed with an impressive 128mm (5in) gun and armour up to 250mm (9.8in) thick, the Jagdtiger was a tactically ineffective vehicle because of its poor manoeuverability.

result for many German soldiers: once it became known that the Americans were shooting any Germans wearing US-issue clothing, several German units gave out orders that no one was to wear any US uniform, and that if anyone had it they were to dispose of it. German troops who had acquired such items with the intention of keeping themselves warm were now forced to go cold again, which was hardly good for morale.

The confusion (and the delays stemming from it) caused by the commandos was out of all proportion to their numbers, despite the fact that they did not have a decisive effect on the battle. Their contribution in the first 24 hours of the Battle of the Bulge was relatively limited, but they still managed to sow the seeds of doubt in the minds of American soldiers of all ranks. This was an important aspect of their contribution to the battle, although it should not be forgotten that they were meant to be the vanguard of the forces that would seize the Meuse crossings – and never made it.

SIXTH PANZER ARMY'S FIRST DAY

The first full day of Sixth Panzer Army's attack produced mixed results. Hitler was euphoric, and spoke of 'good old Dietrich' having forced the Losheim gap. However, this was not the true picture. Dogged defence by the Americans had severely delayed the German advance. Perhaps the most spectacular example of this was provided by Lyle Bouck's I&R platoon, but the 99th Division had stopped the advance at Höfen and along the International Highway. In addition, the use of paratroops had failed completely, while Panzerbrigade 150 had been forced to abandon its supposedly crucial role and deploy as a conventional unit. This did not mean that the German advance had been stopped dead: far from it. The ruthless drive of Joachim Peiper had given the Germans an opportunity to drive through the Losheim gap, while, to the east of Krinkelt-Rocherath, the 12th SS Panzer Division was ready to attack. Despite these possible gains, however, Sixth Panzer Army failed to achieve any of the goals assigned to it for the first day. Hitler's main effort still had a huge amount of work to do if it was to prove that the vision of taking Antwerp could be realized; as subsequent events were to prove, it would not.

The 1st SS Panzer Division's effort was the focus of German efforts to punch through the Allied lines and drive on to the Meuse and Antwerp. Despite the advantages of surprise and concentration of forces, the division did not achieve the goals set out for it on the first day.

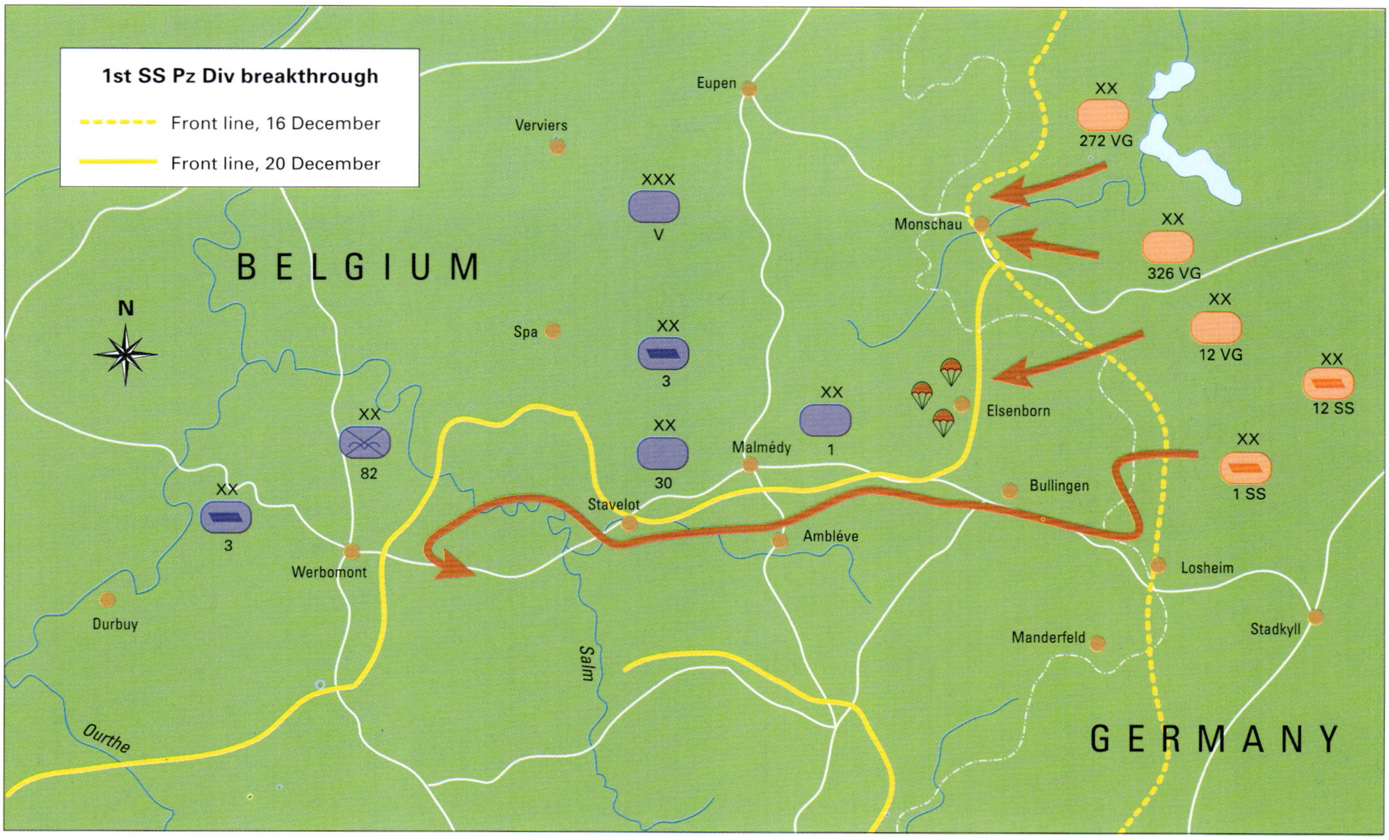

CHAPTER SIX

FIFTH PANZER ARMY ATTACKS

The Fifth Panzer Army's units were not as well-equipped as those of the Sixth Panzer Army, which were designated to carry out the main assault, but they were at least under the command of one of Germany's most capable generals. Largely as a result of his abilities, it was the Fifth Panzer Army that inflicted some of the most serious difficulties upon the Americans. In its path lay the inexperienced 106th Infantry Division, and disaster was to ensue.

FIFTH PANZER ARMY'S COMMANDER, General Hasso von Manteuffel, was one of the most prominent practitioners of tank use and, unlike some of the commanders for whom Hitler had a high regard, well suited for his task in the offensive. Von Manteuffel was a distinctive man, not least since he was only 5 feet 2 inches tall. During officer training, his lack of height meant that his sword had to be shortened to prevent him tripping over it as he walked, but this was about the only deficiency that was noted by his instructors. He had forged a successful career in the army, even though he was no lover of the Nazi party (taking the view that army officers should not dabble in politics). His career had suffered a brief setback when he fell out with Hitler's favourite Walter Model on the Russian front. Model had ordered von Manteuffel, then a colonel, to launch an attack,

A column of Panther tanks rolls across barren terrain, heading for the battle zone. The Panther was one of the best tanks of the war, but was simply not available in anything like enough numbers as the war drew to a close, and was unable to stop the inexorable Allied advance.

but the snow was so deep that von Manteuffel's men had been barely able to move. Von Manteuffel called off the attack, to Model's fury, and it appeared that dismissal might follow. Before anything came of this, however, von Manteuffel had been transferred to France; he then went on to command a division with great distinction in North Africa, before being sent to lead the elite *Grossdeutschland* division on the eastern front. His performance there had so impressed Hitler that the Führer decreed that von Manteuffel should take command of Fifth Panzer Army, even though he had not fulfilled the role of corps commander, which was the normally required stepping-stone for command of an army.

Von Manteuffel was not entirely convinced with the plan as laid down by Hitler and had voiced his concerns. He had managed to persuade Hitler that some of the objectives for his army would best be achieved by the use of infiltration tactics without the use of a large preliminary bombardment, basing these conclusions on his own observations after he had joined some of his men in the front line to reconnoitre the area. He noted that the US 28th Division's positions opposite the Our river were not particularly well held: the 110th Infantry Regiment pulled back from its positions at night, while the gaps between the positions held by the 112th Infantry Regiment persuaded von Manteuffel that his men would be able to make their way between the Americans without the need to alert them with a large barrage. He hoped that, by the time the Americans appreciated the threat, his soldiers would have managed to outflank them, gaining a huge advantage in the process as they headed for the ridge-line known to the Americans as 'Skyline Drive'.

All of these plans were designed to enable Fifth Panzer Army to achieve the key objective of seizing St Vith. This town was crucial to the attack, since if the Germans could capture it they would have access to the road network, enabling them to have a far easier passage to the Meuse and the vital river crossings.

28TH DIVISION

The weaknesses in 28th Division's defences had nothing to do with a lack of attention to detail or basic military logic on the part of its commanders, and everything to do with attrition and lack of manpower. After suffering heavy losses in the Hürtgenwald, the division had been moved to a quiet sector of the front to recuperate. Here the length they held was such that the two panzer corps from Fifth Panzer Army would, in effect, have an advantage of 10:1 over the men at the locations they intended to attack.

The 112th Infantry Regiment was positioned with its back to the river, making the possibility of withdrawal in the face of an enemy assault a difficult proposition, while the 110th Infantry found itself manning the 24km (15 miles) of front at the centre of 28th Division's positions with only two battalions, since the third battalion was the divisional infantry reserve. This meant that Col Hurley Fuller, the regimental commander, was extremely limited in his options for positioning his troops. Defending the whole line was impossible, so he ensured his men held little outposts all along the river, each manned by a squad. After holding the river positions by day, they would patrol the slopes of the Skyline Drive at night. The ridge itself would be defended by the simple expedient of placing a blocking force across the five roads that led up from the Our valley. The troops did enjoy some artillery support, but their supporting battalion had been forced to spread its guns out because it was impossible to concentrate them all in one spot: had this been done, some sections of the front would have been out of range.

A fine commander, General Hasso von Manteuffel was placed in command of Fifth Panzer Army on 1 September 1944. His careful planning made Fifth Panzer Army arguably the most successful of the three German armies employed in the Ardennes.

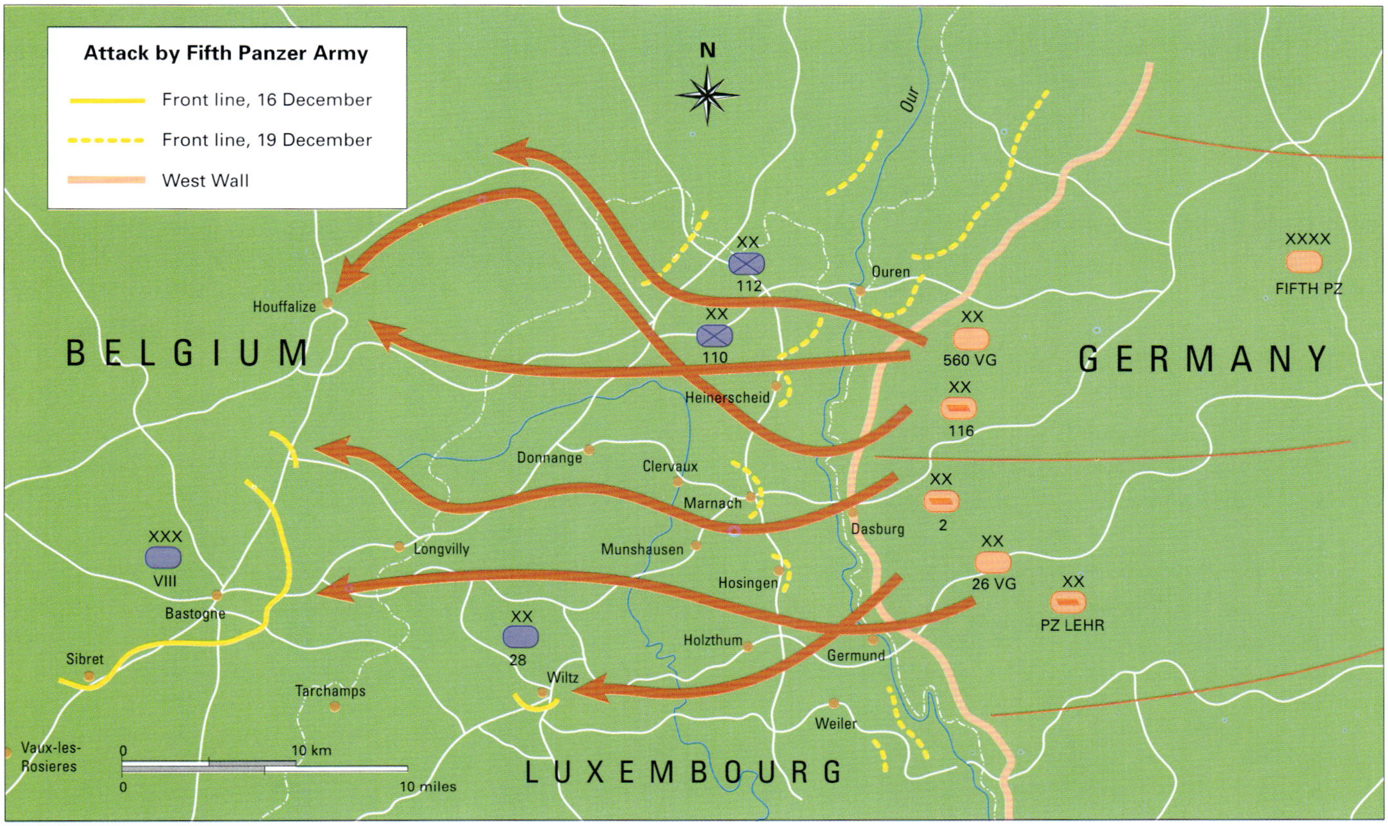

Although dispersing the guns meant a dramatic reduction in the weight of fire that could be brought down on some sectors of the front, this was preferable to leaving some of the line without any artillery support.

The Fifth Panzer Army's attack was marked by the use of innovative tactics which aided its success. The American defensive positions were also thinly held. That said, the American troops fought vigorously, and it took a great deal of effort for the German assault to dislodge them.

106TH INFANTRY DIVISION

Fifth Panzer Army was not confronted by the 28th Division alone, since the sector opposite its northern elements was held by the 106th Infantry Division, commanded by Maj Gen Alan W Jones. The 106th, however, was utterly inexperienced. It had left the United States on 20 October 1944 and upon arrival in Europe had moved up towards the front line. As with the 99th Division, the 106th was assigned a quiet area where it could gain experience patrolling and carrying out limited operations before being thrown into battle against the Germans in a major push. The division took up its position on the left of Gen Middleton's VIII Corps on 11 December, less than a week before the German attack. Totally unaware that a massive assault was about to be launched, the 106th was at a complete disadvantage. Jones and his staff had only just begun to assess their defensive requirements, they had not been able to make any alterations to their dispositions, and had not had the opportunity to lay down a co-ordinated plan for defending in conjunction with their neighbouring units.

As if this were not bad enough, the 106th was also having problems with supplies. There was a shortage of bazooka rounds, and the stocks of 0.3in ammunition needed for the M1 Carbine were at low levels. Stocks were reaching supply dumps, but the nearest ammunition dump was 64km (40 miles) away from the 106th's headquarters at St Vith and the long supply line meant that rapid replenishment was not easy. Although Gen Jones had not had enough time to work out a full defensive plan, he was sufficiently concerned to demand the supply of anti-tank mines to bolster his defences. These took longer than five days to materialize, however, and the division did not have them in place when the Germans launched their assault. The 106th's inexperience also reduced the number of automatic weapons available to it. Experience had demonstrated that automatic weapons were a great help in both attack and defence, and many of the more experienced divisions had taken the opportunity to bolster the number of BARs and light machine-guns that were available to them. This meant ignoring the standard scale of supply of such weapons, as laid down in army documentation, but there appears to have been little opposition to the notion that practical experience should supersede what 'the book' had to say about such matters. Unfortunately the 106th had not yet been in a position to discover that such a variation from regulations was necessary, and still retained the standard proportion of rifles to automatic weapons held in the ranks. Given that it was dealing with a frontage of 34km (21 miles), this was most regrettable, since defence against attacking enemy units would be much more difficult – sweeping automatic fire was generally more effective than rifle fire, no matter how carefully aimed.

The crew of an M7 self-propelled gun prepare to fire in support of the defences. Note the crude makeshift boarding ladder. The crews of the M7s came under attack from German infantry all along the line on 16 December 1944, but provided support for as long as they could.

The 106th's only possible advantage was that the terrain in its sector was not particularly favourable to attackers, since there were a number of places where the enemy would be forced to narrow the width of their attack, possibly placing them in greater danger from defensive fire.

CAVALRY

The last component of the American defences was Col Mark A Devine's 14th Cavalry Group. This was in the unfortunate position of holding an area bisected by the boundary between the Fifth and Sixth Panzer Armies, and was thus positioned next to the 99th Infantry Division. As we have already seen, elements of the 99th Division, in the form of Lyle Bouck's I&R platoon, were operating in the 14th Cavalry Group's area, and this can cause some confusion as to which panzer army was fighting elements of the cavalry when dealing with the history of the battle: to the Americans, the distinction of which particular German formation was facing them was a nicety that could be left to historians – they were facing serious odds, and this was more important to them.

Men of Company B of the 630th Tank Destroyer regiment dig in near Wiltz, having lost their vehicles in the first stages of the German attack. The readiness of American troops from specialist arms to fight on in an infantry role made it hard for the Germans to penetrate the defences.

Within Col Devine's command the 18th Cavalry Reconnaissance Squadron was defending the Losheim Gap with just 800 men. They were concentrated into defensive 'islands' based upon the small farming villages that dotted the region, since this seemed to be the best way to make use of their limited strength. Devine was also concerned that the 18th was lacking one of its three troops (the cavalry equivalent of a company), which had been sent to bolster the defences at the other end of the Schnee Eifel. On the other hand, the cavalrymen did have the support of twelve 3in (76mm) towed anti-tank guns, two reconnaissance platoons from the 820th Tank Destroyer Battalion and some self-propelled guns from the 275th Armoured Regiment.

Overall, then, the American forces facing Fifth Panzer Army were under-strength and in some places were in serious danger of being encircled by an assault.

THE ATTACK

As von Manteuffel had decided against a heavy artillery barrage, the German attacks in this area began with assault companies carefully infiltrating the American positions. In the Fifth Panzer Army's sector around the Losheim Gap, the leading German units began this process between Weckerath and Roth bei Prüm. A battalion of Volksgrenadiers pushed through the gap towards the village of Auw, from where roads led to both the Our and to the Skyline Drive. To the east along the line, the attack at the village of Kobscheid ran into difficulties, since the Americans had established effective defences, boosted by the use of .5in (12.7mm) machine-guns that had been dismounted from armoured cars. The weight of fire provided by these weapons meant that it proved relatively easy to hold the Germans back for most of the 16 December.

The situation at Roth was not so promising for the Americans. The German troops made a vigorous effort to dislodge the defenders, since the village's importance was clear: control of the roads leading from the habitation was needed to push troops, armour and supplies through to support those who had earlier bypassed the village as part of the German infiltration. Roth was defended by the headquarters platoon of the 18th Cavalry Reconnaissance Squadron's A Troop (Capt Stanley E Porché) and two towed anti-tank guns. Their difficult position encouraged Col Devine to send a platoon of light tanks to support the village, but they ran into opposition and were unable to make a breakthrough. By late morning, the light tanks had not managed to advance any further, and it appeared that the defensive position in Roth would shortly become untenable.

Further along the line at Weckerath the headquarters of C Troop was holding the village. Here a platoon of light tanks managed to force its way through to assist, but as it appeared a column of about 15 German assault guns and a battalion of infantry could be seen approaching. It soon became obvious that this formation was not heading directly for the Americans, but was aiming to bypass the village. Although the column was taken under fire, the Germans carried on with little obvious concern. The Americans fought vigorously, but the Germans were able to carry out a methodical advance in this sector, with little hindrance in many places.

The situation was not helped by the fact that 14th Cavalry Group had not been able to confirm a co-ordinated defensive scheme with 106th Infantry Division. The division's recent arrival meant that, on his visit to the divisional headquarters at St Vith, Col Devine had been confronted by staff officers attempting to deal with the details of establishing the 106th's positions and with little time to discuss co-ordination with the cavalry. Devine waited for some time, but once it became clear that he would not be able to talk with Gen Jones he returned to his headquarters to devise his own plan. Once the 106th had bedded into its new positions, this plan would have been superseded by one drawn up between the 14th Cavalry and the 106th, but this notion was overtaken by events.

> If it were not for the will and the determination of these men to stop the superior forces of the German army, a different chapter of history would have been written than the present.
>
> *Maj. Gen. Troy H. Middleton, Commander, VIII Corps*

THE CAVALRY WITHDRAW

Devine's plan was to conduct a fighting withdrawal to the ridgeline upon which the village of Manderfeld stood. He would then bring forward the 32nd Cavalry Reconnaissance Squadron to launch a counterattack, while the men of the 18th Cavalry Reconnaissance Squadron would pull back

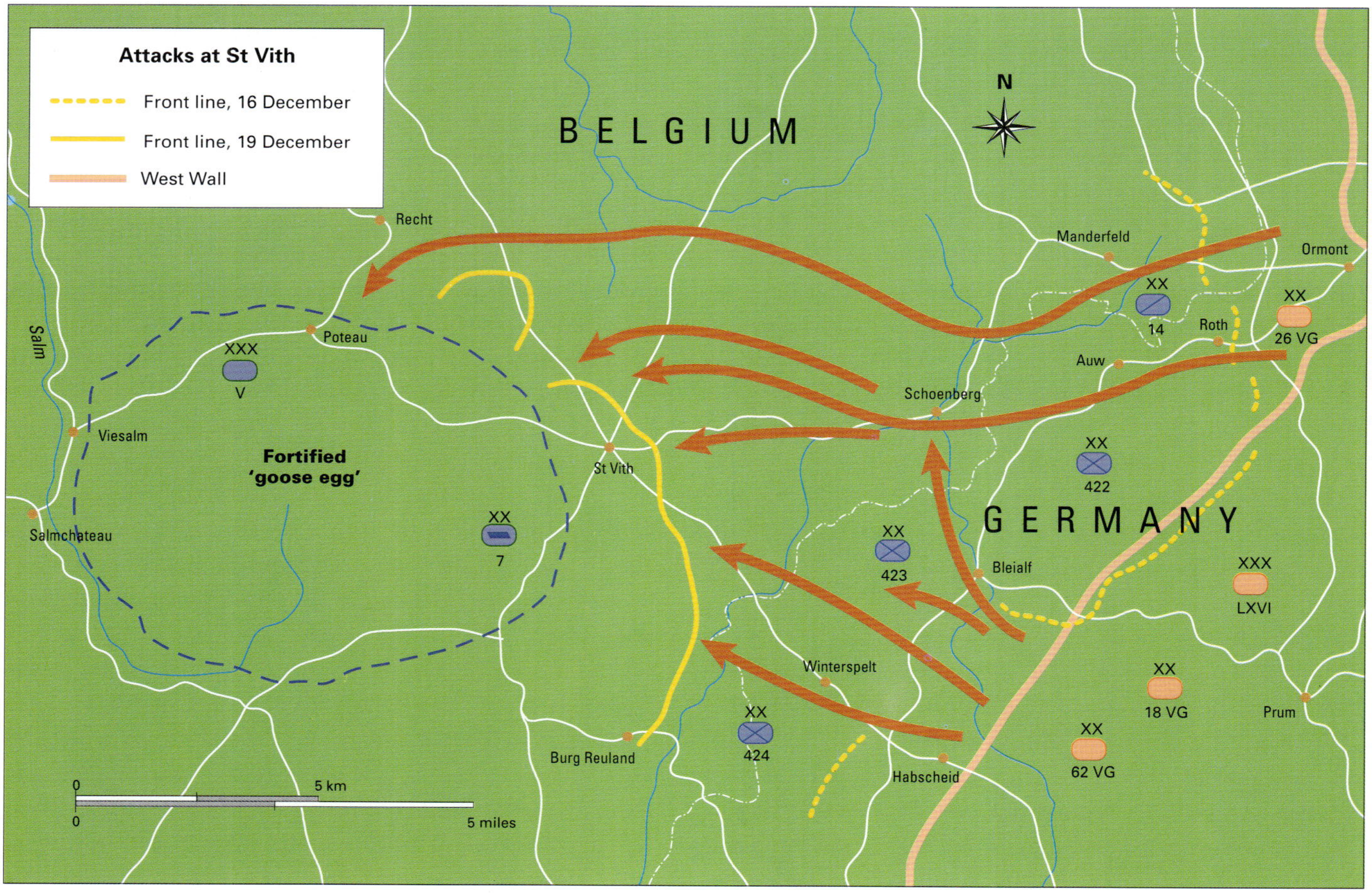

Left: St Vith was a key objective for the Germans, given its position as a major road hub for the Ardennes. It was crucial for the speed of the campaign that it be captured within the first hours of the offensive, but the American defensive line held.

Above: Here, in a still from a propaganda film, German troops pass an abandoned M8 armoured car. Although it has been posed, this photograph provides a good view of the standard dress and equipment of German soldiers towards the end of the war.

further. Thus, when the German attack came on 16 December, Devine ordered the 18th to fall back by 1100, by which time he hoped that the 32nd would have arrived in the area to launch the counterattack.

REQUESTING ASSISTANCE

The responses to the order to withdraw varied. The units at Kobscheid and Roth reported that this was impossible, since the Germans were in too strong a position: any attempt to withdraw in daylight would be suicidal. The Kobscheid garrison thought it might be possible after dark, but the situation at Roth was grave. Capt Porché reported that enemy assault guns were only 68m (75yd) away from his command post, and that the position was untenable. Minutes later, Roth was overrun and the Americans had to surrender. Eighty-seven men were captured.

Devine realized that he would not be able to carry out his defence without help and asked the 106th for assistance. The reply was not encouraging: Gen Jones regretted that he was unable to help, since the enemy was causing terrible problems around St Vith and he simply could not spare the men to aid the cavalry.

Aware that no assistance would be forthcoming, the cavalry began their withdrawal. At Weckerath, Krewinkel and Afst, the cavalrymen pulled back in the face of extremely heavy fire, while the troops at Kobscheid struggled to hold off the Germans until nightfall. Once darkness began to arrive, they sabotaged their vehicles to deny them to the enemy and then left the village, heading for the nearby woods. They spent the next 72 hours carefully working their way through the trees until they made it to St Vith.

As the day drew on, it became obvious that the Germans were trying to outflank the Manderfeld ridge positions. Devine despatched a troop of the 32nd Cavalry Reconnaissance Squadron to Andler, a small village that lay in line with the entrance to the Our valley, while another

GIs from one of the positions attacked on 16 December 1944 recount the story of their escape to interested colleagues. While the Germans took many prisoners during the offensive, several small groups of Americans evaded the enemy by using the dense woodland as cover.

troop from the 32nd, supported by tank destroyers from the 18th Cavalry Reconnaissance Squadron, went towards Lanzerath in an attempt to cover the northern flank of the American positions. The northern flank task force was unable to make a breakthrough, and it was clear that the 14th Cavalry Group's position was in some danger. Devine considered his options and decided that, as the northern flank could not be held, he would have to withdraw. He signalled 106th Division headquarters for permission to withdraw. The cavalry fell back to the next ridgeline, anchoring their southern flank at Andler in order to delay the Germans' entry into the Our valley. While the withdrawal made absolute sense, on a map it appeared that the decision meant that the link between 14th Cavalry Group and the 106th Division's 422nd Infantry Regiment was lost, with the risk of exposing the 106th's northern flank. In fact, the withdrawal had no such effect, since the Germans had already driven so deeply into the American lines between the cavalry and the 422nd Infantry that the flank was exposed anyway. The 106th Division was facing disaster.

DISASTER FOR THE 106TH

The opening barrage against the 106th Division was not as heavy as that fired against American positions elsewhere on the front, but it was effective. The artillery caused great damage to communications lines, ammunition dumps and supply bases. Within minutes, the 423rd Infantry Regiment lost contact with Divisional headquarters and had to rely upon the radio network instead. Worse still, poor visibility meant that it was impossible to see the advancing German troops until they were almost on top of the American positions, giving the defenders little time to react.

The first blow fell against the 424th Infantry Regiment's positions to the north of Heckhuscheid. These were held by K and L companies, with the latter positioned in a small group of houses at the road junction and on a reverse slope, while K Company held a line from the houses in Heckhuscheid itself.

The Germans were able to take the houses quite swiftly, and this enabled them to use the buildings as a firebase to support the attack on the positions on the ridgeline. L Company fell back, regrouped to counterattack, and then regained their position, taking two hundred prisoners. K Company came under heavy artillery and mortar fire, but was able to stop several German attacks and captured the first document referring to Operation Greif – the dissemination of which created some of the panic among security officers noted earlier. Several hundred metres to the south, in the vicinity of Grosskampenberg, the 424th's other forward positions took a heavy toll of forces from the 116th Panzer Division as they passed diagonally in front of the battalion's flank, enabling the defenders to bring down heavy fire.

At Eigelscheid, the Americans were facing the 62nd Volksgrenadier Division, who were hoping to penetrate the American lines and then make a swift advance on St Vith by sending a battalion on bicycles to take the town and seize the fuel supplies. In fact, there were no substantial fuel supplies at St Vith; and as for achieving the first goal, the inexperience of the German troops made that difficult. When they attacked after daybreak, their inexperience was obvious: they rushed forward in tightly clustered groups (which made them easy targets), and fired their weapons without any apparent effort to aim at specific targets. The Cannon Company, under Capt Joseph Freesland, could hear the German NCOs attempting to impose some order on their charges, but with little effect. Freesland called for artillery fire, which inflicted serious casualties. The Germans were not deterred, and every time the artillery fire lifted they would regroup and move forward, only to be hit by heavy fire – the Cannon Company had borrowed several machine guns from the reserve battalion to boost their defences. More artillery would be called for and the Germans would fall back, and the whole process would be repeated. Even

GIs examine a German tank that was knocked out by an M10 tank destroyer near to Wirtzfeld on 17 December 1944. The picture graphically demonstrates that the popular myth that Allied tank guns could not inflict serious damage on German tanks was entirely inaccurate.

GIs make their way cautiously through a wooded area, aware that German troops may be waiting for them somewhere amongst the trees. The woodland meant that it was relatively easy to move without being detected, a factor that was used to advantage by both sides.

though his defences were holding, Freesland could see that the situation was not promising. He took a jeep and went to regimental headquarters to ask for help from the reserve battalion. This, however, was part of the divisional reserve and the regiment could release it only with Gen Jones's permission, which was not forthcoming. Freesland returned to his men to find that the situation had deteriorated: the divisional reconnaissance troop had been overwhelmed at Grosslangenfeld, enabling the Germans to attack from another direction; with them came four assault guns.

Freesland returned to regimental headquarters to request help again, and this time had more luck. The regimental commanding officer, Col Alexander D Reid, had been joined by Brig Gen Herbert T Perrin, Jones's deputy. When he heard Freesland's report, Perrin did not wait to speak with Jones, but ordered that C Company from the reserve should move forward to assist. While C Company headed for Eigelscheid, Perrin contacted Jones to gain approval for the rest of the reserve battalion to move forwards. Jones agreed, but by the time the reinforcements arrived the Germans were close to taking the village. Freesland ordered his men to retreat and the surviving members of Cannon Company, along with the recently arrived reinforcements, headed back towards Winterspelt to join the 1st Battalion's defence. Shortly after darkness the Volksgrenadiers resumed their attack, striking out for Winterspelt. The danger now was clear: if the 424th was forced any further back, the Germans would be in a position to trap both the regiments on the Schnee Eifel.

THE NORTHERN SECTOR

To the north of the 424th, the 423rd Infantry Regiment was in a slightly better position by the end of 16 December,

> My storm battalions infiltrated rapidly into the American front – like rain-drops. At 4 o'clock in the afternoon, the tanks advanced...
>
> *General Hasso Von Manteuffel describes the actions of Fifth Panzer Army on 16 December 1944*

although 'better' was a relative term. After losing its landline communications in the artillery barrage, the 423rd had been attacked all along the line. By 06:00 the Regimental Anti-Tank Company had come under small arms fire at Bleialf, a crucial location since it was the key to the southern route around the Schnee Eifel. The leading elements of the 293rd Volksgrenadier Regiment (18th Volksgrenadier Division) began to filter into Bleialf itself, while another group made its way between the anti-tank gun positions and B Troop of the 18th Cavalry Reconnaissance Squadron, destroying the right-hand platoon of the Anti-Tank Company as they went. The 423rd's commander, Col Charles C Cavender, telephoned Gen Jones to ask that his 2nd Battalion be returned from its duty as the major part of the divisional reserve. Jones did sympathize with Cavender, but felt unable to release half of his meagre reserves. Cavender assembled an ad hoc force from men of the regiment's Service Company, B Company of the 81st Combat Engineer Battalion and as many as could be spared from duty with the Headquarters Company. Some men from the Cannon Company were added to round off the

3-INCH ANTITANK GUN M5

The 3-inch (76.2mm) anti tank gun was a rather unusual weapon in that it combined the components of a number of existing weapons to form a new one. The barrel was taken from an anti-aircraft gun, while the breech and carriage were sourced from the M2A1 105mm howitzer. The gun was rather heavy, and was usually moved around by a 6x6 truck – this made rapid redeployment rather difficult. Nonetheless, the M5 was effective and was widely employed during the Battle of the Bulge. It remained in service for some years after the end of World War II.

The German offensive in the Schnee Eifel area was hampered by the fact that the terrain assisted the defenders. However, the line was only thinly held: American troops held three times the length of frontage that was deemed sound by US Army doctrine.

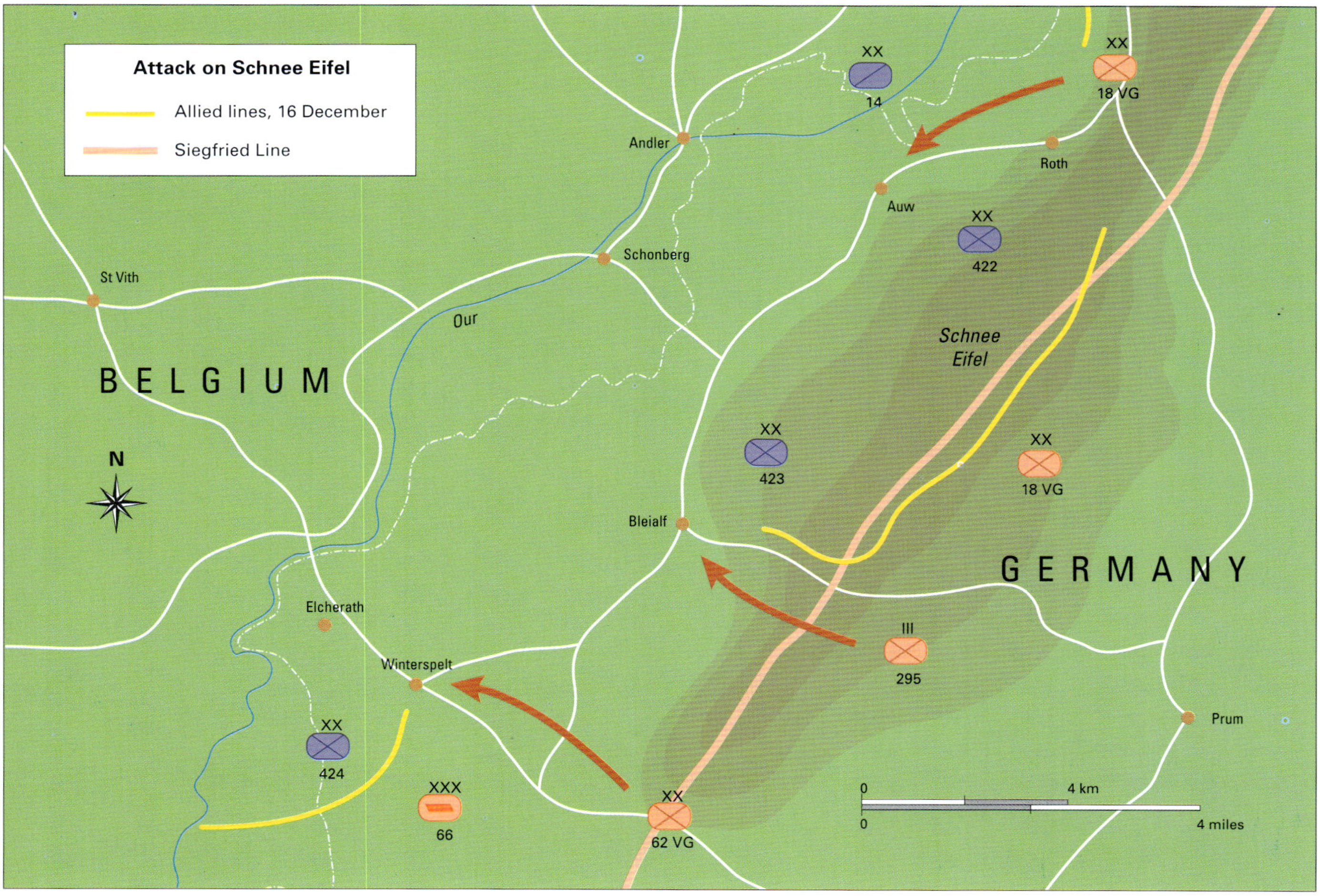

little force and it was sent to Bleialf. After bitter house-to-house fighting, the Germans were almost thrown out of the village entirely, except for those who managed to hold on to some of the houses near the railway line.

422ND WITHDRAW

The final infantry regiment of the 106th Division was the 422nd, which came under sustained attack to its flank and rear from the 294th Volksgrenadier Regiment. Company A of the 81st Combat Engineer Battalion became just as involved in the fighting as their B Company colleagues, since they were billeted in Auw, with its crucial road network. The engineers engaged the leading German column, but the assault guns forced them to fall back. The withdrawal was a desperate affair: 1st Platoon was the last to leave, as the Germans closed within yards of them. Cpl Edward S Withee stayed behind to cover the platoon's withdrawal, armed only with a sub-machine gun. Despite the impossible odds, Withee managed to buy enough time for his colleagues to escape, and – by a near-miracle, given the opposition – survived to become a prisoner; he was later awarded the Distinguished Service Cross.

At midday, the Germans began to move from their new positions in Auw to attack the artillery positions astride the Auw–Bleialf road, with the aim of preventing the guns from firing against the attack into the Our valley itself. The first wave of attacks was driven off by the gunners, using the guns to fire horizontally with short one- or two-second fuzes. This was followed by an American attempt to recapture Auw, for which Col George L Descheneaux jr, the commanding officer of the 422nd Infantry Regiment, despatched a task force at about 13:00. The advance commenced in the teeth of a snowstorm, but just as the task force made contact with the German forward positions it received orders to stop and divert to the regimental command post at Schlausenbach, where it was to establish a defensive line to protect the headquarters, which was under threat from enemy infantry. He had the choice of allowing the attack to continue or protecting the headquarters, since if this fell the regiment's cohesion might collapse as central direction would be lost. The counterattacking forces were recalled. As the task force disengaged from the Germans at Auw to carry out its new orders, the Germans launched another attack against the artillery on the Auw–Bleialf road, this time supported by assault guns. Some of the artillerymen used bazookas to deal with the assault guns, while their colleagues remained with the artillery pieces, firing at the infantry. The attack was driven back, but the gunners suffered heavy casualties.

REINFORCEMENTS

As daylight faded on the 16th, the 106th Infantry Division's troops had lost relatively little ground. This could not disguise the fact that the Germans had managed to make significant penetrations between the positions of the 423rd and 424th; they had also managed to manoeuvre into a position where the flanks and rear of the 422nd were exposed. Once night fell, the Germans resumed their attacks, keeping the Americans occupied and increasing their fatigue while fresh German troops were moved up for a reinvigorated attack the next morning. They were now threatening to encircle the two American regiments on the Schnee Eifel. Gen Jones had sent all his reserves forward, and was waiting for the arrival of reinforcements. The plight of the 106th Division had prompted hurried efforts by VIII Corps, First Army and 12th Army Group to put together some reinforcements. First Army

The crew of a German tank hitch a lift aboard the engine decking of a Panther. They seem relatively cheerful, and their uniforms appear clean, which suggests that they are not being ferried back to friendly lines after losing their vehicle in battle.

A Jagdpanzer IV noses forward over rough ground. Germany infantry relied upon the support provided by assault guns and tank destroyers during the advance, and the relatively small number of these vehicles available for the offensive left many troops bogged down.

released Brig Gen William H Hoge's Combat Command B (CCB) of the 9th Armoured Division to VIII Corps, which allowed Gen Middleton to send his reserve, Combat Command R, forward to support 28th Division. Combat Command B was assigned to the 106th. Hoge set off for St Vith just after 18:00, reaching Jones's headquarters half an hour later. Jones told Hoge that he wanted him to move CCB into the Losheim Gap at Manderfeld, from where he would launch a counterattack to deal with the enemy penetration that threatened the position on the Schnee Eifel.

Shortly after briefing Hoge, Jones received a telephone call from Middleton with the news that he was sending a combat command from 7th Armoured Division as further assistance. This would arrive at 07:00 the next day (17 December) and would be followed by the whole division. This represented an overoptimistic assessment of how swiftly the force would be able to move. While the leading elements of the combat command would be able to reach St Vith by 07:00, the fact that it had to cover almost 100km (62 miles) in a few hours meant that the bulk of the promised reinforcements would not appear until later. Apparently unaware of this, Jones decided to alter CCB's role, which would now be to defend Winterspelt. This made sense, since it would remove CCB from St Vith itself, preventing overcrowding when the 7th Armoured Division's units appeared. Jones also pondered the wisdom of leaving two regiments alone on the Schnee Eifel. He telephoned Middleton to propose a withdrawal, but a poor line and a break in communications for a matter of seconds left Jones thinking that Middleton had ordered him to leave his troops in place while the commander of VIII Corps thought he had just concurred with the decision to withdraw. The 423rd and 422nd Infantry Regiments were left in grave danger.

THE MOUNTING THREAT

The position of these regiments had not been helped by events that befell the cavalry late in the afternoon of 16 December. At about 18:30, the 18th Cavalry Reconnaissance Squadron withdrew to Wereth, leaving A Troop of the 32nd Cavalry Reconnaissance Squadron in a dangerously exposed position. The troop commander tried to obtain permission to withdraw, but was unable to raise his headquarters. An assessment of the situation suggested that the 32nd's position was increasingly tenuous and it was decided to withdraw to Honsfeld. The 32nd duly withdrew towards this village, and into the 99th Division's area of responsibility.

Meanwhile the 32nd's B Troop was assailed at Andler by a German force made up of Tiger tanks and infantry. These were actually elements of Sixth Panzer Army, which had moved into Fifth Panzer Army's area in a search for roads able to take the weight of the Tigers. Troop B withdrew hastily, leaving the 32nd's men at Herresbach isolated; they too were forced to withdraw. B Troop pulled back to Schönberg but was promptly attacked by the German 294th Regiment, which drove the Troop westwards. It fell back looking for a location where it could set up a firm base from which to delay the Germans. It eventually found a suitable spot at a sharp bend in the road near Heuem and held off the pursuing Germans for two hours before receiving instructions to withdraw to St Vith.

SKYLINE DRIVE

Fifth Panzer Army's attacks against the elements of 28th Division holding the other side of the line began with the infiltration of shock troops through gaps in the line. Mortar positions near Sevenig came under fire, but the attacking troops were driven off. An assault on a platoon lining up for breakfast had more success, forcing the Americans to flee. These small indications of an attack were followed at daylight by the sight of German troops marching towards the American lines. One of the attacking shock companies presented itself as a target to elements of the 424th Infantry, who promptly cut the attackers to pieces. This pattern was followed for much of the day and a counterattack through the village of Ouren in the early afternoon by 112th Regiment's 2nd Battalion cleared the Germans from their hard-won positions and restored the line. By the end of the day, the 112th had succeeded in delaying one of the two main columns from Fifth Panzer Army.

While the 112th enjoyed a successful day's defence, the 110th Infantry Regiment had a harder time. A heavy fog made it easier for the troops of the 26th Volksgrenadier Division to move past the defensive positions on the Skyline Drive without being seen. While the defenders heard the

An American column passes through a battered village, in a depressing scene re-enacted across the Ardennes during the winter of 1944–45. The ground is muddy, the weather dull and cold, and the troops are surrounded by scenes of destruction wherever they look.

Volksgrenadiers, they could not be sure whether they were hostile or friendly troops, and dared not open fire. A platoon from K Company was overwhelmed when the Germans emerged from the fog at point-blank range, but the Volksgrenadiers did not press home their advantage as they reached the village of Hosingen. The attack lost impetus and was driven back. The failure to take Hosingen was important, since the Germans could not bypass it – the village offered the best routes westward and toward the bridge at Gemünd.

Further north, the Germans attacking Marnach ran into difficulties when they hit an American minefield just after crossing the Our. Marnach, like Hosingen, could not be bypassed owing to the access it offered to an important road, that to Clervaux. Once the Germans had disentangled themselves from the minefield, they headed for the village but arrived as the fog was lifting. The defenders spotted them and opened fire. Although the attack failed, other German units marched past the village, heading towards Clervaux, leaving the attackers to regroup and renew their assault

DEFENDING THE RIVER

Col Fuller had some difficulty in raising divisional headquarters, but once contact was established, shortly after 09:00, he immediately told Maj Gen Cota that he must have his 2nd Battalion (serving as the divisional reserve) returned to him. Cota demurred, since he did not wish to part with the reserve before he was fully aware of what was going on with all his forces. He did, however, send two companies of Sherman tanks from the 707th Tank Battalion to give Fuller some assistance. The 34 tanks made for a powerful force, but Fuller was compelled to split them into smaller groups to meet the demands for assistance coming from all along the regiment's front. Two platoons went to Marnach, which Fuller regarded as the most important area to defend. Unfortunately events conspired against the speedy despatch of the tanks. Lt Col Donald Paul had sent a patrol from his 1st Battalion's A Company to assist in Marnach, but this had been driven back by the enemy forces bypassing the village. Paul then ordered his reserve, C Company, to drive the Germans from the south of Marnach. The company had begun its march to the village when Col Paul heard that tanks from the 707th Battalion were on their way to Marnach. He requested that they should first head to Munshausen, so they could meet up with C Company. The company, however, had come under heavy fire and left the road to continue its advance cross-country. The tanks missed them and carried on to Marnach. When Paul learned that C Company had not reached its intended destination, he ordered one of the tank platoons to go back to find the missing company; once they had done this, they were to join the defence of Munshausen. The other tank platoon was sent on to Hosingen. The defenders of Marnach were now left without any tank support.

While the 110th carried out its desperate defence, German engineers were busy laying bridges across the Our. The construction was a slow business, since the bridges had to be robust enough to take the weight of a Panther tank. Getting the necessary equipment to the river bank was difficult owing to the steep terrain, while the river itself was swollen from the recent rain and snow. The first bridge was completed just after 13:00, but the eleventh tank to cross it went out of control, struck the bridge and bounced into the river. The bridge had to be repaired, so it was not until 16:00 that the crossings resumed: at the same time, another bridge was completed at Gemünd, enabling the Germans to drive their armour forward into the battle. While the engineers were busy bridging the Our, the Germans maintained heavy pressure along the line, and the defences soon began to suffer. Col Fuller was forced to organize a provisional rifle company from men who happened to be in Clervaux on leave and sent them out to block the road between Marnach and Clervaux, while the headquarters staff were set to work to defend the headquarters itself. Just after nightfall, the defenders of

LIGHT TANK M3/M5

The M3 light tank saw most use in the European theatre as a reconnaissance vehicle, since its main armament of a 37mm (1.45in) gun was unable to counter the armour of German tanks. The M3 first saw widespread use not with the Americans, but with the British, who knew the tank either as the 'Stuart' or the 'Honey'. By the time of the Battle of the Bulge, the M3 had been joined by a development of the original design, the M5, which differed in that it had twin Cadillac engines as opposed to the single engine of the M3. Since the 37mm gun was outmoded, it was not uncommon for the turret to be removed to aid concealment, and extra machine guns were carried in lieu of the main weapon.

The crew of a Panther chat with colleagues at their operating base. The Panther has its gun traversed to the rear so that friendly troops are able to see that it is not a threat as it heads towards them. Crews took this precaution to prevent being mistaken for a hostile tank and fired upon.

Marnach sent their last message, reporting that the village was under heavy attack by infantry supported by half-tracks. Firing continued into the night as the last pockets of defence continued. By the end of the day, Col Fuller had secured the release of his 2nd Battalion from General Cota, planning to retake Marnach with it. Although the situation was serious, the Germans had not progressed particularly well. About two thousand Americans had held off at least ten thousand attackers, an enormous achievement. This had come at a cost, though, since the Americans had suffered hundreds of casualties and were short of ammunition. To make matters worse, just after midnight on 17 December German tanks began to assemble in Marnach – now firmly in their hands – in preparation for an assault on Clervaux.

THE FATE OF THE 106TH

As the first 24 hours of the German offensive drew to a close, the 422nd and 423rd Infantry Regiments were in serious trouble. The Germans were in a position to cut them off from safety and, to add to their problems, communications links with the 106th Infantry Division's headquarters were, at best, patchy. Efforts to assist them failed, and by the early morning of 18 December they were indeed trapped. Gen Jones gave the order to fight their way out, by attacking the enemy at Schönberg. Although they did so the next day, their task was utterly hopeless. The two regiments lost contact with one another as they advanced on their objective and came under heavy fire. By the late afternoon, both Col Cavender and Col Descheneaux understood that their position was utterly hopeless and reluctantly arranged for the surrender of their men. Some eight thousand American soldiers were marched into captivity, and the 106th Infantry Division had been destroyed as a cohesive fighting force.

THE 110TH INFANTRY AT CLERVAUX

Shortly after midnight on 17 December, German artillery fire began to land in Clervaux, providing cover for German patrols to start attacking the American positions in the town, Although the fighting was relatively small in scale, it was enough to make it prudent for the artillery in Clervaux (B Battery of the 109th Field Artillery Battalion) to withdraw, even though it would be unable to support Fuller's proposed counterattack, since the guns were now out of range. Battery A of the 109th artillery fared even worse, since its positions

were overrun by Germans who had made their way behind the Skyline Drive. This left only Battery C and the 110th's Cannon Company in position to support the counterattack, but, since they were already engaged in supporting the defences along the Skyline Drive, it was most unlikely that they would be in a position to contribute.

> We failed because our right flank near Monchau ran its head against a wall.
>
> *General Hasso-Ecard von Manteuffel*

SITUATION CRITICAL

The 2nd Battalion began to advance and immediately ran into difficulties. F Company ploughed straight into German troops emerging from nearby woods and took two hours to drive them away, while E Company managed to advance a little further before it, too, ran into Germans. They were engaged in a fierce fight when Col Fuller ordered one platoon to block the Marnach–Clervaux road, down which German armour was advancing. The platoon could do little to prevent the German advance. The armour from the 707th Tank Battalion ran into German tank destroyers and quickly lost eight out of eighteen vehicles, while infantry-fired Panzerfaust anti-tank rockets accounted for another three. The situation was critical, since the 2nd Panzer Division had gathered momentum and was pushing towards Clervaux, seeking to mount an assault from the rear rather than through a head-on assault. The men in the defensive positions did their best, but were driven back.

The situation in Clervaux itself was little better. At about 09:30, German tanks were seen approaching on the road from Marnach and Fuller sent out his reserve of five Shermans to meet the thrust: there was a vicious exchange of fire in which three of the Shermans were destroyed. The Germans lost four tanks, and the survivors fell back. The two American tanks left for their company headquarters for more ammunition, and this removed them from the rest of the battle. Fuller ordered another tank platoon, under

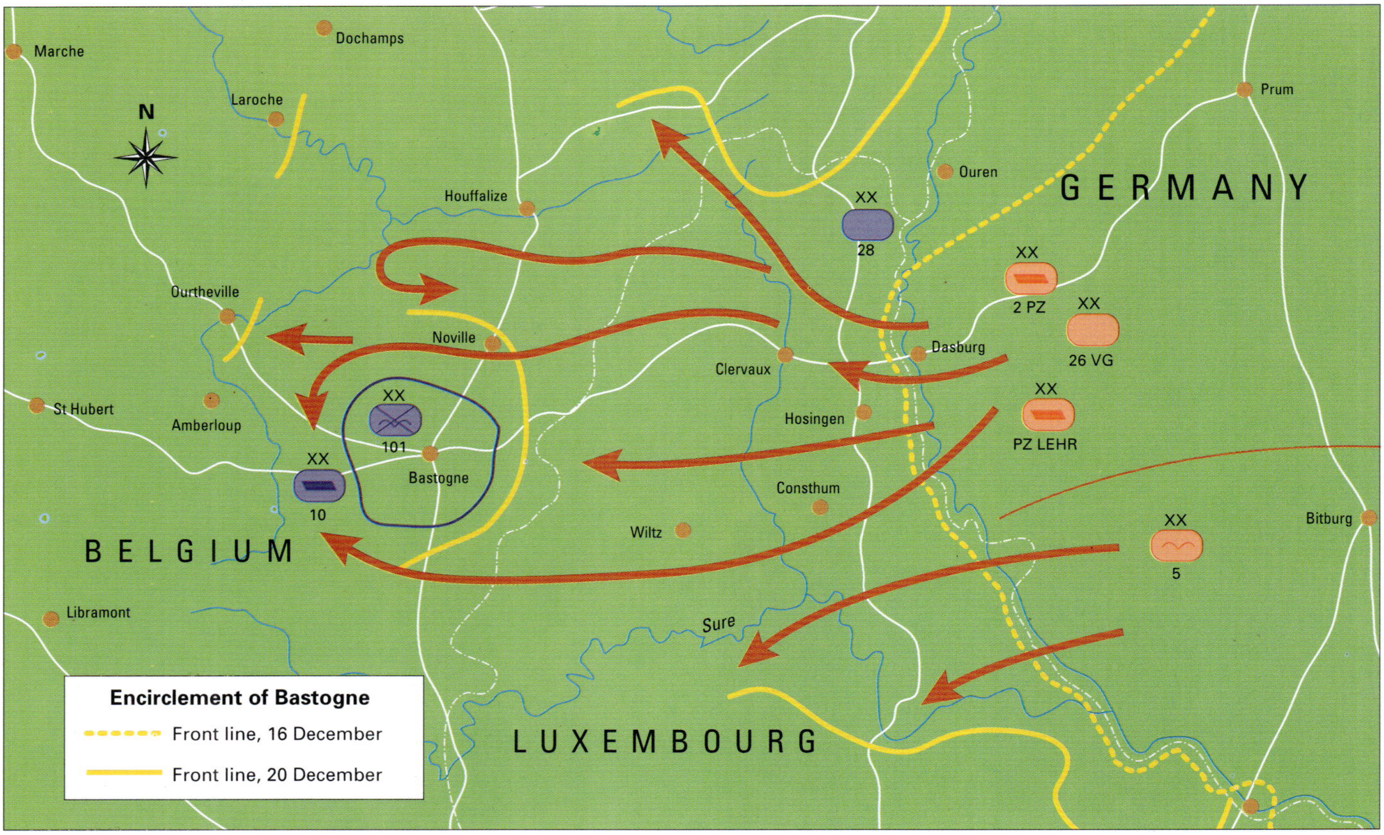

Bastogne, crucial because it was a key road centre, was surrounded by the Germans within a few days of the opening of the offensive. Supported by aerial re-supply once the weather improved, the 101st Airborne carried out an epic defence of the town.

An M4 of the 23rd Tank Battalion comes to grief in a bomb crater. The official caption for the photograph explains that the tank crew reversed when they came under fire from a German gun, without realizing that the crater was behind them. The tank promptly fell into the hole.

Lt Raymond E Fleig, to move from its position at Munshausen to Clervaux. As Fleig reached the road junction, a Panzer IV on the road overlooking Clervaux opened fire. The two tanks exchanged a number of shots, before Fleig's gunner put in the telling blow. The wreck of the panzer formed a perfect road-block on the Marnach–Clervaux road. No other German armour could move towards the town from this direction, but this did not stop attacks from other directions. As the afternoon drew on, Fuller felt obliged to request to be allowed to withdraw. Gen Cota was faced with a dilemma: he did not want to leave a regiment to be destroyed, yet was well aware of the need to prevent the Germans reaching Bastogne. He refused permission to withdraw. At about 18:30, Fuller learned that six German tanks had outflanked the positions on the ridge to the north of the village and were heading for Clervaux. This meant that the 110th was now about to be attacked from its rear. Fuller phoned Cota's Chief of Staff, Col Jesse L Gibney, and again requested to withdraw. Gibney still refused but, as the two men were talking, Fuller was interrupted by a report that German tanks were approaching the command post, located in the Hôtel Claravallis. Fuller returned to the conversation, but was interrupted again, this time by three tank shells crashing into the command post. Telling Gibney that he had no more time to talk, he put the phone down and went to his room to collect his carbine, only to find it occupied by ten of his men taking cover; the room was then hit by a *Panzerfaust* round that wounded half the men. As Fuller was bandaging a blinded man's eyes, a military policeman appeared to show them how to leave the building by a fire escape. Once they were safely away, Fuller paused to catch his breath and then led his group (now 14 strong) to the village of Esselborn, where he hoped he might find a telephone: he did not. The first intimation of the loss of Clervaux at 28th Division headquarters was when the switchboard operator reported that a tank had just thrust its main armament into the hotel lobby, and that he thought it a good idea to shut down the switchboard. As 17 December drew to a close, the Germans were in a good position to drive on to Bastogne: they would find the 101st Airborne Division waiting for them, and participate in a battle that was to become the stuff of legend.

CHAPTER SEVEN

SEVENTH ARMY

The final German formation involved in the offensive was the under-equipped and poorly resourced Seventh Army. Hitler had shown little concern about this element of the assault, convinced that his other armies would advance at such a pace that the Seventh Army's role would be nothing more than a formality. He was to be sadly mistaken in this view.

THE SEVENTH ARMY, under General der Panzertruppen Erich Brandenberger, was by far the least well equipped of the three Armies attacking on the Ardennes front. Brandenberger had three Volksgrenadier divisions and one parachute division under his command, with which he was expected to provide protection to the southern flank of the offensive from the German border to the Meuse. Assuming that the Army met its objective of reaching the river, each division would have to hold a sector of about 32km (20 miles) in length. This would hardly be an obstacle to a determined attack by Patton's Third Army. To compound the Seventh Army's problems, it was heavily reliant on horse-drawn transport and was unable to move at the same pace as would have been possible with motor vehicles. Hitler had not shown much concern for the problems facing the Seventh Army, since he believed that the Fifth and Sixth Panzer armies would be across the Meuse before the Americans could organize a counterattack.

Although taken on the Eastern Front in 1943, this photograph illustrates a major problem for the German army, namely a lack of motor transport. Much of the army's logistic train relied upon horses, which were slow-moving and in need of large amounts of fodder.

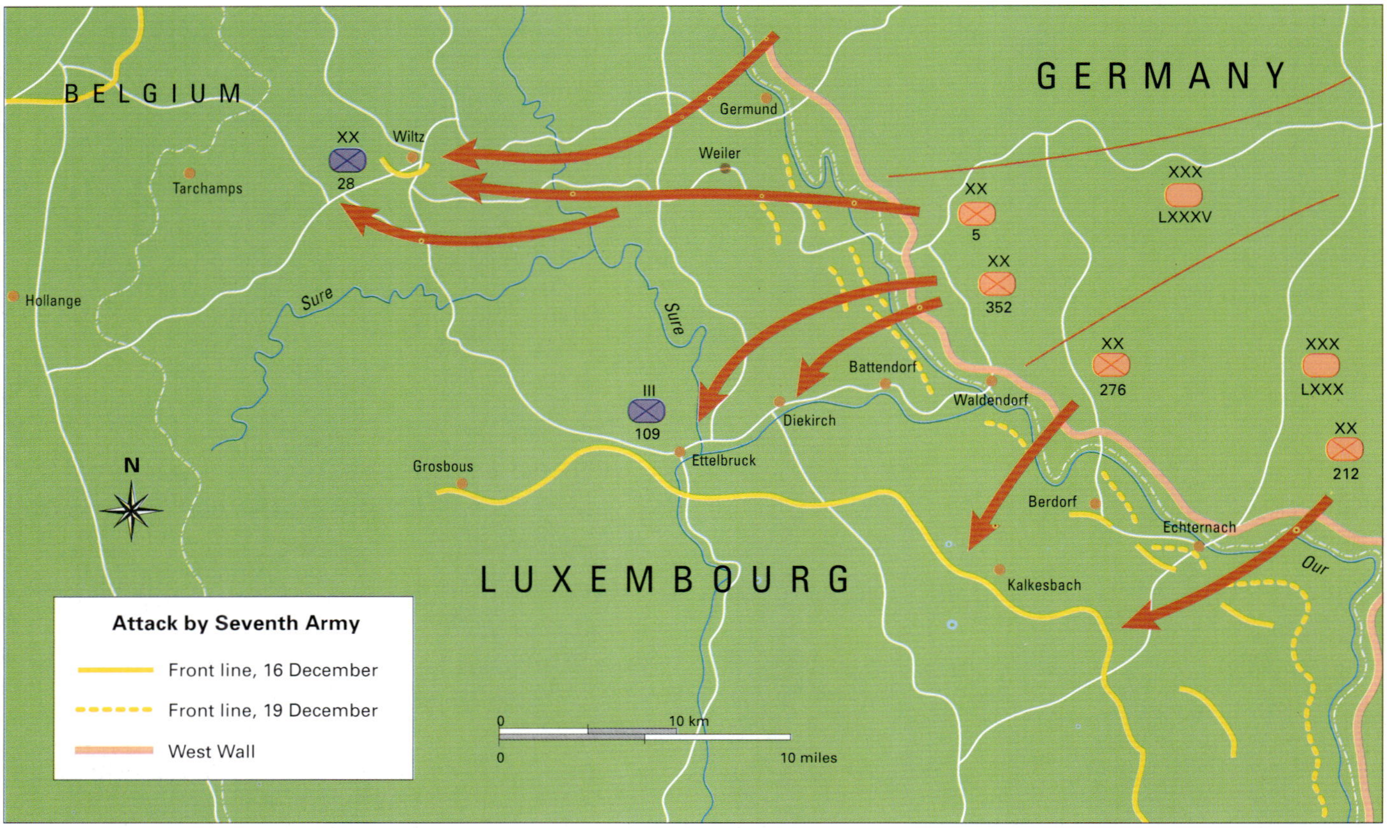

Seventh Army was the 'poor relation' of the other attacking armies in terms of manpower and equipment, and it is said that Hitler did not concern himself with the details of its plan. Von Rundstedt and Model could not convince the Führer that more troops were needed for success.

This opinion was not shared by many of Hitler's generals. They were all too aware that the recognized solution to deal with an enemy offensive was to hold the 'shoulders' of the offensive (the forces alongside the main effort – the 'head') as this would prevent the enemy penetration from widening. Once the shoulders of the assault were held in place and the line stabilized, the next step was to cut the penetration off at the base. If the Seventh Army were not strong enough to prevent the Americans from driving through it, the offensive would be cut off. Both von Rundstedt and Model urged Hitler to strengthen the forces available to Brandenberger, but were ignored. This left Brandenberger with an army that was short of men and lacking key equipment. He had less than half the artillery pieces and rocket launchers that had been made available to Sixth Panzer Army: a mere 30 assault guns and no tanks at all. With such limited forces, how could he accomplish the aims that Hitler had set? His answer, quite simply, was that he would not. He could probably achieve a limited penetration using one of his corps in the region of Echternach, and then position his forces as a defensive barrier about 16km (10 miles) short of Luxembourg. His other corps could, if it kept close enough to Fifth Panzer Army, derive sufficient impetus from the advance to place it to the south of Bastogne, where it could set up defensive positions. Brandenberger had absolutely no illusions about reaching the Meuse: it was, he thought, impossible.

On the Germans' north wing, the assault would be led by LXXXV Corps, under General der Infanterie Baptist Kneiss. His 5th Parachute Division (again, operating in an infantry role and with relatively few qualified paratroops) would drive across the Wiltz river, head west towards the town of the same name and bypass the 28th Division's headquarters. They would then take up a blocking position to the south of Bastogne. LXXXV Corps' other division, the 352nd Volksgrenadier, would move across the Our, push on to the western end of the Sûre river and then build defensive

American infantry occupy a shallow defensive position. These trenches lack overhead cover, which was valued when the Battle broke out. Shell bursts amongst the trees showered the ground beneath with deadly shards of wood.

> **LIGHT ARMORED CAR M8**
>
> The M8 was the most important American armoured car of the war, 11,667 having been built by the time production ended in April 1945. The M8 was a roomy vehicle, with a crew of four. The main armament of a 37mm (1.45in) gun was accommodated in an open turret, while a 0.5-inch (12.7mm) machine gun was often carried on a ring mounting above the turret itself. The British also used the M8 (naming it the 'Greyhound'), but considered it to be too vulnerable to mines. This was a relatively minor shortcoming, and outweighed by the M8's ability to negotiate almost any terrain that it encountered.

positions on the high ground beyond the river. To help with these objectives, most of the assault guns were assigned to LXXXV Corps, while two-thirds of the artillery available to Seventh Army was also to go to this corps in order to bombard the 109th Infantry Regiment's positions.

VULNERABILITIES

As for the southern wing, LXXX Corps would use its 276th Volksgrenadier Division to cross the Sûre and, after destroying the American forces ahead of it, would take the high ground where it too would build defensive positions. The exact location for the positions was not specified, since Brandenberger could not be certain of the depth to which the 276th Volksgrenadiers would penetrate: he was hoping that the line would be 13km (8 miles) south of Luxembourg City, but was prepared to shift the location if necessary. The most important consideration was that a blocking position needed to be established, and this did not have to be done at the exact point that Brandenberger hoped to reach. The other division in LXXX Corps was the 212th Volksgrenadier Division, which Brandenberger considered to be his best. He therefore gave it the task of anchoring the army's southern flank and providing the army's reserve regiment. Although there was no doubt that the 212th Volksgrenadier Division was more capable than the others – after its mauling on the eastern front, it had been rebuilt with experienced officers and NCOs and using soldiers assessed to be above average – it had just four assault guns and limited artillery support.

It was not all doom and gloom for Brandenberger, however. While his forces were far fewer than he would have liked, he did at least have more men than the Americans units facing the Seventh Army. These comprised the 109th Infantry Regiment (the third regiment in 28th Division with the 110th and 112th); a regiment from the 4th Infantry Division, the 12th Infantry, and the 60th Armoured Infantry Battalion from the 9th Armoured Division. The latter held a plateau between the Sûre and a stream known as the Ernz Noire. The gorge of the Ernz Noire offered no benefits to the defenders, since there were three roads leading across it, one of which ran right into the rear of the battalion's headquarters at Beaufort. Much to the concern of Lt Col Kenneth W Collins, the battalion commander, the Ernz Noire itself was not part of the 60th Armoured Infantry Battalion's area of responsibility. Instead its defences were the concern of the 12th Infantry, which was so overextended that there were only a few men to block any German advance up the gorge.

The northern flank also worried Col Collins, since there was a gap of more than 1.6km (1 mile) between his men and the nearest positions of the 109th Infantry. He therefore sent a squad to fill the gap, although he had no illusions that they could do more in the face of an attack than raise the alarm. The remainder of the line was less of a concern, since most of Collins's positions had good fields of fire into the Sûre valley, providing some means of offsetting the numerical superiority enjoyed by the attacking Germans. Further along the line, the 109th Infantry had been able to move a battalion into reserve with the arrival of the 60th Armoured Infantry, while a medium tank company from the 707th Tank Battalion had been assigned to support the 109th. As for the 12th Infantry Regiment, it had the prospect of gaining support from two regiments holding the line to the south, but the divisional commander, Maj Gen Raymond O Barton, would have to take into account the likelihood of a German assault in their part of the line, and might not be able to release them to support the 12th Infantry.

FIRST ASSAULT

The lack of artillery available to the Seventh Army meant that the bulk of the guns and rocket projectiles was assigned to support the assault by LXXXV Corps, with most of the fire landing in the 109th Infantry's sector, hitting the headquarters and artillery positions. The assault companies advanced under the protection of the heavy fog that hung along the entire front and, as elsewhere, were able to move without being spotted by the defenders. In one or two places, the first the Americans knew of the German attack was when they were taken under fire by enemy troops who were only a matter of metres away. The paratroops operating against the northern wing of the 109th Infantry followed instructions to bypass the opposition wherever possible. At Vianden,

F Company saw nothing of the paratroops, who left them alone as they moved towards the southern parts of the Skyline Drive. Another column of troops entered the village of Walsdorf, which had been left undefended. In the afternoon, they moved on towards the village of Brandenbourg, which was the headquarters for the 109th's 2nd Battalion. This prompted the battalion commander, Lt Col James E Rudder, to order a company of the regimental reserve to support the headquarters troop. Rudder also had to worry about E Company, which was defending the village of Fouhren. The road running through Fouhren led down the Sûre valley and on to the town of Diekirch and was needed by the Germans. The village, however, was on the interdivisional boundary between the 5th Parachute Division and the 352nd Volksgrenadier Division, and there seems to have been some confusion on the German side as to who was to deal with it. Small parties made forays against the village, but no co-ordinated assault was launched and E Company remained in possession of the village as the day drew to a close. Although the Germans may not have posed as great a threat to the defenders in Fouhren as they might have done, they did not necessarily need to take Fouhren – instead, they took two small, undefended villages that gave them road access to the Sûre valley. Col Rudder was aware that if the Germans pressed on down to the valley they would cut off the supply route to the 3rd Battalion. Just after midday, he sent a company from the reserve battalion, supported by a platoon of tanks, to remove the Germans from the villages. He later added the last elements of the reserve to support this force. The two reserve companies reached the outskirts of the two villages before they dug in, blocking the roads leading into the Sûre valley. The Germans, however, remained in control of the villages, from which they were certain to move out before long.

Third Battalion itself had been attacked, but its defensive positions were good. The eventual German assault was vigorous, but was repelled. The failure to make progress and

A German truck uses a bridge laid by American engineers and abandoned in the withdrawal. The Germans had destroyed many river crossings when they had pulled back towards their frontier, only to find that they needed them for the offensive.

take the ground meant that artillery observers could direct fire on the engineers trying to throw a bridge across the Our. As the day ended, the 109th seemed to be in a good position and had not suffered heavy losses in either men or armour.

> On the evening of 16 Dec 1944, Seventh Army was satisfied with the tactical successes achieved. If it was true that the goals reached – above all in the centre and on the left wing – were not all that had been planned and expected, it was also true that the penetration of the enemy front, especially on the strategically important right wing of the army, had succeeded.
>
> *General Erich Brandenberger*

SLOW PROGRESS

The 60th Armoured Infantry, meanwhile, was not subjected to a particularly heavy barrage when the offensive began and most of the rounds fell on the headquarters at Beaufort. By the time the fog lifted, it was obvious that the Germans were crossing the Sûre in some numbers and artillery fire was called for. Although this was heavy, it did not prevent them crossing the river and they quickly took the positions at the village of Hogenberg. By the end of the day, as with the 109th, the 60th Armoured Infantry's positions were still intact. The same was largely true for the 12th Infantry. The Germans made initial progress around Echternach, as Brandenberger had hoped they would, but they ran into trouble as the Americans fell back from their outposts to the main defences in Osweiler and Dickweiler. The assault at Osweiler was driven back with the loss of 50 men, while at Dickweiler the German effort lacked any drive. This was rectified by another assault in the late afternoon, but by then the defences had been reinforced by three tanks, which engaged the Germans at point-blank range. Fifty were killed, another thirty-five surrendered and the remainder retreated. Although the position of F Company at Berdorf looked precarious, they were still in place as the day came to a close.

By the end of 16 December, Seventh Army had failed to take any of the bridges needed to get its armour across the river, but all the attacking units had succeeded in breaking into the American front somewhere along the line, even if they had not managed to dislodge the defenders from their positions. Brandenberger believed that this was because the Americans had been able to commit their reserves, so the Seventh Army now had the opportunity to break through

A squad of German troops advances along a ditch, past a column of abandoned American vehicles. This is another of the propaganda shots purporting to show German troops in the thick of battle, but which were taken some time after the convoy had been engaged.

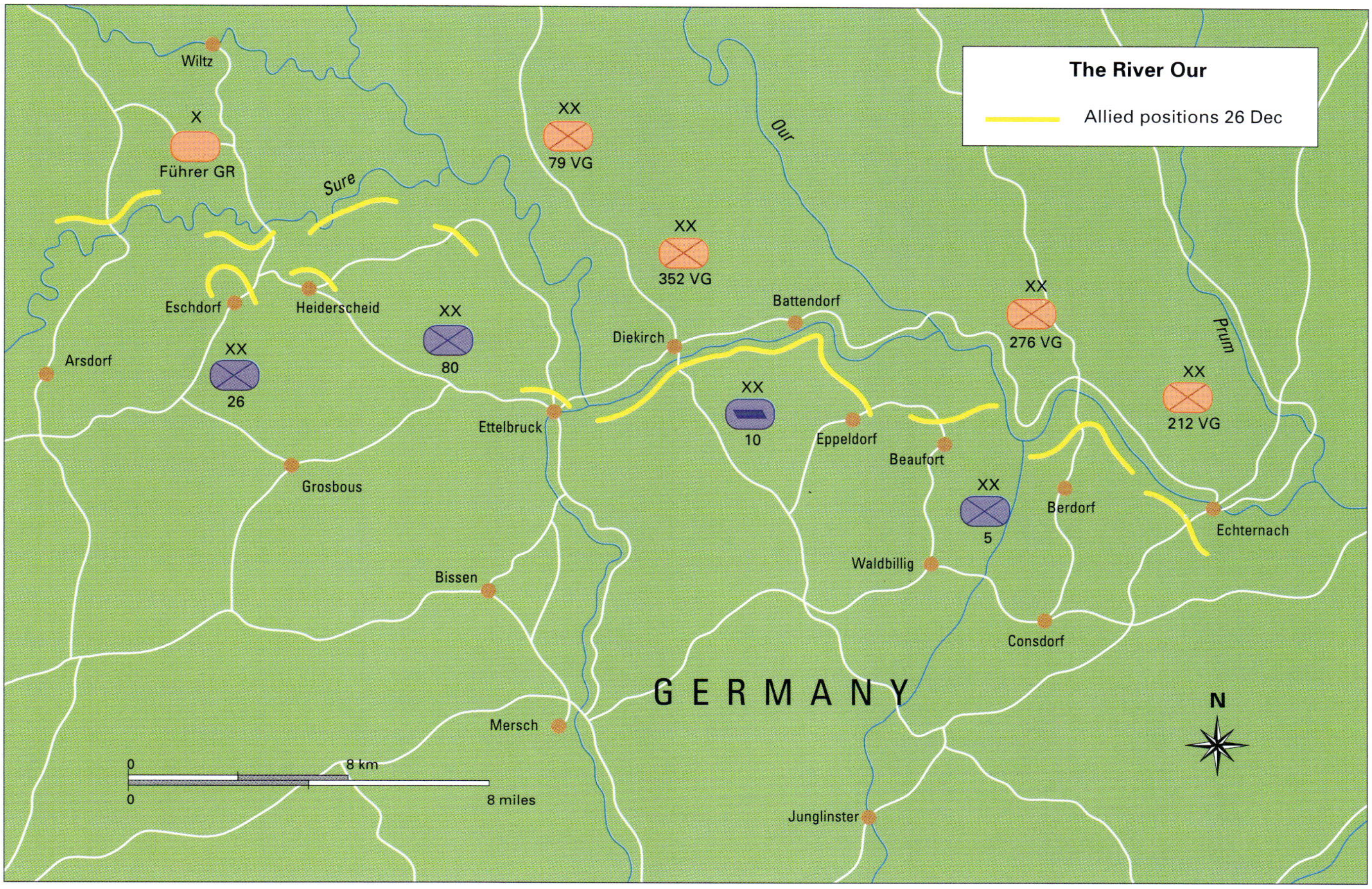

The Our river played a key part in the plan for the offensive, since capture of the river crossings was vital if the Germans were to be able to drive on for Antwerp. Although the Germans enjoyed some success, their progress was too slow, which allowed the Americans time to react.

before any more were brought up. Even as Brandenberger was contemplating this, however, Gen Middleton was telling Gen Barton on the telephone that he was sending a combat command from the 10th Armoured Division to assist with the defences, and that they would leave their assembly area at daybreak.

The combat command sent to aid the 106th Infantry Division had been thwarted by the distance it had to travel, but the combat command heading for 4th Division had just 56km (35 miles) to cover from Third Army's zone before it would reach the 12th Infantry. Brandenberger's troops would face far stronger opposition than anticipated.

17 DECEMBER

Brandenberger had underestimated the strength of the American position, since Col Rudder still had a company of tanks from the 707th Tank Battalion that had not been committed. The Germans, meanwhile, were having difficulty in bringing their own forces forwards, since by dawn on 17 December the engineers had not managed to bridge either the Sûre or the Our. This denied the Germans their fire support.

East of the Ernz Noire, the reserve battalion from 12th Infantry had been sent to defend the road linking Echternach and Luxembourg City, leaving the battalion commander, Col Robert H Chance, without any more troops to commit. As compensation, Gen Barton had arranged for a company of medium tanks from Combat Command A of the 9th Armoured Division to provide support and brought forward the reserve battalion from the 22nd Infantry Regiment (the southernmost of his units). 10th Armoured Division's CCA had also begun to leave its positions to join the battle and would be ready to start fighting by daylight on 18 December. The prospect of this support meant that Barton and his unit commanders intended to use 17 December to relieve pressure on units that had been surrounded, bolster the defences in areas that appeared to be under threat and block the exits from the gorge of the Ernz Noire.

An American soldier watches carefully for enemy movement from his defensive position. The photograph gives a particularly good view of the M1 Garand rifle, the standard arm of the US forces. The Garand was an accurate weapon, and was employed well into the 1950s.

ATTEMPTING RESUCE

In the 109th Infantry's sector, Col Rudder attempted to rescue the men of E Company trapped in Fouhren. The rescue did not go to plan. Although two companies backed by a platoon of tanks had been sent to relieve the company, they were unable to break through the German positions. The relief column fell back and Rudder ordered that a patrol should attempt to reach the village at nightfall, but this too failed. Eventually a tank and a patrol from the 109th's I&R platoon reached a position from which they could observe the village on the morning of the 18th. The company command post had been destroyed and the Germans were in the village in strength. By the middle of the day, it was clear that their advance could not be stopped, since they were simply moving through the gaps between American positions. The next day, Col Rudder decided that he had to withdraw to a new line, and secured permission to do so from General Cota.

The 60th Armoured Infantry Battalion faced the problem of German advances along the roads leading to the rear of their positions, and this prompted Col Thomas L Harrold, the commanding officer of CCA from 9th Armoured Division, to send a company of light tanks to protect the northern flank. A troop of tanks was given the task of patrolling the road between the Ernze Noire and Beaufort, while another troop and a company of tank destroyers was sent to block the other two roads that led up from the gorge. While these steps were eminently sensible, they could not prevent the Germans from infiltrating through the American positions. The Germans first took the village of Mullerthal, which gave them access to a road that bisected the gorge and the ability to threaten the firing positions of the Americans' artillery pieces. An attempt to dislodge the Germans failed in the early afternoon when the lead tank was knocked out, blocking the road. By nightfall, the Germans had entered Beaufort and Col Collins gave the order to withdraw.

STRUGGLING TO HOLD

The 12th Infantry were in a rather better position, since with the arrival of the reserve battalion they now enjoyed equality of numbers with the Germans, and had more artillery and armour. The 212th Volksgrenadier Division had only four assault guns and these were still on the other side of the river. Although their engineers had made two attempts to throw a bridge across the Sûre, the first construction had been destroyed by artillery fire before a single vehicle had managed to cross it, while an attempt to build another one after dark on 16 December had been aborted when the engineers came under heavy artillery fire; it would take another 24 hours for the bridge to be completed.

After the fall of Mullerthal, which was not far away, and while the Germans awaited their armour, Gen Barton sent reinforcements to the high ground above the Ernz Noire. This was done by creating Task Force Luckett, under the command of Col James S Luckett, who had joined the divisional headquarters staff after moving on from commanding 12th Infantry Regiment. He was given eight Sherman tanks to support his ad hoc force, together with the tank battalion's mortar platoon. They would also be able to make use of the reserve battalion from the neighbouring 8th Infantry Regiment.

When the force arrived, however, they sat puzzled as the German troops made no effort to attack the 12th Infantry, unaware that these were actually from the 276th Volksgrenadier Division, who were attacking along a different axis. The rest of the 12th Infantry spent the day trying to rescue those units that required help or reinforcing the line where it appeared that the Germans might be in a position of advantage.

Company B, accompanied by four Shermans and a platoon of light tanks, was sent to rescue Company F in Berdorf. The force made its way through the village house by house until it reached the troops holding out in the local hotel. Although the Germans were pushed back, they were not driven out of the village before nightfall brought a halt to proceedings. While the men at Berdorf had been reinforced, those at Echternach remained isolated, since Companies A and G were unable to make much progress before darkness fell.

By the end of the first full day of the battle, the Americans were still holding on, although they had been forced to adjust their defensive line. The positions in Osweiler and Dickweiler were firmly held to the extent that the Germans decided against further attacks there, while Task Force Luckett had succeeded in anchoring the front along the Ernz Noire. The weakest point of the American defences was in the centre of their position, for it was clear that there was a gap along the road that led from Luxembourg City to Echternach.

Reinforcements were on their way, however, and the position was not at all bleak. It would be too much to say that the German assault had been stopped, since Seventh Army was still in a position to press on with its attack. Rather, the Americans had not crumbled in the face of the onslaught, leaving the situation in doubt for both sides. Instead of the rapid advance anticipated by Hitler (if not his generals), Seventh Army, just like Fifth and Sixth Panzer Armies, had made progress, but nothing like enough to suggest that Hitler's goals were attainable.

GIs advance through the snow on a patrol around Wiltz early in 1945. The man nearest the camera carries a Thompson sub-machine gun, and his colleague an M1 Carbine. Both weapons were prized by their users, though they were less effective over long ranges than the Garand.

CARRIAGE, MOTOR, 105MM M7 'PRIEST'

The US Army began searching for a self-propelled howitzer even before the American entry into the war, mounting 105mm (4.1in) howitzers aboard half-tracked vehicles. Initial experience with these mounts suggested that a fully tracked gun carriage would be a better option, and this led to the decision to produce a vehicle based on the M3 tank chassis. The first examples of the M7 went to the British Army, who gave the vehicle the nickname 'Priest' from the prominent 'pulpit' which housed the 0.5-inch (12.7mm) machine gun. The next examples joined the US Army, and were employed for the remainder of the war. Unlike the German decision to use self-propelled guns in the assault role, the Americans used the Priest as mobile field artillery, providing indirect supporting fire.

ASSESSMENT OF 16/17 DECEMBER

Hitler's plans for the Ardennes offensive were overoptimistic, a fact recognized by almost all of his senior commanders. They fully understood that the Americans were unlikely to be struck by the paralysis that Hitler anticipated, and appreciated that this created many problems. Although able to assemble an attacking force in the Ardennes that outnumbered the defenders, the generals knew that the task of taking Antwerp was almost impossible. They would be able to give the Allies cause for concern, however, and possibly reach the Meuse. There was a possibility that the Germans might be able to strike a considerable blow that would create major problems for the Allies' attempt to invade Germany from the west. Thus, the offensive was not doomed if it failed to take Antwerp. The first 24 hours of the assault would indicate how close the Germans would come to their goals. The result suggested that they would have more difficulty than Hitler anticipated. On 16 and 17 December 1944, the Germans put in heavy attacks against lightly defended American positions all along the front. The traffic jams that affected Sixth Panzer Army scuppered Operation Greif before it had even started and had an adverse effect on Kampfgruppe Peiper. Some attacks failed because they were not pursued with sufficient vigour; others failed for various reasons, including a lack of armour and sheer bad luck.

A German Kubelwagen passes through the detritus of war in a Belgian village. The shell casings littering the foreground suggest that artillery, probably American, had recently been in the area.

However, the most potent obstacle to the Germans' goal of a rapid breakthrough on the first day was the American soldier. Despite the often tenuous nature of their positions, the Americans put up stout resistance. The image of American units losing cohesion and running in the face of a determined enemy has persisted, but has no basis in fact. It may be true that individuals deserted and that small groups of soldiers retreated in disorder, but the three German armies did not fulfil many of their objectives on the first day, and the advance was delayed. This delay was important, since it gave the Allies time to organize their response and left them in a position from which they could begin to deal with the enemy threat. This is not to say that the Battle of the Bulge was won and lost on the first full day. The first 24 hours of the battle were not decisive, and to suggest that the ultimate outcome of the offensive can be divined from the events of 16–17 December would be to place a greater burden on the historical evidence than it can bear. What can be said, though, is this: the day's events demonstrated that the German generals had been correct to assume the offensive would be difficult, and the grandiose objectives next to impossible to achieve. As far as reaching the Meuse was concerned, however, only time would tell. The first day of the Battle of the Bulge demonstrated that the fight would not be over quickly, would be hard and would be bloody.

The M7B1 self-propelled howitzer was the main Allied mobile fire-support weapon from 1942 onwards. It was based on the chassis of the classic M4 Sherman tank.

CHAPTER EIGHT

AFTERMATH

The failure to achieve any of the first day's objectives did not mean that the offensive had collapsed. The Allies remained concerned about several key parts of their front for some days to come, not least in the area around Bastogne. The gallant action of the US 101st Airborne Division at Bastogne became part of military legend, and would serve as a springboard for bringing about the final defeat of Hitler's plans.

ONCE PEIPER'S TROOPS had dealt with the positions at Buchholz station, they moved on towards Honsfeld. Their tanks ran into American vehicles that were heading for the town as well, and attached themselves to the traffic. The American vehicles rolled into Honsfeld in a continuous stream, oblivious that the enemy was literally just yards behind them. The column passed an armoured car situated just beyond the last house in Honsfeld, placed there to spot any approaching enemy vehicles. Its commander, Sgt George Creel, had to look twice to make certain that his eyes were not playing tricks: just ahead of him was a man with a white flag leading a German tank down the road in the pre-dawn darkness. Creel jumped into his armoured car, but it was towing a trailer – and this blocked the field of fire from his gun. Further down the road, firing broke out as the Americans and Germans came into contact. The infantry had little chance of success against armour and headed for the rear. Creel and his crew abandoned their vehicle and ran back to Honsfeld to raise the alarm, but were unable to reach the centre of the village.

Men of the 101st Airborne move from the village of Haufelige to take up defensive positions at Bastogne, 19 December 1944. The vehicles in the background include two half-tracks and at least one M7 Priest. Despite the best efforts of the Germans, the 101st refused to give in.

> After the Ardennes failure, Hitler started a corporal's war. There were no big plans – only a multitude of piecemeal fights.
>
> *General Hasso von Manteuffel*

The first two Panther tanks made their way into the village, followed by three half-tracks. As they neared the centre of Honsfeld, they opened fire against houses, parked vehicles and any American soldiers unfortunate enough to be in their way. The lead elements were followed by more half-tracks, bringing with them Panzergrenadiers. The Americans in the village were taken by surprise and some were left with no chance of escape. A number surrendered, but the SS troops now in the town were not prepared to observe the legal obligations pertaining to prisoners of war and shot some in cold blood. A group of about 100 surrendered personnel from the 612th Tank Destroyer Battalion was then fired upon, and witnesses claimed that at least thirty were killed. These brutal scenes were not the first time that the SS had operated without any regard for the laws of war, and they were not the last; Kampfgruppe Peiper would make its own contribution to this array of war crimes.

After taking Honsfeld, Peiper headed towards Büllingen, using the route assigned to the 12th SS Panzer Division (he was able to do so since that unit was still caught in traffic jams around the start line for the offensive). By 07:00, Peiper's men had overwhelmed the Americans in Büllingen and used their prisoners to help refuel their vehicles. The column moved off once more, but it was pounced upon by American fighter-bombers, exploiting a break in the weather, which shot up a number of vehicles and then shot down half-a-dozen German fighters that attempted to interfere. Peiper restored order on the ground and then carried on to the Baugnez crossroads.

MASSACRE

At the crossroads, Peiper's lead tanks ran into Battery B of the 285th Field Artillery Observation Battalion and attacked it with vigour. The Americans, armed only with rifles and machine guns, were unable to resist and were compelled to surrender. The prisoners were rounded up and marched to a field near the crossroads, where they were left milling around, chatting. There were about 130 prisoners and the Germans ordered them into rows, hands above their heads. Two Panzer IVs were moved into a position where they were covering the Americans: then, to the horror of the captives, an officer ordered one of the tank commanders to open fire. He did not do so, instead leaving this to his assistant gunner, Private Georg Fleps, who shot one man, and then another. The machine guns on the tanks opened up, and the prisoners began to fall to the snowy ground. Some survived, burrowing beneath the dead bodies of their comrades; the SS men, apparently satisfied with their handiwork, carried on. For the next few hours, passing Germans fired into the pile of bodies lying by the road. Just as the area fell silent, the survivors heard German voices. Men from the 3rd SS Pioneer Battalion had arrived, and began wandering through the lines of dead men, shooting those they thought were still alive. As the SS troops left the field, the remaining survivors of the massacre decided that they had to flee the scene and rose as one, running as hard as they could. Some were cut down as they ran, while others headed towards the apparent safety of a nearby café building, only for the Germans to set fire to it; when the y escaped from the flames, they were shot down.

Despite the considerable efforts of the SS, they had not managed to kill all of the prisoners. The few survivors did not have long to wait for rescue. At the edge of the nearby town of Malmédy, Lt Col David E Pergrin, the commanding officer of the 291st Engineers, had heard the firing, knowing that the artillery unit he had just seen had been attacked by the enemy. When the firing died away, he decided to see what had happened there, heading for Baugnez in his jeep, accompanied by his communications sergeant, William Crickenberger. They climbed out of the jeep when they saw the flames emanating from the burning café and walked carefully towards the village. As they did so, three of the survivors emerged from the forest and rushed towards them. Pergrin and Crickenberger helped the men back to the jeep and rushed them to Malmédy.

The survivors were in deep shock and it took Pergrin more than 90 minutes to ascertain what had happened. He immediately signalled the terrible news to Gen Hodges. As the day ended, more survivors left their hiding places, walking, crawling or staggering to friendly positions, or to houses where local civilians assisted them. Altogether, some forty-three survivors made their way back to American lines. Eighty-six of their colleagues lay dead, most in the field where the shooting had begun. Their bodies lay in the open until two days before Christmas, when a heavy snowfall covered them in a white shroud.

Another propaganda shot taken at the site of the ambushed American convoy: an SS NCO waves his men forward against an enemy that is not actually present. Armed with an StG 44 assault rifle, he wears one of the camouflage smocks often seen in photographs of the SS.

The Battle of the Bulge is noted for the number of atrocities carried out by German troops. This picture shows Belgian civilians murdered at Stavelot. Discovery of atrocities increased the determination of the Americans to resist and then repel the German attack.

The reason for the massacre of the Americans was never adequately explained: the SS men had killed some of their prisoners before reaching Büllingen, but did not do so when they were there; then, on the road once more, they murdered the next batch of captives. Whatever their motives, they were counterproductive. Within hours, Gen Hodges's report of the massacre had circulated throughout the American forces in the Ardennes and beyond, filling them with even greater determination than they had displayed on the first day of the offensive. Very few SS troops survived to become prisoners after the Malmédy massacre. Gen Hodges's signal also reached the headquarters of Maj Gen Elwood 'Pete' Quesada, the commander of the IX Tactical Air Command, who made sure that every one of his fighter-bomber pilots heard of the massacre. They were outraged. And the weather – so helpful to the Germans on 16 December by keeping the pilots grounded – was starting to clear.

HOLDING THE NORTHERN SHOULDER

In the north, the 99th Division was holding on against the German attack. Although a request from Gen Gerow of V Corps, that he be allowed to call off the attack by 2nd Division in the direction of Wahlerscheid and fall back to the Elsenborn ridge, was refused, the 2nd Division brought its reserve battalions up to the twin villages of Rocherath and Krinkelt. The advancing Germans ran into stiff resistance here and by 18 December the twin villages had still not fallen. General Priess of I SS Panzer Corps launched an attack early that morning and fierce fighting continued for the rest of the day. Although the Germans made some progress, the defences held firm and they were thrown back. Another assault the next day, aided by a new division of Panzergrenadiers, was stopped in its tracks, and a third effort met a similar fate. The 12th SS Panzer Division, which was now 72 hours behind schedule as a result of the fighting and had suffered heavy losses, was ordered to bypass Krinkelt and Rocherath, following in the wake of Peiper's advance. On the evening of 19 December, the men of the 99th, 2nd and 1st US Division fell back from the villages to the better defences of the Elsenborn ridge, where they dug in to hold the northern shoulder of the Bulge. They were never dislodged.

ALLIED REACTIONS

As the German advance continued, the Allied high command began to appreciate the size of the offensive and take steps to counter it. As the threat to the towns of Stavelot and Bastogne became obvious, Eisenhower released two airborne divisions to Bradley. The absence of several of the senior commanders in the XVIII Airborne Corps (arranged when the Allies were quietly confident that there was little threat of an attack) meant that the youthful Maj Gen James Gavin of the 82nd Airborne Division was acting as corps commander. He reported to Gen Hodges and was told to send the 82nd to join V Corps at Werbomont, while the 101st was to go to Bastogne. In the absence of the 101st's commander, Gen Maxwell D Taylor, who was in Washington, it was placed under the divisional artillery commander, Brig Gen Anthony C McAuliffe. He was given orders to hold Bastogne against the Germans, and was to guarantee himself a place in military history as he carried out this task. Bastogne would also enjoy the protection of a battalion of recently arrived M36 tank destroyers; armed with a 90mm gun, these derivatives of the M10 tank destroyer could deal with any German tank that they were likely to encounter.

An SS NCO recovers rations from an abandoned M8 armoured car, in another propaganda shot taken of the ambushed American convoy. The man here unwittingly demonstrates another aspect of the war – short of rations, the Germans eagerly 'liberated' American supplies.

As the 82nd and 101st made their way to their new positions, Gen Hodges pulled VII Corps out of the line from its location at Düren, and ordered Gen Lawton J Collins to prepare to deliver a counterattack from the north of the Ardennes with two armoured and two infantry divisions. In 21st Army Group, Field Marshal Montgomery moved Gen Brian Horrocks's XXX Corps to a position from where it would be able to attack any German crossing of the Meuse, while the 29th Armoured Brigade was sent to protect the river crossings near Dinant.

On 19 December, Eisenhower held a conference of his senior commanders to discuss the situation. This was a far swifter reaction than Hitler anticipated. Eisenhower was in no mood for gloom, telling his subordinates that he did not want to see long faces at the conference table; as far as he was concerned, the German offensive might be a temporary setback, but it represented a great opportunity for damaging the Germans, perhaps fatally. He made clear his intentions: there would be no withdrawal behind the Meuse, and Patton was to prepare to strike against the German southern flank, while Gen Simpson's Ninth Army was to be ready to attack the northern flank. Patton would launch the first thrust, driving to Bastogne where he would then link with the First Army. Eisenhower then turned to Patton and asked when he thought he could be ready to attack. Patton immediately replied 'in three days', adding that he could do so with three divisions. Unimpressed, Eisenhower told him not to be flippant, but Patton was, in fact, deadly serious. He explained that he had already drawn up three plans to deal with the problem, and that he only had to telephone his headquarters and give the order for the plan that dealt with a drive on Bastogne.

> After 24 December 1944, heavy air attacks made impossible almost all daytime transport, either of troops or of their supplies. Even regrouping of troops in occupied positions was rendered extremely difficult by the bombardment.
>
> *Field Marshal Gerd von Rundstedt*

Two German soldiers take a rest under an abandoned M8 armoured car. The man nearest the camera has been identified by the Belgian historian Jean Paul Pallud as SS-Untersturmführer Steiwe, although his colleague remains unknown.

MONTGOMERY IN CONTROL

At the end of the conference, Eisenhower returned to his headquarters at Versailles to be met with calls for another decision. His staff officers had reached the conclusion that Gen Bradley was too far away from the First and Ninth Armies to control them from his headquarters, since he was separated from these formations by the German penetrations. They suggested that the solution lay in temporarily transferring control of troops north of the bulge to Montgomery, while Bradley

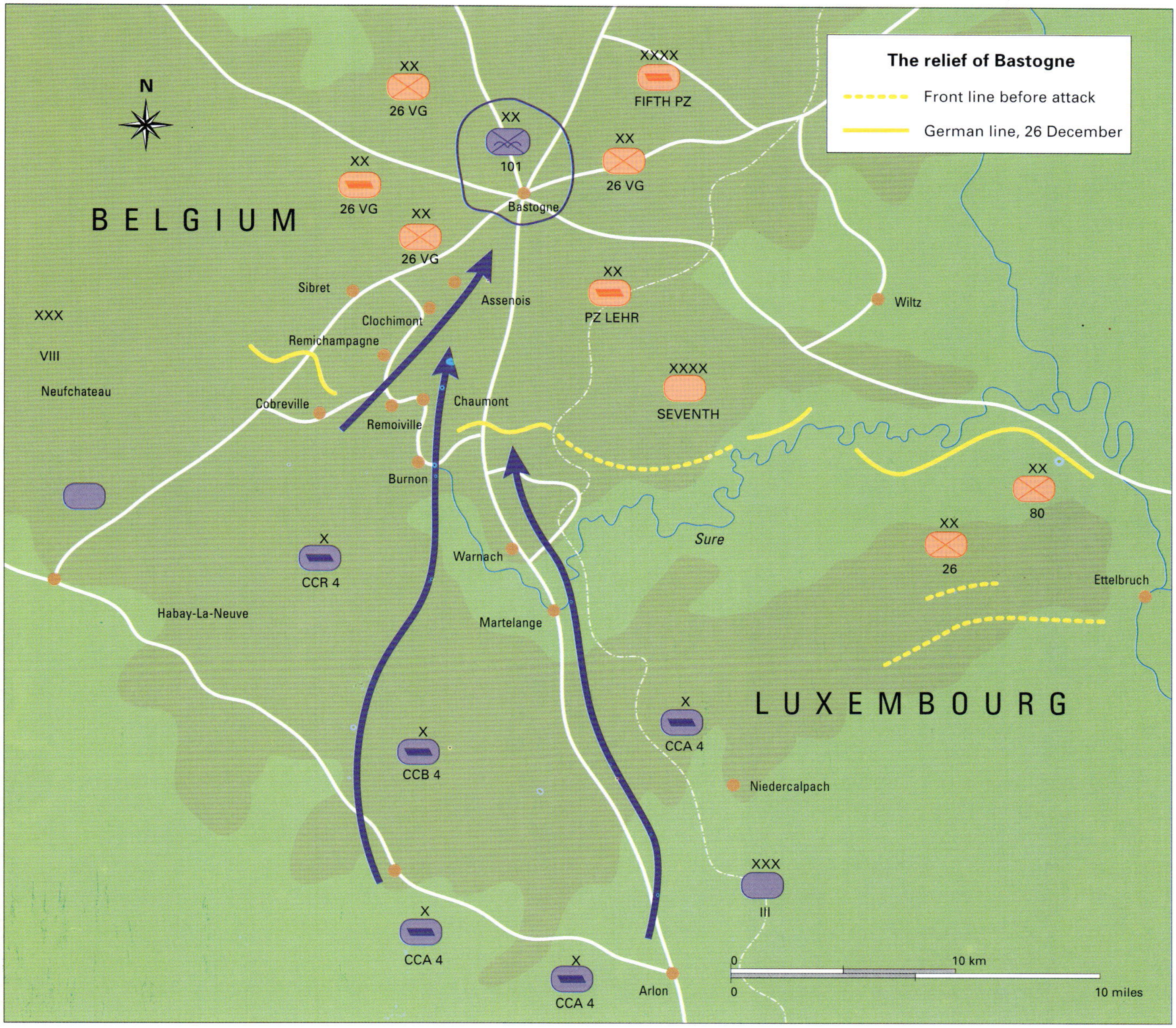

After several days heavy fighting, an American relief column drove from south of the town, and joined up with the 101st Airborne on the late afternoon of 26 December 1944. This ensured that the town would not fall to the Germans, denying them a vital transport hub.

would lead those to the south of the German thrust. This was a sensitive decision, as it might be taken as a comment on Bradley's abilities as a commander. There was also a danger that Montgomery would use such an action as ammunition in his continuing attempts to be given overall command of the land campaign in northern Europe. Eisenhower, though, saw the sense in the move and gave his consent. Orders to this effect were issued the next morning – with predictable results. Bradley was furious, while Montgomery seemed to revel in his greater command responsibility. With his customary lack of tact, he descended on First Army headquarters 'like Christ come to cleanse the temple', as one of his own staff officers put it, confirming every suspicion (not all of them unfair) held by the Americans about the British Field Marshal. Neither Bradley nor Montgomery, however, was unprofessional enough to place personal feelings above professionalism. Bradley conceded that the decision made sense, while Montgomery moderated his attitude. Although he thought a withdrawal from St Vith made sense, he was

GENERAL OMAR N BRADLEY

Omar Bradley was in the same class as Eisenhower at West Point, and his career was inextricably linked with that of his friend. He first came to prominence in North Africa, when Eisenhower employed him to assess the quality of American forces. He recommended the relief of the commander of II Corps, and was made deputy corps commander to George Patton. When Patton left this post, Bradley succeeded him, and led II Corps for the remainder of the North African campaign, and then in Sicily, where the corps served as part of Patton's Seventh Army. Eisenhower then gave Bradley command of the US First Army, in which capacity he oversaw the American landings on D-Day. Bradley then took command of the 12th Army Group on 1 August, when US forces were expanded with the arrival of Patton's Third Army. As 12th Army Group commander, he was responsible for leading the American response to the German offensive in the Ardennes, although part of his Army Group was temporarily assigned to Field Marshal Bernard Montgomery to facilitate tighter command of the northern sector of the battlefield. 12th Army Group became the largest formation ever commanded by an American General; Bradley left this post in August 1945. He was given responsibility for veterans' affairs by President Truman. In early 1948, he succeeded Eisenhower as the Chief of Staff of the Army and after eighteen months in this position, he became the first Chairman of the Joint Chiefs of Staff. He served two terms in this position, being promoted to General of the Army (five star rank). He oversaw American operations in the Korean war, and retired in 1953. He became involved in industry in a consultancy role, and died in April 1981, at the age of 88.

sufficiently sensitive to American opinion not to press the point when they made clear their determination to make a stand there.

DEFENDING ST VITH

The six main roads that made St Vith the centre of the road network in the Ardennes were the reason the Americans insisted on remaining there. This was also exactly why it was important to the Germans. Combat Command B from 7th Armored Division was sent to St Vith on 17 December, but ran into a massive traffic jam as it encountered vehicles withdrawing to the west. By the end of the day, a defensive position had been established around St Vith. This was done with some rapidity, although there was time to make the best of the situation, since the Germans were also having fearsome difficulties with traffic jams, which left them unable to thrust forward as swiftly as they would have hoped. The American defences held despite several heavy attacks, and their success contributed to their decision to turn down Montgomery's suggestion of a withdrawal to 'tidy up the battlefield' on 20 December. Montgomery's decision not to push for this was tactful, but the question became nugatory the next day, when the German LXVI Corps launched a full attack. By nightfall, the Germans had entered St Vith and a new defensive line had to be set up to the west of the town. This held out against renewed attacks, but by the morning of 22 December, the two Combat Commands in the defence had lost half their tanks (both were Combat Command B – one from 7th Armored Division, the other from 9th Armored Division). A withdrawal in contact with the enemy was undertaken, and the Americans retreated in good order behind the Salm river on 23 December. The Germans were unable to make much of their success, since their transport columns became hopelessly entangled in the narrow streets of the town. On top of this, the freezing soldiers began to break into houses to loot clothing and food – and to stay indoors for a while. This meant that units lost their cohesion as men disappeared for some time. To compound the problem, elements of Sixth Panzer Army entered St Vith in the hope of using it as a means to get around the traffic jams in the Losheim gap. Field Marshal Model fell victim to all this traffic – when he entered St Vith, he did so on foot, having abandoned his staff car some miles away.

BASTOGNE

The fighting at St Vith occurred in parallel with that around the equally vital road centre at Bastogne. On 19 December, even before all the defenders were in place, von Manteuffel began to have serious doubts as to whether he would be able to succeed in his task. By the next day, the forces that would defend Bastogne were ready. The main element of the

Taken on 22 January 1945, this photograph demonstrates the importance of Bastogne as a road hub. Vehicles roll through the town to supply the 90th Infantry Divisions and bring back the wounded. The logistic support available gave the Allies the edge over their opponents.

defending force was the 101st Airborne, with just over 10,000 men. Combat Command B of the 10th Armored Division was in support, although it had taken heavy losses when two of its combat teams had been badly mauled east of Bastogne. It was still in a better state than Combat Command R from the 9th Armored, which had only its field artillery battalion in something like one piece. The tanks were placed under the command of Capt Howard Pyle, in Team Pyle, while the remainder of CCR – a mix of infantrymen, tank crews who had lost their vehicles, support staff and other assorted troops – was formed into another makeshift taskforce. With dark humour, this was christened Team SNAFU (standing for 'Situation Normal, All Fouled Up', or something a little pithier when not in polite company). The defenders were better off for artillery, since they had the 101st's Cannon Company with 105mm (4.1in) howitzers, plus 75mm (2.95in) pack howitzers. There were also four battalions of 155mm (6.1in) guns. This gave a total of about 130 guns. Gen McAuliffe was careful to position the weapons so that they could cover every part of the defensive perimeter around Bastogne, extending to the outlying villages that made up the outposts.

Two tired-looking members of the 110th Infantry Regiment, 28th Division take a short break in the middle of Bastogne on 19 December, having withdrawn to the relative safety of the town after their positions were overrun by the enemy.

'AW, NUTS!'

That afternoon (20 December), Gen McAuliffe visited Gen Middleton at his headquarters in nearby Neufchâteau. Asked how long Bastogne could be held, McAuliffe replied that he was confident he would be able to hold the town for at least two days if the Germans were to totally encircle the town. It was Middleton's opinion, however, that he was not entirely certain the town could be held, so it was vital that the Germans did not cut the road between Neufchâteau and Bastogne. If this happened, the 101st would be surrounded. When he left, McAuliffe ordered his driver to travel at top speed, in case the road had already been taken. This was good thinking:just thirtyminutes after he reached his head-

Brigadier General Anthony C McAuliffe, the legendary commander of the 101st Airborne Division at Bastogne. McAuliffe took command while Major General Maxwell D Taylor was elsewhere, and entered history with his one-word response to a German demand for surrender: 'Nuts!'.

quarters, the road was cut by German units. Bastogne was surrounded.

For the next two days, the Germans made several probes, but did not attack, instead massing their forces for an assault. The men of the 101st were not at all daunted at the prospect of being surrounded: as Capt Richard Winters of the 506th Parachute Infantry Regiment so famously said, paratroops *expected* to be surrounded. McAuliffe was concerned, however, since it was clear that ammunition stocks were not adequate, and the ammunition for the artillery had to be rationed. Food and medical supplies were running short. Nonetheless, the defenders waited. Then, at about midday on 22 December, men in the forward positions were startled to see four German soldiers approaching under a white flag. Two NCOs left the command post, taking a German-speaking soldier with them to find out just what these new arrivals wanted.

The four men were two officers and two private soldiers. One of the officers explained, in good English, that they wished to speak with the commanding general of the defending forces. The Germans were led to the farmhouse that served as the command post for their section of line. There the enlisted men were left under guard while Lt Leslie E Smith took the officers to the company command post. They then handed an ultimatum to the company commander, Capt James F Adams, insisting that the Americans surrender. If they did not, the Germans would level Bastogne with artillery. This was a rather bold claim, since Fifth Panzer Army did not have the guns to make good the threat, but McAuliffe was not to know this. The message passed up the chain of command, and was presented to McAuliffe by his chief of staff, Lt Col Ned D Moore. McAuliffe asked what was in the ultimatum.

'They want us to surrender', Moore said.

'Aw, Nuts!' McAuliffe replied.

McAuliffe called his staff together to ask how to respond to the ultimatum. None of them could think of a suitable response until the operations officer, Maj Harry Kinnard, told his general that it was difficult to think of a response better than his first comment. The staff agreed, and McAuliffe produced perhaps the most famous reply to an ultimatum in military history. It read:

To the German Commander:

Nuts!

From the American Commander

The German emissaries were taken back to the farmhouse, accompanied by Col Joseph H Harper, the commander of the 327th Glider Infantry Regiment. He handed the reply to the Germans, who politely asked what it contained. Although the English-speaking officer had an excellent grasp of the language, his comprehension did not extend to this. Harper

> The re-iterated order of the Führer to 'stay and hold' advanced positions caused very heavy losses of armoured fighting vehicles and artillery which could not be withdrawn. Here were the germs of the later collapse on the Western Front.
>
> *Field Marshal Gerd von Rundstedt*

American transport aircraft head for Bastogne to drop supplies. Allied air superiority meant that the greatest danger often came from the weather, not the Germans. Most of the supplies fell inside the American perimeter, ensuring that the garrison was not starved into surrender.

noted his bemusement and explained that, in plain English, 'nuts!' equated to 'go to hell'. He then dismissed the rather perplexed Germans, sending them back to their lines.

The ultimatum had been drawn up without the knowledge of Hasso von Manteuffel, who was furious when he learned of it. As he pointed out to the officer responsible, Gen Luttwitz of XLVII Panzer Corps, he did not have the guns to carry out the threat. If he proved unable to do so, there was a serious danger it would make the Germans look ridiculous. The only solution was to ask the *Luftwaffe* to bomb Bastogne. He put in the request that night.

AIR POWER

Although von Manteuffel was himself anxious to see aircraft above the battlefield, his desire was nothing compared to that of the Allies. The weather on 16 December had been appalling, thus grounding flights, but it had slowly improved over the next few days. Then, on 23 December, the defenders of Bastogne awoke to a beautiful morning. On the airfields of the US Ninth Air Force, aircraft were prepared, and by midday an armada of fighters and bombers, followed by C-47 transports, was filling the skies.

For the troops in Bastogne, the first intimation that aircraft were at last able to fly came when parachute pathfinders dropped into the city just after breakfast. Three hours later, the C-47s appeared over the town, dropping supplies. With the exception of Christmas Day, nearly 1000 sorties were flown and 850 tonnes of cargo were dropped to supply Bastogne over the next five days. The Boxing Day resupply mission included gliders that brought surgeons and medical supplies. The Germans shot down 19 transports, but they could not prevent the vital supplies from getting through.

The transports were not the only aircraft to support the 101st and its fellow defenders, since the fighter-bombers went looking for targets. The snowy ground meant that finding enemy vehicle tracks was a simple matter; finding the vehicles that made them was an equally easy task. The fighter-bombers, backed by B-26 Marauder medium bombers, caused havoc among the German vehicles, adding to their already notable difficulties.

THE FINAL ASSAULT

In response to von Manteuffel's request, the *Luftwaffe* attacked Bastogne on Christmas Eve, causing heavy damage. This only made the defenders more determined, which was not good news for those who attacked on 25 December. An all-out assault was launched at 03:00 and the Germans broke through in two places near the village of Champs. The panzers rolled through, but ran into four tank destroyers of the 705th Tank Destroyer Battalion. Two of the American vehicles were knocked out, but the others destroyed three German tanks, while the airborne troops, heartened by this performance, disabled another with a bazooka. A fifth tank fell victim to another bazooka team, while a sixth headed for the village, but was knocked out on arrival. The crew of a seventh tank abandoned it at Hemroulle and surrendered. The Christmas Day attack was not going to succeed.

The commander of the 26th Volksgrenadier Division, Col Heinz Kokott, agreed to another attack on the morning of Boxing Day, but only after pressure from von Manteuffel. He knew there was a serious danger of American reinforcements arriving. And that very afternoon the men of the 4th Armored Division did indeed near the town, having fought their way through the German lines for the past four days. The lead elements of 4th Division were the 37th Tank Battalion and the 53rd Armoured Infantry Battalion. By 15:00 on 26 December, they had reached a road junction just short of Clochimont, where they were meant to swing northwest to the next village, Sibret, known to be occupied in force by German units.

The commanding officers of the two units, Lt Col Creighton W Abrams and Lt Col George L Jacques stopped to confer at the road junction. Both were concerned at the prospect of fighting their way through Sibret. The sight of a C-47 coming in low, heading for Bastogne, brought it home

New Year's Eve, 1944 and tanks of General Patton's Third Army await orders to begin their advance from Bastogne. On the side of the tank are additional armour plates covering vulnerable areas of the hull: skilled German tank gunners realized this, and used the plates to aim.

to Abrams that relieving Bastogne was more important than fighting through Sibret, so he proposed that they should ignore that village and head for Bastogne by a back route. Jacques agreed, and they set off – neglecting to tell Col Wendell Blanchard, the commander of Combat Command R (to which they belonged) that they had slightly altered his plan. Abrams's men led the way, and at dusk a group of six Sherman tanks, headed by Lt Charles P Boggess, made their way towards Assenois, which lay between them and Bastogne. Boggess and his formation of tanks (accompanied by half-tracks carrying the infantry) swept through the town, but the following elements ran into opposition and a fierce fight broke out. Boggess and his tanks, meanwhile, headed past Assenois and along the road through the woods that lay beyond the town. The first three tanks passed through so quickly that the Germans in the woods were able to lay a few mines on the road just in time to catch the half-track that was following them.

Abrams's operations officer, Capt William A Dwight, who was riding with the second group of Boggess's tanks, ordered them off the road to pin down the Germans in the trees with their machine guns. The infantry in the accompanying half-tracks bailed out, removed the mines and then jumped back

Men of the 101st Airborne meet under a sign commemorating the resistance by the division against the enemy. The 101st were relieved on 26 December 1944, but as the historian Stephen Ambrose noted, no 'Screaming Eagle' would concur that the division needed rescuing.

> Each step forward in the Ardennes offensive prolonged our flanks more dangerously deep, making them more susceptible to counterstrokes. I wanted to stop the offensive at an early stage, when it was plain that it could not attain its aim, but Hitler furiously insisted that it must go on. It was Stalingrad No.2.
>
> *Field Marshal Gerd von Rundstedt*

into their vehicles to follow the leading group. As Boggess emerged from the woods, he noticed a small pillbox a few hundred yards ahead, which apparently was about to be assaulted by American troops. He decided to help and his gunner fired a single round into the pillbox, knocking it out. The Americans dived for cover. Boggess opened his turret hatch and waved to the Americans, who turned out to be from the 326th Airborne Engineer Battalion. It was 1650 on 26 December 1944 and the siege of Bastogne had been lifted.

THE FINAL PHASES

The relief of Bastogne was arguably the point at which German hopes of victory faded. Of course, Hitler did not see it quite like this: he agreed that the offensive to the east of the Meuse should be contained, but would not countenance any thought of abandoning Antwerp as the objective. Hitler's decision was rooted in misplaced optimism. His forces had done their best, but had been unable to inflict the shattering blow against the Allies that Hitler had hoped for. All along the line, the American and British forces were inflicting serious casualties. By Christmas, all the armoured formations had suffered severely. Allied air superiority meant that it was extremely dangerous for the Germans to move during the day. During fighting around the Celles pocket between 25 and 28 December, the German 2nd and9th Panzer and Panzer Lehr Divisions were badly mauled by air attack, with the RAF's Typhoon fighter-bombers causing considerable damage. At the end of three days' fighting, the Germans had lost 82 tanks and 441 vehicles, as well as a number of artillery pieces. They also lost more than three thousand men killed, wounded or taken prisoner.

Once Christmas had passed, the Allies became ever more confident that the worst was over. Hitler, still insistent on the goal of Antwerp, ordered his commanders to launch Operation Nordwind (North Wind), with the intention of attacking enemy forces in the Saar. The plan was intended to make Patton turn his forces to meet this offensive, thus relieving the threat to the German units on the southern flank of the Ardennes. After this had been achieved, Hitler instructed, the offensive would be resumed, aiming once more for the goals laid down in the original plan. Had Hitler known it, he might have been encouraged to learn that part of this plan had succeeded: the Battle of the Bulge had caused enmity between the Allied commanders – however, it was not the success of the German assault that had done this, but disagreement over how the offensive should be brought to an end.

DISAGREEMENT

The Americans were eager to see an attack against the enemy salient, but Montgomery demurred: he was concerned that the Germans might be able to make one last thrust, and did not wish to be caught out by it. Finally, on Boxing Day, he intimated to Eisenhower that he had begun to consider a thrust against the Germans. The two agreed to discuss it on 28 December. Eisenhower discovered that Montgomery was not in a helpful mood, reiterating his view that the Germans had sufficient strength left for one more attack. Such caution did not accord with the intelligence information from Bletchley Park's decryptions, which suggested that the Germans were desperately short of fuel and that their armoured units had sustained heavy losses. When Eisenhower suggested that Montgomery's assessment might be unduly cautious, he secured agreement from the Field Marshal that he would launch an attack on 3 January 1945 if the German assault did not materialize.

This seemed to settle the matter, but, before Eisenhower left, Montgomery took the opportunity to raise the matter of his appointment in overall command of ground operations when the Allies resumed their advance. Montgomery thought that he had managed to gain Eisenhower's agreement,

A member of the 101st Airborne division ferries rations back to his position. He wears standard US Army issue cold-weather kit, but has placed a towel under his helmet as protection from the biting cold that was experienced by the 101st at Bastogne.

A GI keeps guard over three German PoWs. The Battle of the Bulge was marked by the large numbers of prisoners taken by both sides. The Germans lost around 50,000 men to captivity in December alone, a drain on their resources that they could ill-afford.

and followed it by writing a letter to clarify the details. Difficulty arose in that Montgomery used the letter to tell his supreme commander what to do: he criticized Eisenhower's policy to date and even wrote the signal confirming his appointment as the ground commander. It is almost certain that he thought he was doing nothing more than helping Eisenhower – but it is easy to see why such an interpretation of his actions was not shared by anyone else. Montgomery's letter was simply too much.

Eisenhower drafted a letter to the Combined Chiefs of Staff explaining that he had 'had enough' of the whole matter and wished to place the question in their hands. The implication was clear – either Montgomery or Eisenhower would have to go. There was, of course, no choice: given Eisenhower's role, it would be Montgomery who was sacked. Montgomery's chief of staff, Maj Gen 'Freddie' de Guingand, learned of this impending disaster from friends on Eisenhower's staff. He reasoned that he might be in a position to defuse the situation caused by his Field Marshal's supreme self-confidence – not for the first time. De Guingand headed for Eisenhower's headquarters to discuss the matter, emphasizing that Montgomery was blissfully unaware of the distress caused by his letter. He asked Eisenhower to delay sending his ultimatum to the Chiefs of Staff for 24 hours while he spoke with Montgomery. Eisenhower agreed.

De Guingand arrived back at Montgomery's headquarters just as the latter was having afternoon tea. Montgomery finished his cup before his chief of staff and headed upstairs to his office. De Guingand drained his cup, and followed. He came straight to the point, explaining that Montgomery's letter had caused such consternation that it was likely to lead to his dismissal. As de Guingand later recalled, Montgomery was utterly amazed. For the first – and only – time, he appeared to be completely at a loss as to what to do. De Guingand had the answer in a letter he had already drafted for Montgomery to send to Eisenhower. It amounted to a full and gracious apology that could satisfy both parties: Montgomery was to explain that he gave his frank views to the supreme commander only because he assumed that this was what Eisenhower wanted. He was anxious to make clear, he added, that he supported Eisenhower absolutely. He was very distressed if his letter had caused any upset (which, of course, it had), and hoped that Eisenhower would tear it up and forget about it.

The letter did the trick. Eisenhower was mollified, and his letter to the Chiefs of Staff joined Montgomery's first missive in the wastepaper bin. This was the closest to splitting the Allied high command that Hitler came with his offensive.

NORDWIND

Operation Nordwind began on 31 December 1944, just before the arrival of the New Year. When Eisenhower heard of the attack, he inadvertently precipitated another near-crisis in command, giving orders that Gen Devers abandon Strasbourg. The French were not at all impressed and made it clear that they would leave their forces there to defend their territory, no matter what the supreme commander had to say about the matter. This caused an argument between Gen de Gaulle's staff and Eisenhower's chief of staff, Gen Walter Bedell Smith. The matter was resolved at a conference on 3 January. Although the atmosphere was heated, with Eisenhower threatening to cut supplies to the French if they failed to cooperate, it is unlikely that this was a serious threat since the German offensive had already been checked by the US Seventh Army by the end of New Year's Day. Eisenhower told de Gaulle that he would make adjustments to the boundaries of his armies so that the French could defend Strasbourg, and the Frenchman departed, relieved.

The desperate nature of the German attacks had now become obvious: on 1 January, the *Luftwaffe* launched Operation Bödenplatte, an all-out assault on allied airfields by more than 1000 aircraft. Although the attack destroyed numerous Allied aircraft, the Germans lost over 300 of their own, along with many pilots. The Allies replaced every single aircraft that had been lost within days. The *Luftwaffe* never recovered – another casualty of Hitler's Ardennes offensive.

Nordwind continued until 25 January 1945 in appalling weather. Although the Germans got within 16km (10 miles) of Strasbourg, this was the closest they came. Twenty-five thousand more Germans became casualties of the offensive, and it did nothing to reduce American efforts in the Ardennes.

REMOVING THE BULGE

On 8 January 1945, Hitler showed the first signs that he accepted his plan had failed, giving permission for the withdrawal of some units from the Bulge. On 12 January, he ordered that the SS units be withdrawn, supposedly to act as a guard against an American attack along the base of the Bulge – but, in reality, as the precursor for Sixth Panzer

Early in 1945, the crew of this Sherman take a break between fire support missions. The tank has been driven onto a makeshift timber mount to enable the gun's angle of elevation to be increased. The additional sandbag 'armour' can be seen to advantage.

Army's withdrawal. As Hitler reached these decisions, the Americans, with often-ignored assistance from British and Commonwealth units, drove the Germans back. When the skies cleared again on 22 January after more inclement weather, Allied pilots found the roads packed with retreating German vehicles and 'did fearful execution' among them. By 28 January 1945, the last German units had been destroyed.

The Battle of the Bulge was over.

Once the 'Bulge' had been flattened, the Allies turned their attention once more to the final defeat of Germany. The first step was to cross the Roer (a process rudely interrupted by the offensive) and then to drive on to the Rhine. On 15 January, the British XII Corps attacked along the whole of their front in the area known as the Roermond Triangle. They were confronted by two German divisions, which were dug into heavy defences. The battle that followed was, of necessity, a hard-fought struggle of attrition as the British forces attempted to break through the belts of mines and concrete pillboxes. It took ten days, but eventually the Germans were dislodged.

VERITABLE AND GRENADE

Eisenhower's plan called for 21st Army Group to clear the way to the Rhine opposite Wesel. The first part of the plan, Operation Veritable, would call for Horrocks's XXX Corps to advance from Nijmegen through the forests of the Reichswald; US Ninth Army would then drive through Mönchengladbach and link up with the British troops – this was Operation Grenade. The army group would then consolidate for a period before launching an assault crossing of the Rhine, which would enable it to outflank the Ruhr and push on to the North German Plain. The Plain was good tank country, which would enable Montgomery to head for Berlin for the next phase of operations.

While 21st Army Group was attacking in the north, 12th Army Group would carry out Operation Lumberjack, advancing to the south of Montgomery's forces and clearing the approaches to the Rhine from Cologne to Koblenz. Patton would then take his Third Army to link up with 6th Army Group around Mainz. The next step would be to take bridgeheads across the Rhine. Both Patton and Bradley objected to the relatively small role given to US forces in the overall plan, which was to prompt a change in emphasis from Eisenhower after the first phase was complete.

Operations commenced on 8 February 1945 and XXX Corps ran into fierce resistance. The Germans opened the Ruhr dam, preventing any movement in the US Ninth Army's area of operations, and enabling them to transfer troops to meet the British attack. XXX Corps had to engage in a hard attritional slog, while Operation Grenade was delayed until the Ruhr floodwaters had subsided. When it eventually started, on 23 February, it ran into relatively weak German resistance. The link-up with the British and Canadian forces finally occurred on 3 March, and the Allies had a clear approach to the Rhine. Montgomery then started to formulate his plans for crossing the Rhine, which was scheduled for the last week in March. Since there were no bridges available, it became obvious that an assault crossing of the river would be required in the north.

12th Army Group began its operations on 28 February, and made good progress as many German units had been sent to the north to meet 21st Army Group's attacks. Cologne fell on 6 March and the advance concluded with the seizure of the bridge at Remagen the next day. The bridge was not expected to be taken intact and had not been factored into the overall plan. Nonetheless, it was impossible to ignore the opportunity to use the bridge, and American troops pushed across it until it collapsed on 17 March. The capture of the bridge inspired a degree of envy in Patton, who ordered some of his men to cross the river: On 22 March, the 11th Infantry Regiment paddled across in small boats. Montgomery, meanwhile, was still laying the preparations for his crossing. Patton was among those who gleefully pointed out the relative slowness of Montgomery's approach, but this was rather unfair criticism: the Germans had expected the attack to come in the northern sector and had sent many of their units there. Montgomery therefore took the view that it

> The failure of the Offensive may be attributed to the following reasons:
> a. The chief fact was the improper grouping (by the High Command) of troops and the insufficient number of divisions places at the disposal of the army commanders;
> b. Inadequate fuel supplies and unsatisfactory transportation;
> c. The absolute air supremacy of the Allies in the Offensive and rear sectors was a decisive factor, and, later, the failure to capture Bastogne played a most important role;
> d. The numerous reserves of the Allies, their good road net, their high class motorization and important reserves of fuel and ammunition were decisive factors.
>
> *Field Marshal Gerd von Rundstedt*

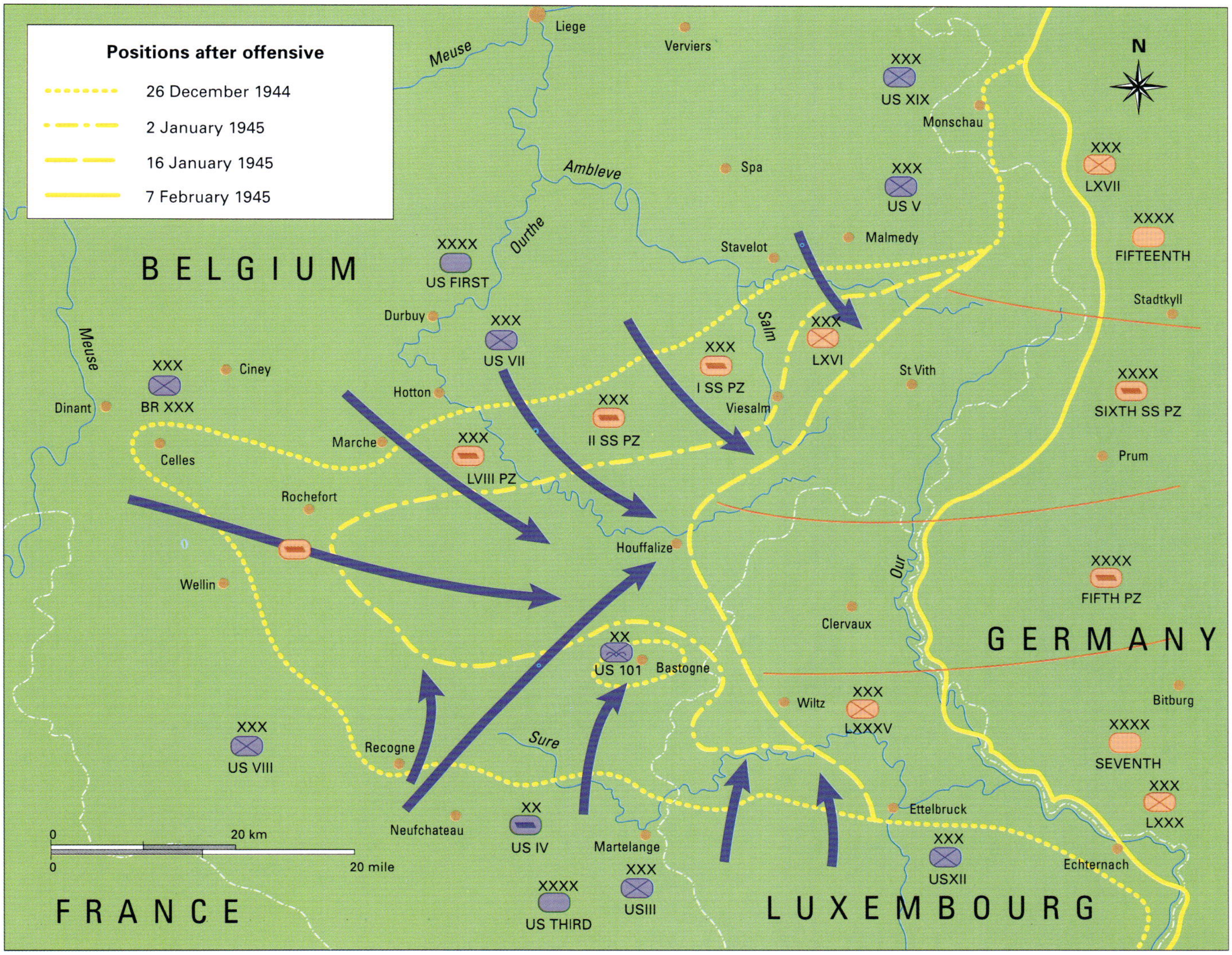

The initial thrust from the south to relieve Bastogne was swiftly followed by an Allied assault along the whole front, driving the German forces back and substantially reducing the size of the 'bulge' in the process.

would be irresponsible to launch his attack without preparing the battlefield by a mixture of artillery fire and aerial bombardment. The weight of preparation was such that the eventual crossing on 23 March was not especially dramatic. By dawn on 24 March, five bridgeheads had been established across the Rhine. An airborne assault consolidated the gains, and by the next day the Rhine had most assuredly been crossed. The end of the war was, at last, in sight. The Allies advanced towards Berlin, heading for a rendezvous with the Russians, who were applying deadly pressure from the East.

THE RUSSIAN ADVANCE

While the western Allies were crossing the Rhine, the Red Army was not far away from Berlin. At the beginning of 1945, the Russians had almost cleared German troops from their territory and were advancing through Poland, Czechoslovakia and Hungary. The Russians enjoyed massive superiority in numbers by this point and there was, realistically, little that could be done to stop them reaching their goal. This was not to say that the Germans had given up: their fear of the Russians meant that every metre of ground would be gained at heavy cost to both sides. The Russian attack began on 13 January and within six days the Russians had cut off the German garrison at Königsberg. This was an impressive achievement, but was nothing compared to the advances made by Marshal Georgi Zhukov's forces on the 1st Belorussian Front. They advanced behind a massive

An M16 half-track/anti-aircraft gun combination keeps watch over the approaches to the bridge at Remagen, the first Rhine crossing seized by the Allies. The M16 mount had four 0.5-inch (12.7mm) machine guns in a one-man turret mounted on the rear of the half-track.

bombardment along the line from Warsaw to Berlin (with a concentration of 400 artillery pieces per mile, supported by rocket batteries) and had made advances of 16km (10 miles) within the first day. The Russians did even better in the southern area of the assault, where they penetrated up to 50km (30 miles). The First Polish Army entered Warsaw on 17 January. Zhukov had now forced a breach 290km (180 miles) wide through the German lines and sent his armoured forces racing forwards. The Russians ploughed through the German forces in their path and reached the Oder river on the last day of the month. Within a week, the sound of Russian artillery fire could be heard in Berlin. Zhukov's army was joined a few days later by troops from Marshal Koniev's 1st Ukrainian Army.

ON TO BERLIN

The task of taking Berlin fell to the Russians, since Eisenhower felt that they were better placed to seize the German capital. Consequently, on 16 April, another massive artillery bombardment fell upon German forces opposite the Oder and Neisse rivers, and vicious fighting began. The Germans fought with great tenacity, desperately trying to keep back the Russians.

Zhukov's forces made little progress, advancing a maximum of 12km (8 miles) on the first day. Koniev's soldiers faced less opposition and made at least this distance, following this up with vigorous thrusts towards the suburbs of Berlin. On 19 April, Zhukov, anxious not to leave the capture of Berlin to Koniev's forces alone, drove his troops forward. They advanced 32km (20 miles) and almost annihilated the German Ninth Army in the process. On 25 April, with Berlin surrounded by Russian troops, American and Russian forces met at Torgau on the Elbe. Five days later Hitler retired to his room with his new bride, Eva Braun. His aides heard a shot and entered the room to find her dead from poison and the Führer lying dead on the couch with a single bullet wound to his head.

The war was almost over. Berlin surrendered unconditionally on 2 May, while two days later Montgomery took the surrender of all German forces in the North. On 7 May the unconditional surrender of Germany was arranged, and VE-Day was declared on 8 May 1945. The war in Europe was over. The 'thousand-year Reich' had lasted a little over twelve.

SUMMING UP THE BULGE

Hitler's decision to attack American forces in the Ardennes was a gamble and the goals he set were far too ambitious, as his generals tried to point out. He ignored them, and the result was a loss of men and equipment that Germany could ill afford. Antwerp was never threatened, although there were times when it appeared that the attacking army might gain some truly significant success. The battle ended with the Germans falling back, assailed by Allied air power. The campaign demonstrated that Hitler's grasp of reality was tenuous at best. The Americans had fallen back under the weight of the assault, but they did not dissolve into inchoate mobs, as Hitler predicted. Nor did the offensive destroy the alliance. It was, however, responsible for 81,000 American and more than 100,000 German casualties, and it succeeded in causing irreparable damage to the German army in the west. The events on 28 January may have been the last of the fighting, but they were not quite the last act.

> I would say the German as a military force on the Western front...is a whipped enemy.
>
> *General Eisenhower, Press conference, 28 March 1945*

Forty-three SS men, including Peiper and Dietrich, were tried for war crimes relating to the Malmédy massacre. Peiper was sentenced to death, but after considerable controversy over the trial and the interrogation of the defendants, the

A mound of jerry-cans litter the side of a road in Belgium. The Americans had vast supplies available, while to the Germans low levels of fuel were a constant concern, and one they could not overcome; Kampfgruppe Peiper for one ground to a halt for want of fuel.

A significant factor in the defeat of the German offensive was overwhelming Allied air superiority, here demonstrated by these American P-51 Mustang fighter aircraft over Germany in early 1945.

sentence was commuted to 35 years in prison. Peiper was released in 1956 and retired to Alsace. His house was firebombed in 1976, two weeks after a newspaper article revealed he was living there. Police and fire services sifted through the remains and discovered the body of the former commander of Kampfgruppe Peiper. His death was not widely mourned.

The final act of the Battle of the Bulge occurred in 1981. In *The Bitter Woods* (1969), his masterful account of the Battle of the Bulge, John S D Eisenhower told the story of Lyle Bouck's I&R platoon for the first time. This led to a campaign to honour the men who had put up such a fierce struggle, including demands for the award of the Medal of Honor to William Tsakanikas; this continued even after Tsakanikas's death in 1977. The authorities decided that the action of the I&R platoon merited recognition.

Although the recommendation for a Medal of Honor for Tsakanikas was not accepted, the award of a Distinguished Service Cross was approved. Bouck refused to accept any honour for himself, but the authorities had the good sense to ignore his protests. At a medal ceremony in 1981, the surviving members of the I&R platoon and the families of those who had died were presented with four DSCs, five Silver Stars and nine Bronze Stars, making the I&R platoon one of the most highly decorated military units in American military history.

The Battle of the Bulge was filled with courageous action by soldiers of both sides, interspersed with the peculiar brutality of the SS towards their prisoners. Despite the grandiose plans laid down by Hitler, it did not succeed. Perhaps the final word should be left to Winston Churchill, who addressed the House of Commons on the subject on 18 January 1945. He was doing so partly to deal with yet more offence caused by Montgomery (who at a press conference had effectively claimed for himself the credit for the victory in the Ardennes) and by the British press, who were keen to criticize Eisenhower in order to promote Montgomery. His remarks to the Commons, whatever the reason behind them, were genuine enough:

'[The Battle is] undoubtedly the greatest American battle of the War, and will, I believe, be regarded as an ever famous American victory.'

It is impossible to disagree.

ORDER OF BATTLE

16 December 1944

Wehrmacht

OB WEST
Field Marshal Gerd von Rundstedt

ARMY GROUP B
Field Marshal Walter Model

Fifth Panzer Army
General Hasso von Manteuffel

XLVII Corps *(von Luttwitz)*
- 2nd Panzer Division *(von Lauchert)*
- 26th Volksgrenadier Division *(Kokott)*
- Führer Begleit Brigade *(Remer)*
- Panzer Lehr Division *(Bayerlein)*

LXVI Corps *(Lucht)*
- 18th Volksgrenadier Division *(Hoffman-Schonborn)*
- 62nd Volksgrenadier Division *(Kittel)*

LVIII Panzer Corps *(Kruger)*
- 116th Volksgrenadier Division *(von Walenburg)*
- 560th Volksgrenadier Division *(Langhauser)*

Sixth Panzer Army
SS General 'Sepp' Dietrich

I SS Panzer Corps *(Priess)*
- 1st SS Panzer Division *Leibstandarte Adolf Hitler (Mohnke)*
- 3rd Parachute Division *(Wadehn)*
- 12th SS Panzer Division *Hitler Jugend (Kraas)*
- 12th Volksgrenadier Division *(Engel)*
- 150th Panzer Brigade *(Skorzeny)*
- 277th Volksgrenadier Division *(Viebig)*

II SS Panzer Corps *(Bittrich)*
- 2nd SS Panzer Division *Das Reich (Lammerding)*
- 9th SS Panzer Division *Hohenstaufen (Stadler)*

LXVII Corps *(Hitzfeld)*
- 272nd Volksgrenadier Division *(Kosmalla)*
- 326th Volksgrenadier Division *(Kaschner)*

Seventh Army
General Erich Brandenberger

LXXX Corps *(Beyer)*
- 212th Volksgrenadier Division *(von Sensfuss)*
- 276th Volksgrenadier Division *(Mohring)*

LXXXV Corps *(Kniess)*
- 5th Parachute Division *(Heilmann)*
- 352nd Volksgrenadier Division *(Schmidt)*

The following order of battle represents the assignment of forces to the American Corps that faced the initial German assault on 16 December 1944. As the battle progressed, some divisions were assigned to the command of other corps, while divisions from elsewhere arrived to bolster American forces engaged in the fighting.

Supreme Headquarters Allied Expeditionary Force (SHAEF)

General of the Army: Dwight D. Eisenhower

US ARMY

12 ARMY GROUP
Lieutenant-General Omar N. Bradley

First Army
Lieutenant-General Courtney H. Hodges

V Corps *(Gerow)*
- 1st Infantry Division *(Andrus)*
- 2nd Infantry Division *(Robertson)*
- 78th Infantry Division *(Parker)*
- 99th Infantry Division *(Lauer)*

VII Corps *(Collins)*
- 3rd Armored Division *(Rose)*
- 5th Armored Division *(Oliver)*
- 9th Infantry Division *(Craig)*
- 83th Infantry Division *(Macon)*

VIII Corps *(Middleton)*
- 4th Infantry Division *(Barton)*
- 7th Armored Division *(Hasbrouck)*
- 9th Armored Division *(Leonard)*
- 10th Armored Division *(Morris Jr)*
- 28th Infantry Division *(Cota)*
- 106th Infantry Division *(Jones)*

BIBLIOGRAPHY

ARNOLD, JAMES R. *Ardennes 1944: Hitler's Last Gamble in the West.* London: Osprey, 1990.

COLE, HUGH M. *The Ardennes: Battle of the Bulge.* US Dept of the Army, 1965.

CROOKENDEN, NAPIER. *Battle of the Bulge 1944.* Shepperton: Ian Allan, 1980.

CROSS, ROBIN. *The Battle of the Bulge 1944: Hitler's Last Hope.* Havertown, Penn: Casemate, 2002.

EISENHOWER, JOHN D. *The Bitter Woods: the Dramatic Story of Hitler's Surprise Ardennes Offensive.* London: Hale, 1969.

ELSTOB, PETER. *Hitler's Last Offensive.* London: Secker & Warburg, 1971.

FORTY, GEORGE. *The Reich's Last Gamble: the Ardennes Offensive, December 1944.* London: Cassell, 2000.

MACDONALD, CHARLES B. *Battle of the Bulge: the Definitive Account.* London: Weidenfeld and Nicolson, 1985.

MERRIAM, ROBERT E. *The Battle of the Ardennes.* London: Souvenir Press, 1958.

NOBECOURT, JACQUES. *Hitler's Last Gamble: the Battle of the Ardennes.* London: Chatto & Windus, 1969.

PALLUD, JEAN PAUL. *Battle of the Bulge, Then and Now.* London: Battle of Britain Prints International Ltd, 1984.

PARKER, DANNY S. *To Win the Winter Sky: the Air War Over the Ardennes, 1944–1945.* London: Greenhill Books, 1994.

PARKER, DANNY S (ed). *The Battle of the Bulge, the German View: Perspectives from Hitler's High Command.* London: Greenhill Books, 1999.

PARKER, DANNY S. *Battle of the Bulge: Hitler's Ardennes Offensive, 1944–1945.* London: Greenhill Books: 1999.

RUSIECKI, STEPHEN M. *The Key to the Bulge : The Battle for Losheimergraben.* Westport, Conn.: Praeger Publishers, 1996.

SCHADEWITZ, MICHAEL. *The Meuse First and then Antwerp: Some Aspects of Hitler's Offensive in the Ardennes.* Winnipeg: J J Fedorowicz Publishing, 1999.

STRAWSON, JOHN. *The Battle for the Ardennes.* London: B T Batsford, 1972.

INDEX

Page numbers in *italics* refer to illustrations and maps; those in **bold** refer to special profiles or biographies.